Lecture Notes in Computer Science   8651

Commenced Publication in 1973
Founding and Former Series Editors:
Gerhard Goos, Juris Hartmanis, and Jan van Leeuwen

More information about this series at http://www.springer.com/series/7410

Nitesh Saxena · Ahmad-Reza Sadeghi (Eds.)

Radio Frequency Identification

Security and Privacy Issues

10th International Workshop, RFIDSec 2014
Oxford, UK, July 21–23, 2014
Revised Selected Papers

 Springer

Editors
Nitesh Saxena
Computer and Information Science
University of Alabama at Birmingham
Birmingham, AL
USA

Ahmad-Reza Sadeghi
Technische Universität Darmstadt
Darmstadt
Germany

ISSN 0302-9743   ISSN 1611-3349 (electronic)
Lecture Notes in Computer Science
ISBN 978-3-319-13065-1   ISBN 978-3-319-13066-8 (eBook)
DOI 10.1007/978-3-319-13066-8

Library of Congress Control Number: 2014955536

LNCS Sublibrary: SL4 – Security and Cryptology

Springer Cham Heidelberg New York Dordrecht London

Printed on acid-free paper

Springer International Publishing AG Switzerland is part of Springer Science+Business Media
(www.springer.com)

Preface

This volume contains the proceedings of the 10th International Workshop on RFID Security (RFIDSec), held at St. Anne's College, Oxford, UK, from July 21 to 23, 2014. For a decade, RFIDSec has been the primary forum where international experts from academia, industry, and government present, debate, discuss, and advance the security and privacy aspects of RFID. First time in the history of RFIDSec, the workshop was colocated with the WiSec conference, an established venue centred on wireless security. This conglomeration of the two communities led to a synergistic development and discussion of new cross-disciplinary ideas.

This year, we assembled a diverse program of nine regular papers and four short papers selected by the Program Committee. All submissions received three reviews from the 23 members of the Program Committee chosen by the Program Co-chairs, assisted by the 13 external reviewers. The conference opened up with an invited talk "Clustering Distance Bounding Protocols" by Prof. Gildas Avoine, INSA Rennes, a known expert in RFID Security and Privacy. The talk focused on distance bounding protocols, a widely studied topic within the RFIDSec community. The second talk was a keynote speech given by John O'Donnell, Cisco Systems's Internet of Everything (IoE) Pre Sales Consultants Manager. His talk "IoT – Connecting the Unconnected Securely" examined real-world security problems within the IoT field. The highlights of this year's technical program were timely and fundamental topics such as RFID power-efficiency, privacy, authentication and side channels, and key exchange.

We thank the General Chairs, Andrew Martin and Ivan Martinovic, both from the University of Oxford, UK, for their dedicated work and the excellent local organization of the workshop, the RFIDSec Steering Committee members for their guidance and support, all the authors for the high-quality submissions, and all the Program Committee members and the external reviewers for contributing their expertise to the selection of the papers for the program. Without their service and contribution, setting up such a conference would have been impossible.

July 2014

Ahmad-Reza Sadeghi
Nitesh Saxena

Organization

Program Committee

Gildas Avoine	Université catholique de Louvain, Belgium
Lejla Batina	Radboud University Nijmegen, The Netherlands
Mihai Bucicoiu	University Politehnica of Bucharest, Romania
Srdjan Capkun	ETH Zürich, Switzerland
Mauro Conti	University of Padua, Italy
Bruno Crispo	University of Trento, Italy
Roberto Di Pietro	Roma Tre University, Italy
Thomas Eisenbarth	Worcester Polytechnic Institute, USA
Aurélien Francillon	Institut Eurécom, France
Tzipora Halevi	Polytechnic Institute of New York University, USA
Gerhard Hancke	City University of Hong Kong, Hong Kong
Jaap-Henk Hoepman	Radboud University Nijmegen, The Netherlands
Mehran Kermani	Rochester Institute of Technology, USA
Karl Koscher	University of Washington, USA
Kari Kostiainen	ETH Zürich, Switzerland
Farinaz Koushanfar	Rice University, USA
Yingjiu Li	Singapore Management University, Singapore
Mark Manulis	University of Surrey, UK
Bart Preneel	Katholieke Universiteit Leuven, Belgium
Pankaj Rohatgi	Cryptography Research Inc., USA
Ahmad-Reza Sadeghi	Technische Universität Darmstadt, Germany
Nitesh Saxena	University of Alabama at Birmingham, USA
Babins Shrestha	University of Alabama at Birmingham, USA
Joshua Smith	University of Washington, USA
Ersin Uzun	PARC, USA
Jonathan Voris	Columbia University, USA
Avishai Wool	Tel Aviv University, Israel

Contents

Lightweight Authentication Protocols on Ultra-Constrained RFIDs - Myths and Facts

Frederik Armknecht, Matthias Hamann$^{(\boxtimes)}$, and Vasily Mikhalev

University of Mannheim, Mannheim, Germany
{armknecht,hamann,mikhalev}@uni-mannheim.de

Abstract. While most lightweight authentication protocols have been well analyzed with respect to their *security*, often only little (or even nothing) is known with respect to their *suitability* for low-cost RFIDs in the range of $0.05 to $0.10. Probably this is mainly due to the fact that open literature rarely provides information on what conditions need to be met by a scheme in practice, hindering a sound development and analysis of schemes.

We provide a comprehensive collection of several conditions that should be met by lightweight authentication schemes if deployed in low-cost RFID systems. Afterwards, we show that none of the existing authentication protocols that are based on the hardness of the Learning Parity with Noise (LPN) problem complies to these conditions, leaving the design of an LPN-based protocol for low-cost RFIDs as an open question.

Keywords: Lightweight authentication protocols · Low-cost RFIDs · Real world conditions · Learning parity with noise

1 Introduction

For economical reasons low-cost RFID tags (e.g., in the production cost range of $0.05 to $0.10) are particularly interesting for industry. This cost pressure directly translates into severe hardware restrictions for the targeted devices. Consequently, the search for appropriate lightweight authentication protocols has become an important topic in cryptography during the last years with high relevance for academia and industry.

While there is quite a good understanding with respect to the *security* of most of these schemes, often only very little is known about their *applicability* for real-world systems. One main reason is the apparent lack of commonly accepted criteria for a scheme to be considered as lightweight. Of course one might argue that developments in technologies continuously enable *more possibilities* at the *same price*. However, experience shows that for economic reasons advances in technology are rather used for developing hardware that possesses about the *same capabilities* as existing devices but at a *lower price*.

In this work, we concentrate on authentication protocols between an RFID reader and ultra-constrained tags. More precisely, we target devices in the cost

© Springer International Publishing Switzerland 2014
N. Saxena and A.-R. Sadeghi (Eds.): RFIDSec 2014, LNCS 8651, pp. 1–18, 2014.
DOI: 10.1007/978-3-319-13066-8_1

range of \$0.05 to \$0.10. The reasons for this specific choice are twofold: Firstly, RFID tags which can be produced at costs of \$0.1 or cheaper, like (variants of) *Electronic Product Codes* (EPCs), have been a common motivation for existing work (see, e.g., [6,9,20,28]). Secondly, if one allows for only few additional costs, standard cryptographic primitives like AES become in fact feasible, thus practically removing the need for alternative solutions altogether (see, e.g., [9] or also Sect. 2 - *Area*). Our contributions are:

Set of Conditions. Our first contribution is that we specify and argue several conditions that need to be satisfied by authentication protocols to be suitable for ultra-constrained RFID devices. These conditions have been derived partly from open literature but most importantly from various discussions with experts from industry. Although these experts were working for different companies and were aiming for RFID-based authentication in different areas, all of them share more or less the same view on what "lightweight" means in the context of ultra-constrained devices and when a scheme can be considered to be relevant for real-word applications. As these conditions mostly result from long lasting experience in hardware production and have not (or only partly) been comprehensively described and summarized in open literature, we think that this information will be very helpful for assessing the suitability of existing protocols and for providing guidance in the development of new ones.

Evaluation of LPN-Based Protocols. Our second contribution is the application of the gained knowledge for evaluating the suitability of *LPN-based protocols*. This branch of research represents the most prominent non-proprietary approach for designing lightweight authentication protocols. It has been initiated by HB [18] and HB$^+$ [20], which became the prototypes for a whole family of protocols that base their security on the hardness of the learning parity in the presence of noise (LPN) assumption (or variant problems). To this end, we extracted concrete parameter choices for almost 20 proposals in this work and verified whether these comply to the derived set of conditions. As it turned out, none of the existing LPN-based protocols meet the requirements, i.e., none of them can actually run on current low-cost RFID hardware.

2 Hardware Constraints of Lightweight Authentication Protocols for Low-Cost RFID-Systems

In this section, we discuss hardware limits imposed on the design of lightweight authentication protocols by typical factors like, e.g., chip size, power consumption and clock speed. Due to their prevalence in the field of lightweight authentication hardware, we focus on *Application-specific Integrated Circuits* (ASICs) in this work. As a platform, low-cost RFID tags (i.e., ultra-constrained devices) in the range of \$0.05 to \$0.10 like *Electronic Product Codes* (EPCs) are targeted, as is done, e.g., by Juels and Weis in [20]. In [19], Juels additionally points out that while "it is tempting to dismiss this computational poverty a temporary state of affairs, in the hope that Moore's Law will soon render inexpensive tags more computationally powerful [...] pricing pressure is a strong countervailing force". And indeed, it seems that most of the limits described in, e.g., [20] and [19], still apply today as our numerous discussions with experts from industry have revealed. Hence, the numbers presented in the following paragraphs can be expected to remain valid also in the medium term.

Operating Frequency and Transmission Bandwidth. The operating frequency of RFID tags and, closely related, their maximum available transfer rate is determined by several factors. One of the most important is the targeted reading distance implied by, inter alia, a tag's purpose. Table 1 is based on the data provided in [44]. Hence, corresponding authentication solutions are limited to exchanging data at a rate of at most 200 kb/s (100 kb/s in the very common HF band) between a tag and a reader[1]. Based on the common notion that the whole process of authentication should not take more than 150 ms (cf. next paragraph), this implies that 30,000 bit can be considered as the upper bound for an authentication protocol's communication complexity. Furthermore, this number is even lowered by the fact that, within those 150 ms, the respective data must be processed by the tag and that not only non-volatile memory but also volatile memory (e.g., Juels and Weis assume 32–128 bits in [20]) is a scarce resource, which heavily limits buffering incoming data.

Table 1. Application fields, transfer rates, and range by waveband (cf. [44]).

Waveband	Utilization	Bandwidth	Distance
Low frequency (LF), 30–300 kHz	Animal identification	<10 kb/s	0.1–0.5 m
Medium frequency (MF), 300 kHz–3 MHz	Contactless payment	<50 kb/s	0.5–0.8 m
High frequency (HF), 3–30 MHz	Access control	<100 kb/s	0.05–3 m
Ultra HF (UHF), 300 MHz–3 GHz	Range counting	<200 kb/s	1–5 m
Super HF (SHF), 3 GHz–30 GHz	Vehicle identification	<200 kb/s	ca. 10 m

Timing. Perhaps surprisingly, we were told the aforementioned upper timing bound of 150 ms by various hardware producers on the basis of rather different reasons. These ranged from human interaction in the presence of additional tag functions to regulations by the automotive industry w.r.t. timing restrictions for component interaction. From a technical point of view, UHF regulations would impose a maximum of 400 ms due to channel hopping but "user performance requirements establish a time limitation on a label operation since at least 100–300 labels must be read per second" [37]. For example, Feldhofer et al. designed their AES-based authentication protocol such that each tag has 18 ms

---

[1] In [6], it is stated that "in accordance with C1G2, a maximum tag to reader data transmission rate of 640 kbps and a reader to tag data transmission rate of 126 kbps based on equi-probable binary ones and zeros in the transmission can be calculated" and that "performance criteria of an RFID system demand a minimum label reading speed in excess of 200 labels per second".

time, hence "a maximum of 50 tags can be authenticated per second" [9]. Consequently, the upper bound of 150 ms told to us by several industrial sources is probably already very generous and, depending on the use case, might actually be much lower by factors of 10–50. Keep in mind that this would directly translate to vastly reduced upper bounds for communication (e.g., a maximum of 600 bit instead of 30,000 bit per authentication) or available clock cycles (e.g., only 300 instead of 15,000; cf. Sect. 2). However, we will evaluate the (in-)feasibility of the protocols in Sect. 3 using the generous upper timing bound of 150 ms and the respective limits for communication and computation.

Area (in GE). Juels and Weis [20] stated the "Security Gate Count Budget" of an EPC tag to be "200–2000 gates" and, even today, this upper bound of 2000 GEs is still commonly considered to be the magic number for lightweight cryptographic implementations. From an academic perspective, this conclusion can be drawn based on the fact that many recent works (see, e.g., [29,36,42,46]) still assume 2000 GEs to be the upper bound w.r.t. tag area. Some other works assume between 200 and 4000 GEs [6,37] but are sometimes not clear about whether they are actually referring to the total area of a low-cost RFID tag or just the amount of GEs available for security purposes. Apart from academic publications, all experts from industry we spoke to confirmed that 2000 GEs still constitute a plausible security gate count budged for low-cost RFIDs, nine years after [20] was published in 2005. For comparison, one of the currently smallest known AES implementations due to Feldhofer et al. [8] requires about 3,400 GEs, which implies that newly suggested approaches requiring even more area should at least be obliged to justify what additional benefit they bring. This obligation to justify even the need for a single additional gate has straightforward monetary reasons as, according to [6], 1,000 additional gates of silicon logic increase a tag's price by $0.01, which amounts to considerable sums given production volumes of hundreds of millions in the case of low-cost RFID tags. It should also be noted that, in addition to the number and placement of logic gates, other (security-related) components contribute to the chip area of an RFID tag as well. Most notably, one way to fix constant bit values (e.g., cryptographic keys) on individual tags is to use fuses/antifuses and "burn" a corresponding selection of them before a tag leaves the factory. As it has to be ensured that no other (i.e., normal logic) components get damaged during this process of burning fuses, considerable area is needed, rendering the technique infeasible when it comes to storing large amounts (i.e., thousands) of constant bits at production time. Finally, providing acceptable side channel security can also significantly increase the number of required GEs, depending on the structure of the protocol.

Power. Low-cost RFID tags are commonly powered via an electromagnetic field radiated by the reader (i.e., passively), limiting the total electric energy available during a single authentication run. As the transmission power of an RFID reader is limited by factors like regulations (e.g., for the EPC Gen 2 band, to 4 W EIRP in the U.S. and 2 W EIRP in Israel [38]), the more power a tag consumes, the smaller the maximum (legally possible) reading distance becomes. In [20], Juels and Weis give a general upper bound of 10 μW. Saarinen and Engels emphasize that power peaks should be below $3\,\mu W$ to $30\,\mu W$ [42]. Keep in mind, however, that a tag's power consumption depends on multiple design specific factors, e.g. it increases with higher clock speeds and EEPROMs play an important role, too, as we will elaborate below. Hence, analyzing the power consumption of a given authentication protocol is difficult if no reference implementation is given.

Clock Speed and Clock Cycles. Ceteris paribus, the higher the clock speed of a tag is, the more clock cycles can be safely consumed by the cryptographic authentication process. But as pointed out in the previous paragraph, factors like the power budget of a passively powered RFID tag impose an upper bound on its clock frequency. Many works consider 100 kHz to be the prevalent clock speed feasible on ultra-constrained RFID tags, e.g., [9,32,35]. This value is in line with the information we obtained from the RFID hardware producers who demanded confidentiality. Hence, assuming an upper bound of 150 ms for executing a full authentication instance, a clock speed of 100 kHz immediately implies an upper bound of 15,000 clock cycles on the tag's side to authenticate successfully. Keep in mind, however, that none of the protocols in Appendix B are deemed infeasible w.r.t. ultra-constrained devices solely due to their computational complexity. Still, it should be noted that many of them exceed our upper bound of 15,000 clock cycles even by magnitudes (e.g., MAC_1 and MAC_2) and, hence, would be clearly infeasible also for higher clock rates like 1 MHz.

Random Number Generator (RNG). The hardware means of generating random numbers on a lightweight RFID tag can probably be considered the "magic bullet" with respect to authentication protocols and are most likely the main reason why all of the hardware producers we interviewed demanded to remain unnamed. In [20], Juels and Weis state that the random noise bit ν (and probably also the blinding factors required as part of each protocol round; see Sect. 3) "can be cheaply generated from physical properties like thermal noise, shot noise, diode breakdown noise, metastability, oscillation jitter, or any of a slew of other methods". While the listed physical properties can undoubtedly serve as a source for the generation of random bits, ensuring a sufficient level of entropy in these cases still constitutes a difficult task and is subject to research areas on its own. For example, [45] presents a metastability-based *True Random Number Generator* (TRNG) fabricated in $0.13\,\mu m$ bulk CMOS technology, which requires $0.145\,mm^2$ of area and consumes $1\,mW$ of power (at a clock speed of 200 MHz). Even for lower clock speeds (and, hence, lower power consumptions), the required area of $0.145\,mm^2$ would still render this TRNG infeasible as a component (i.e., one of many parts) of a low-cost RFID tag considering that "10 US cents RFID read only chips have design sizes ranging from $0.16\,mm^2$ to $0.25\,mm^2$" [37] and that the RNG's "circuit should not occupy more area than $100 \times 100\,\mu m$" [2].[2] TRNGs designed particularly for passive RFID tags exist, too, but we are only aware of those like [2], which focus on generating

---

[2] In [2], a $0.13\,\mu m$ CMOS process is used. For comparison, the AES implementation in [8] is based on a $0.35\,\mu m$ CMOS process and occupies $0.25\,mm^2$, which "compares roughly to 3400 gate equivalents" in this context.

16-bit-long random numbers mainly meant for resolving collisions during communication. Hence, it is unclear to what extend such low-cost RNGs are actually suitable for generating large, continuous amounts of random bits (with sufficient entropy) in time as needed by many HB-type protocols for each authentication instance. For the sake of completeness, we would like to mention that there are also *Pseudorandom Number Generators* (PRNGs) aiming at low-cost scenarios, but, e.g., LAMED [32] still consumes roughly 1,600 GEs, which is about 600 GEs more than the lightweight block cipher PRESENT [41], which can be used straightforwardly to realize (one-way) authentication in the spirit of [9] without the need for any random numbers at all on tag side. As none of the above TRNG/PRNG solutions seems to fit the scenario implied by HB-type protocols on ultra-constrained devices, at this point, we have resort to information provided to us by different experts from industry, who all agree that generating more than 128 true random bits per authentication on an RFID tag in the price range of \$0.05–\$0.10 seems currently implausible. Note, however, that none of those protocols in Appendix B which are currently unbroken were ruled infeasible only because they require more than 128 bits per authentication and, in addition, many protocols exceed this number even by magnitudes. Finally, another problem particular to HB-type protocols is that they depend on a specific probability distribution w.r.t. the noise bit ν and deriving such a fixed distribution from the aforementioned sources is also everything but a trivial task.

Non-Volatile Memory (NVM). While the cost of volatile memory is often implicitly included in the numbers for area in the form of flip-flops/latches (respectively the components needed to build those), non-volatile memory is commonly provided through the use of EEPROMs. One drawback, however, to employing EEPROMs is their high latency. Moreover, from the first EEPROM memory unit on, corresponding charge pumps have to be included in the design in order to supply the high voltages necessary for memory programming. Hence, EEPROMs are not only a major cost driver in terms of money and area but also have a significant impact on a tags power budget when it comes to ultra-constrained RFID devices. Concretely, Ranasinghe and Cole state in [6] that, for low-cost RFID tags, the power required for a read operation amounts to 5–10 μW while "a write operation to its EEPROM will require about 50 μW or more", which would practically allow only read operations (in the field) given the aforementioned power limitations of, e.g., EPC UHF tags, and, hence, inhibit a tag from keeping values across a loss of power (for example, between two separate authentication instances). With respect to area requirements, Nuykin et al. propose a low-cost 640-bit EEPROM for passive RFID tags fabricated in a 0.18 μm CMOS process, which requires a total area of 0.04 mm^2. They also compare their design to several other recent suggestions, which all require at least twice the area and mostly even offer less memory (i.e., 192 bit). It is therefore not surprising that, as compared to the targeted low-cost EPC-like devices, even significantly more expensive RFID tags like the HITAG 1 by NXP do not provide more than 2048 bit of EEPROM. In line with this, Juels and Weis assume "128–512 bits of read-only-storage" and "32–128 bits of volatile read-write memory" to be realistic memory resources available on low-cost RFID tags, not considering non-volatile read-write-storage at all [20]. Finally, our sources from industry also all agreed that 2048 bit constitute a plausible upper bound for current EEPROM sizes on ultra-constrained RFID tags in the $0.05 to $0.10 range.

3 Evaluation of LPN-Based Protocols

In this section, we revisit existing protocols that are based on LPN (or related problems) and that have been suggested for lightweight applications. More precisely, we evaluate their suitability for low-cost RFID systems based on the conditions presented in Sect. 2. Our respective results for almost 20 HB-type protocols are summarized in tabular form in Appendix B. The conclusion one can draw from these results is that each of the considered protocols would induce costs that are significantly outside of the derived bounds. Furthermore, many of the protocols are insecure against MITM attacks. Although one may debate whether MITM attacks are actually relevant in certain low-cost use cases, note that there are straightforward authentication schemes on the basis of prevalent lightweight ciphers (cf. the full version of this work), which are perfectly feasible and do not only provide active but also MITM security.

A short overview of the most important proposals for lightweight authentication protocols based on the LPN problem is given in Appendix A. As this branch of research has been initiated by the introduction of HB [18] and HB$^+$ [20], which became the prototypes for this family of protocols, these are explained in further detail (Sect. 3.1). Moreover, at the example of HB$^+$, we discuss the main parameters which influence the security and the hardware characteristics of HB-type protocols. This allows us to identify the general cost drivers common to the HB family (Sect. 3.2). Subsequently, we present our evaluation results for popular follow-up protocols of HB$^+$ (Sect. 3.3). In the full version of this paper, we give a more detailed analysis for each of the considered protocols.

3.1 The Procotols HB and HB$^+$ and the Main Parameters

The HB protocol [18] was originally developed to be used by humans and with this aim was designed to be very simple. Both the reader (verifier) and the tag (prover) share a secret $x \in \{0,1\}^{k_x}$. The protocol is composed of several rounds that are conceptually all the same. At the beginning of round i, the verifier chooses a random challenge $a^{(i)} \in \{0,1\}^{k_x}$ and sends it to the prover, who replies with $z_i = (a^{(i)} \cdot x) \oplus \nu_i$, where $\nu_i \in \{0,1\}$ represents a biased random noise bit satisfying $Prob[\nu_i = 1] = \eta$ for a fixed probability $\eta \in (0, 0.5)$. Then, the reader verifies whether the received bit z_i is equal to $a^{(i)} \cdot x$. If this is the case, the response is called correct and otherwise incorrect. The security of HB against passive attacks relies on the LPN problem with the parameters η, k_x [26].

The HB$^+$ protocol [20] was developed to resist active attacks in the detection-based model. In extension to the HB protocol, the tag and the reader share an additional secret y. At the beginning of round i, the tag generates a random blinding factor $b^{(i)} \in \{0,1\}^{k_y}$ and sends it to the reader. Afterwards, similar to the HB protocol, the reader generates a challenge $a^{(i)} \in \{0,1\}^{k_x}$ and sends it to the tag. Then, the tag computes $z_i = (a^{(i)} \cdot x) \oplus (b^{(i)} \cdot y) \oplus \nu_i$ and sends it to the reader for verification. In the original proposal [20], the challenge $a^{(i)}$, the blinding factor $b^{(i)}$ and the secrets x, y all have the same length $k_x = k_y = k$, which is implied by the LPN problem. However, later it was shown in [26] that, when striving for 80-bit security in the detection-based model, the x-component of the common secret key (x, y) can be restricted to a length of $k_x = 80$ bits while the security of HB$^+$ still relies on the hardness of LPN with parameters η and k_y, where $k_y > k_x$ as we will explain shortly.

As already mentioned, both protocols, HB and HB$^+$, run in r rounds. Each additional round increases the confidence of the verifier. To this end, both protocols fix a parameter $u \in (\eta, 0.5)$, such that the authentication is considered to be successful if the number of incorrect answers is less than $t = u \cdot r$. Otherwise, the reader rejects the tag. If the noise probability η is chosen too close to 0.5 then a huge number of rounds is required in order to make the protocol reliable. At the same time, if η is close to 0, then for obtaining the necessary level of security of the protocols, extremely large key lengths k_x, k_y are inevitable. Hence, an appropriate tradeoff needs to be found, which is specified by the choice of η.

However, besides security considerations, there are also practical aspects that impact reasonable choices for η. Usually, random number generators are assumed to produce uniformly distributed random bits. In this case, it is much easier to implement instantiations where $\eta = 2^{-j}$, $j \in \mathbb{N}$, as j uniformly distributed bits are sufficient for the generation of one noise bit ν_i. However, for other values of η, many more uniformly distributed random bits may be needed to realize a corresponding random bit generator on top of those. Therefore, in this paper we restrict η to the values 0.25 and 0.125, which are in fact typical choices for HB-type protocols [26].

The reliability of the protocols depends on the probabilities of the possible errors. On the one hand, an honest tag may be rejected with probability P_{FR} (false rejection probability or completeness error). On the other hand, an adversary answering randomly at each round will be authenticated with probability P_{FA} (false acceptance probability or soundness error). For HB and HB$^+$, these values are computed as follows [13]:

$$P_{FR} = \sum_{i=t+1}^{r} \binom{r}{i} \eta^i (1-\eta)^{r-i}, \qquad P_{FA} = \frac{1}{2^r} \sum_{i=0}^{t} \binom{r}{i}$$

According to [26], P_{FA} should be less than 2^{-80} for 80-bit security and P_{FR} should be less then 2^{-40}. In order to achieve such bounds for soundness and completeness errors, an appropriate combination of the parameters η, r, u needs to be chosen. In [26], for each value of η suitable values for u and r were computed, leading to the following two choices:

- Variant 1: $\eta = 0.25$, $u = 0.348$, $r = 1164$
- Variant 2: $\eta = 0.125$, $u = 0.256$, $r = 441$

In one of the protocols proposed afterwards [14], the following trick has been suggested based on ideas from [21]: if the tag computes in advance r noise bits and keeps them only if the number of 1s is less than $u \cdot r$, then the completeness error P_{FR} will be equal to 0. The advantage of this approach is that the number of rounds r can be reduced, while the soundness error is kept small. Our evaluation takes this approach into account as well and uses the parameters provided in [14]: $r = 256, \eta = 0.125, u = 0.1875$ (variant 3). Summing up, in this paper we evaluate, where possible, each protocol in all three explained variants.

As mentioned above, the protocols' security relies on the LPN problem. The proofs of security for HB against passive attacks and for HB^+ against active attacks were simplified by Katz et al. and extended to the parallel versions of the protocols [21,22], which means that several rounds can be performed at the same time. Based on the state-of-the-art heuristic algorithm for solving the LPN problem [26], reasonable parameter choices for achieving (almost) 80-bit security are $k_x = 512$ for HB and $k_x = 80$, $k_y = 512$ for HB^+. In these cases, solving the LPN-problem would take 2^{89} bytes of memory if $\eta = 0.25$ and 2^{77} bytes of memory if $\eta = 0.125$.

3.2   Cost Drivers of LPN-Based Protocols

In Sect. 2, we have established a concrete notion of the term *lightweight* in the RFID context by providing actual hardware limits for low-cost tags. As our goal is to assess for (allegedly) lightweight authentication protocols whether they in fact comply to all of the respective hardware limits, we first need to identify the major cost drivers of such schemes. In particular, we will discuss for each of the following protocol properties how it is linked to the hardware properties of RFID tags in the \$0.05 to \$0.10 cost range discussed in Sect. 2.

Symmetric Key. All HB-type authentication protocols use symmetric keys[3]. Consequently, the full shared secret, must permanently be available on the (passively powered) tag, hence implying the need for some non-volatile *key storage*. Depending on the deployment scenario, multiple (e.g., batches of) RFID tags might share a single key or, in other cases, tag-individual secrets may be required.

Closely related, but even more restrictive w.r.t. key storage options, is a potential need to set or change the secret key of a tag that is already in the field, as compared to irreversibly fixing the key once at production time. In the latter case, key-dependent masks may be used in the factory to apply the secret keys directly to so-called wafers in the process of creating *Integrated Circuits* (ICs) for low-cost RFID tags. However, while this can alleviate the need for additional components like EEPROMs or fuses (cf. Sect. 2 - *Area*), it inevitably results in

---

[3] For the sake of simplicity, in this subsection, the term *key* will always be used to refer to the shared secret's unique representation as a binary vector in the corresponding scheme, irrespective of potential blow-up measures like, e.g., the use of Toeplitz matrices. In particular, the key size lower bounds the size of the individual key storage required on each tag.

the potentially dangerous situation that large quantities of tags will now share the same irreversible key. Concretely, as production costs increase with each new mask (by thousands of U.S. dollars), the size of per-mask-batches must be big enough (i.e., hundreds of thousands or even millions of devices) to allow for per-tag savings (e.g., by removing the need for EEPROMs) which compensate for the additional costs of using multiple masks. At the same time, an attacker's outlook on, e.g., counterfeiting large amounts of items who are all protected by tags using the same key, may now easily justify the costs for retrieving the respective key by means of reverse engineering (for instance, through etching and the use of an electron microscope).

Ultimately, if the deployment scenario requires fully individual keys, the use of masks is clearly not feasible anymore and two other, more flexible options remain: EEPROMs and fuses, whose major hardware properties and limitations w.r.t. low-cost RFID tags were summarized in Sect. 2. These general preconditions will now be compared to the requirements imposed by how symmetric keys are chosen and used in HB-type protocols. Clearly, EEPROMs offer the highest degree of flexibility as a key storage, allowing, e.g., to redeploy existing tags after changing their keys. On contrast, when resorting to fuses, keys are irreversible and need to be written already at production time. However, unlike masks, fuses allow for individual keys on a per tag basis. Hence, as fuses neither suffer from the high power consumption nor from the latency problems characteristic of EEPROMs, they are a viable option when individual but fixed keys are required.

Unfortunately, in the context of HB-type authentication protocols, key storage options are further restricted by the large key size common to these schemes. In [23], key sizes for multiple HB-type protocols are specified on the basis of the parameter l denoting the length of an LPN secret. For example, the key size of the original HB$^+$ protocol, i.e., the variant suggested by Juels and Weis in [20], is given by $2l$ along with $l = 500$ described as a "typical parameter". Please note that the resulting key length of 1000 bit is even at the lower end of the protocols summarized in [23] (which range from l bit for the original HB protocol [18], over $4.2 \cdot l$ bit for AUTH [23], up to $80 \cdot l = 40000$ bit for a MITM-secure protocol also suggested in [23]; see Sect. 3.3 for further details). However, e.g. due to area requirements, already for 1000 bit it seems highly questionable whether fuses can still be considered a feasible option for storing the secret key on a low-cost RFID tag. Moreover, it is easy to see that, similar to (or even worse than) masks, fuses fail to provide substantial physical security. Ultimately, it depends on the deployment scenario whether this is an actual thread, hence requiring the use of, e.g., EEPROMs instead. Bring to mind, however, that in the context of low-cost RFID devices, EEPROMs typically do not allow for storing more than 2048 bit. As a result, it must be suspected that many of the HB-type protocols discussed in Sect. 3.3 are already precluded by their key size from practical application on RFID tags in the $0.05 to $0.10 range.

Challenges, Blinding Factors, and Noise Bits. Another property characteristic of HB-type protocols is their heavy use of challenges and what is often referred to as blinding factors. For most HB-type protocols, the following three phases per round can be identified: (1) The prover creates a vector of random bits, the so-called blinding factor, which is then transmitted wirelessly to the verifier. (2) Just alike, the verifier now also creates a random bit vector and sends it to the tag. (3) Depending on the specific protocol, the prover deterministically computes some 1-bit value based on the blinding factor in (1), the challenge in (2), as well as the secret/shared key. Finally, he needs to produce one more random bit, which, on contrast to the aforementioned challenge and blinding vectors, is not based on the uniform but some other, fixed distribution. Adding this so-called noise bit to the 1-bit value yielded by the previous operation is crucial to the security of HB-type protocols, as described in Subsect. 3.1. The resulting bit is then sent to the verifier, who will check whether it is correct or not. In the following paragraph, we will denote the number of protocol rounds per authentication run by r and, for reasons of simplicity, assume that the blinding vector in step (1) as well as the challenge vector in step (2) are both of length l, i.e., the size of the secret key (as done in the original HB$^+$ paper [20] and popular follow-up works like [23]).

Apparently, the protocol scheme we just outlined makes heavy use of at least two hardware resources previously identified as potential bottlenecks for low-cost RFID tags: the transmission bandwidth (cf. Sect. 2) and the generation of random numbers. Concretely, in each round of the above archetypical example, the communication complexity amounts to $2l + 1$ and the prover needs to obtain l uniformly random bits and 1 differently distributed random bit from his RNG. Hence, a single authentication procedure consisting of r rounds has a communication complexity of approximately $2 \cdot l \cdot r$ bit and requires at least $r \cdot l$ random bits on the prover's side. As in the previous paragraph about key sizes, let us exemplify the actual consequences of these complexities for HB-type protocols using parameters described as "typical" in [23]: $l = 500$ and $r = 250$. Moreover, as justified in Sect. 2, let us consider 150 ms to be the maximum time available for a complete authentication. As a result, at least $2 \cdot 500 \cdot 250 = 250,000$ bit would need to be transmitted within 150 ms, corresponding to a vastly implausible transmission rate of $250,000/0.15$ bit/s ≈ 1.66 Mbit/s (as compared to actual values between 10,000 bit/s and 200,000 bit/s as given in Sect. 2). Similarly far from reality is the idea that an RFID tag whose production costs are in the \$0.05–\$0.10 range could actually feature an RNG delivering as much as $500 \cdot 250 = 125,000$ uniformly distributed random bits within just 150 ms. Apart from the apparent bottlenecks transmission bandwidth and generation of random numbers, the generalizing description of HB-type protocol at the beginning of this paragraph contained a third aspect worth investigating. Concretely, depending on the involved operations, the first computation in step (3) can easily turn out to consume (possibly too) many clock cycles, especially in view of the fact that three operands of bit-length 500 are involved. As this is highly protocol-specific and implementation-dependent (e.g., parallel vs. serial processing in step (3) of HB$^+$) though, the question of computational complexity will be treated, where of importance, in the corresponding paragraphs of Subsect. 3.3 (and the full version of the paper, respectively).

3.3   Evaluation Results

In the following, we explain how the evaluation results of the considered protocols (as presented in Appendix B) have been derived at the example of HB, HB^+ and HB^{++}. For these, we first provide a short protocol description in the respective paragraphs and, afterwards, justify the chosen parameters. Even though we implemented the discussed protocols, we do not provide the exact values here due to the variety of possible implementation choices, which lead to different performance results. Explaining all of these options would fill several papers on its own. Consequently, to keep the description as simple and readable as possible, we explain only the reasons why, either way, the protocols are infeasible on ultra-constrained low-cost RFID hardware, independent of the implementation choices. In this section, we use the notations explained in Table 2.

Table 2. Considered cost factors.

Cost	Meaning
St_k	Key storage complexity
NR_n	# uniformly distributed random bits for generating noise (prover's side)
NR_b	# uniformly distributed random bits for generating blinding factors (prover's side)
CC	Total communication complexity

HB and HB^+. The protocols HB and HB^+ have been described already in Sect. 3.1. Hence, we provide only the formulas for computing the parameters listed in Table 2. For HB, the costs are calculated as follows:

$$St_k = k_x, \quad NR_n = -\log_2(\eta) \cdot r, \quad NR_b = 0, \quad CC = (k_x + 1) \cdot r \qquad (1)$$

In the case of HB^+, the respective formulas are:

$$St_k = k_x + k_y, \quad NR_n = -\log_2(\eta) \cdot r, \quad NR_b = k_y \cdot r, \quad CC = (k_x + k_y + 1) \cdot r \quad (2)$$

HB^{++}. In 2006, Bringer et al. [5] proposed the HB^{++} protocol, where reader and tag share one secret of 768 bits, which is used for generating session keys. The protocol consists of two steps. During the first step, the reader and the tag exchange 80-bit nonces, which, together with the shared secret, are used as the inputs for a hash function h. The output of this function are four temporary keys $x, y, x', y' \in \{0,1\}^{80}$ of total length 320 bit. The second step of HB^{++} can be considered as running HB^+ twice with correlated challenges (see [5] for details) and blinding factors and independent temporary keys x, y, x', y'. Similarly to HB^+, tag and reader exchange a blinding factor $b^{(i)} \in \{0,1\}^{80}$ and a challenge $a^{(i)} \in \{0,1\}^{80}$ (i.e., like in the original version of HB^+ [20], both are of the same length). Afterwards, the tag computes and sends the two values

$$z_i = \left(a^{(i)} \cdot x\right) \oplus \left(b^{(i)} \cdot y\right) \oplus \nu_i,$$
$$z_i' = \left(rot_i\left(f\left(a^{(i)}\right)\right) \cdot x'\right) \oplus \left(rot_i\left(f\left(b^{(i)}\right)\right) \cdot y'\right) \oplus \nu_i',$$

where $rot_i(\beta)$ denotes the rotation of β by i bits to the left and f is a function with special properties (again, we refer the reader to [5] for further details).

Parameter choices: Bringer, J. et al. [5] gives an exact specification of the hash function, which results in secrets of 80 bits length. However, no concrete values have been recommended for the noise rate η and the number of rounds r. According to [13], the completeness and soundness errors for HB^{++} are given by

$$P_{FR} = 1 - \left(\sum_{i=0}^{t} \binom{r}{i} \eta^i (1 - \eta)^{r-i} \right)^2, \quad P_{FA} = \left(\frac{1}{2^r} \sum_{i=0}^{t} \binom{r}{i} \right)^2.$$

We calculated the smallest number of rounds r such that $P_{FR} \leq 2^{-40}$ and $P_{FA} \leq 2^{-80}$. The results are the following: $r = 282$ if $\eta = 0.125, u = 0.285$, and $r = 731$ if $\eta = 0.25, u = 0.368$.

Security: In 2008, a MITM attack was presented by Gilbert et al. [13], who broke HB^{++} with and without the first protocol step (i.e., with and without renewed secrets).

Implementation cost considerations: In order to store the temporary session keys generated in step 1 and used during step 2 of the protocol, 320 additional flip-flops are needed (on top of the logic for, e.g., operations, counters etc.). Please note that using one flip-flop of the smallest size increases an ASIC's area by approximately 6 GEs. This already precludes HB^{++} from satisfying the area limits justified in Sect. 2. Moreover, e.g., the non-linear function f applied to $b^{(i)}, a^{(i)} \in \{0,1\}^{80}$ significantly increases the required area even further. The formulas for determining the costs are:

$$St_k = 768, \; NR_n = -\log_2(\eta) \cdot r, \; NR_b = 81 \cdot r, \; CC = 80 \cdot 2 + (k_x + k_y + 2) \cdot r$$

Further HB-Type Protocols. The protocols HB-MP [30], HB-MP$^+$ [25], HB* [7], HB$^{\#}$ [14], RANDOM-HB$^{\#}$ [14], Trusted HB [4], HB-MAC [40], HB^N [3], GHB$^{\#}$ [39], HB^b [43], NL-HB [27], PUF-HB [16], AUTH/MAC$_1$/MAC$_2$ [23], and Lapin [17] were also analyzed for this work in the same way as demonstrated at the example of HB^{++} in the previous paragraph. The table given in Appendix B contains a summary of the most important results w.r.t. feasibility and security, while the respective details like formulas and implementation considerations will be provided in the full version of the paper.[4]

4   Conclusion

As our analysis reveals, building authentication protocols which are based on the LPN problem has, so far, not led to any practical solutions feasible for

---

[4] At the current state, Lapin was omitted from the table in Appendix B as, according to its authors, it is actually "targeting lightweight tags that are equipped with (small) CPUs" as compared to "ultra constrained tokens (such as RFIDs in the price range of few cents targeting the EPC market)" [17]. (See also [11] for a very recent suggestion of an FPGA implementation for Lapin, which, however, is still not feasible when transferred to low-cost ASICs. Again, the details of this will be discussed in the full version of the paper.)

ultra-constrained devices. While this neither questions the significance nor the security of such designs, it indicates that for real-world applications in the context of low-cost RFID tags other approaches should be considered. This is particularly true as we show in the full version of this work that straightforward applications of suitable lightweight ciphers yield appropriate authentication schemes.

Acknowledgment. We would like to thank the anonymous reviewers of RFIDSec 2014 and Gildas Avoine for their helpful comments. Finally, we would also like to express our special thanks to Peter Fischer and Michael Ritzert, who supplied us with the necessary technical means and additional valuable information for actually implementing the discussed protocols.

A   Overview of the Considered Protocols

In 2000, the HB [18] protocol was proposed, which is proven to be secure against passive attacks [22]. In order to resist active attacks, HB^+ [20] was introduced that is provably secure in the detection-based model (where the adversary is able to communicate only with the tag before attempting to authenticate itself to the reader). However, if the attacker is given the ability to modify messages which go from the reader to the tag (GRS model), the HB^+ protocol is not secure anymore as it was shown in [12]. As a result, many new HB-type protocols were proposed in order to overcome this and other types of Man-in-the-middle (MITM) attacks. In 2006, the HB^{++} protocol was introduced [5], which can be seen as running HB^+ twice with correlated challenges and independent secrets. Later, [30] proposed the HB-MP protocol, which was designed to be more efficient than HB^+ but turned out to be vulnerable w.r.t. certain MITM attacks [13], which is why HB-MP$^+$ [25] has been suggested. Another attempt to improve the performance of HB^+ and to make it resistant against GRS-type MITM attacks was the HB^* protocol [7]. In 2008, the $HB^\#$ and RANDOM-HB$^\#$ protocols were proposed, where the keys were extended from vectors to matrices [14]. Another proposal called Trusted-HB [4] is based on the idea of using a hardware efficient hash function for verifying the integrity of the data in order to resist MITM attacks. PUF-HB [16] is a construction which relies on Physically Unclonable Functions (PUFs) as a hardware primitive. In the protocols NLHB [27] and GHB# [39], the linear functions are replaced by non-linear functions, while HB^N [3] can be seen as a bilinear variant of HB. In 2011, AUTH [23] was proposed, where the security is based on a modified LPN problem, called the *subspace LPN problem* [33]. One year later, a more efficient proposal building on the ideas from [23] called Lapin [17] was introduced, whose security relies on assumed hardness of the *Ring LPN-problem*.

B Evaluation Results for the Considered Protocols

Table 3. Evaluation results for the considered HB-type protocols.

Protocol	Parameters	St_k	NR_n	NR_b	CC	Suitability** and Security
HB [18]	$\eta = 0.25, k = 512, r = 1164$	512	2328	0	597132	$CC \geq 30000, NR_b + NR_n \geq 128$ for all sets of parameters. Active attacks [18].
	$\eta = 0.125, k = 512, r = 441$	512	1323	0	226233	
	$\eta = 0.125, k = 512, r = 256$	512	770*	0	131328	
HB$^+$ [20,12]	$\eta = 0.25, k_x = 80, k_y = 512, r = 1164$	592	2328	59568	690252	$CC \geq 30000, NR_b + NR_n \geq 128$. MITM attacks [12].
	$\eta = 0.125, k_x = 80, k_y = 512, r = 441$	592	1323	225792	261513	
	$\eta = 0.125, k_x = 80, k_y = 512, r = 256$	592	770*	131072	151808	
HB^{++} [5,13]	$\eta = 0.25, r = 731$	768	2924	58560	118582	$CC \geq 30000, NR_b + NR_n \geq 128$. MITM attacks [13].
	$\eta = 0.125, r = 282$	768	1692	22640	45844	
HB-MP [30,13]	$n = 1, k = 513, m = 512, r = 1164$	1026	0	893952*	1191936	$CC \geq 30000, NR_b + NR_n \geq 128$. Passive attacks [13].
	$n = 2, k = 513, m = 512, r = 441$	1026	0	395136*	451584	
HB-MP$^+$ [25]	$n = 2, k = 512, m = 224, r = 1164$	1024	0	391104*	521472	$CC \geq 30000, NR_b + NR_n \geq 128$.
HB* [7,34,13,43,26]	$\eta = 0.5k, = 256, r = 80$	1024	80	20480	41200	$CC \geq 30000, NR_b + NR_n \geq 128$.
HB^{*1} [7,34,13,43,26]	$\eta = 0.25, k = 512, r = 1164$	1536	3492	595968	598296	$CC \geq 30000, NR_b + NR_n \geq 128$. MITM attacks [34,13].
	$\eta = 0.125, k = 512, r = 441$	1536	1764	225792	226674	
Trusted HB [4,10,24]	$\eta = 0.25, k_x = 80, k_y = 512, r = 1164$	693	2328	595968	690353	$CC \geq 30000, NR_b + NR_n \geq 128$. $\approx 7 \cdot 10^5$ clock-cycles (max. available $1,5 \cdot 10^5$). MITM attacks [10].
RND-HB$^{\#}$ [14,31]	$\eta = 0.25, k_x = 80, k_y = 512, r = 1164$	689088	2328	512	1756	$NR_b + NR_n \geq 128$. MITM attacks [31].
	$\eta = 0.125, k_x = 80, k_y = 512, r = 441$	261072	1323	512	1033	
	$\eta = 0.125, k_x = 80, k_y = 512, r = 256$	151552	770*	512	848	
HB$^{\#}$ [14,31]	$\eta = 0.25, k_x = 80, k_y = 512, r = 1164$	2918	2328	512	1756	$NR_b + NR_n \geq 128$. MITM attacks [31].
	$\eta = 0.125, k_x = 80, k_y = 512, r = 441$	1472	1323	512	1033	
	$\eta = 0.125, k_x = 80, k_y = 512, r = 256$	1102	770*	512	848	
HB-MAC [40,31,14,24]	$\eta = 0.25, k = 160, r = 1164$	186240	4656	160	2808	$St_k \geq 2048, NR_b + NR_n \geq 128$. MITM attacks [40].
	$\eta = 0.125, k = 160, r = 441$	70560	2646	160	1362	
GHB$^{\#}$ [39,14,15]	$\eta = 0.25, k_x = 80, k_y = 512, r = 1164$	689088	2328	512	1756	$St_k \geq 2048, NR_b + NR_n \geq 128$.
	$\eta = 0.125, k_x = 80, k_y = 512, r = 441$	261072	1323	512	1033	
	$\eta = 0.125, k_x = 80, k_y = 512, r = 256$	151552	770*	512	848	
HB^N [3]	$\eta = 0.25, n = 513, r = 3921$	263169	7842	2011473	4026867	$St_k \geq 2048, NR_b + NR_n \geq 128, CC \geq 30000$.
	$\eta = 0.125, n = 513, r = 522$	263169	1566	267786	536094	
HB^b [43,31]	$\eta = 0.25, k_x = 80, k_y = 512, r = 1164$	689088	Unclear	512	1756	$St_k \geq 2048$. Noise generation mechanism is unclear.
	$\eta = 0.125, k_x = 80, k_y = 512, r = 441$	261072	Unclear	512	1033	
	$\eta = 0.125, k_x = 80, k_y = 512, r = 256$	151552	Unclear	512	848	
NL-HB [27,1]	$\eta = 0.25, k = 512, r = 1164$	512	2328	-	597132	Similar to HB, the conditions $CC \geq 30000, NR_b + NR_n \geq 128$. Active attacks [27,1].
	$\eta = 0.125, k = 512, r = 441$	512	1323	-	226233	
	$\eta = 0.125, k = 512, r = 256$	512	770*	-	131328	
AUTH [23,14]						Depending on trade-off parameter c, either CC, St_k, or both not feasible (cf. [23] and [14]).
MAC$_1$ [23,14]						Same as AUTH + $CompC$ of $\Theta(m^2)$, $m = 600$, imposed by pairwise independent permutation (cf. [23]).
MAC$_2$ [23,14]						Same as AUTH + $CompC$ of $\Theta(m^2)$, $m = 1200$, imposed by pairwise independent permutation (cf. [23]).

St_k - Key storage complexity.

NR_n, NR_b - Number of uniformly distributed random bits (generated by the prover, i.e., an RFID tag) required for noise (NR_n) or for blinding factors (NR_b).

CC - The total communication complexity.

$CompC$ - The total computational complexity.

* - Is used when the average number of random bits is given.

** - As the bounds given in Sect. 2 are not always tight, only severe violations (often by magnitudes) are indicated in this column (Table 3).

References

1. Abyaneh, M.R.S.: On the security of non-linear HB (NLHB) protocol against passive attack. In: 2010 IEEE/IFIP 8th International Conference on Embedded and Ubiquitous Computing (EUC), pp. 523–528. IEEE (2010)
2. Balachandran, G.K., Barnett, R.E.: A 440-nA true random number generator for passive RFID tags. IEEE Trans. Circ. Syst. I: Regular Pap. $55(11)$, 3723–3732 (2008)
3. Bosley, C., Haralambiev, K., Nicolosi, A.: HB^N: An HB-like protocol secure against man-in-the-middle attacks. IACR Cryptology ePrint Archive 2011, p. 350 (2011)
4. Bringer, J., Chabanne, H.:. Trusted-HB: A low-cost version of HB^+ secure against man-in-the-middle attacks. arXiv preprint (2008). arXiv:0802.0603
5. Bringer, J., Chabanne, H., Dottax, E.: HB^{++}: A lightweight authentication protocol secure against some attacks. In: Second International Workshop on Security, Privacy and Trust in Pervasive and Ubiquitous Computing, 2006, SecPerU 2006, pp. 28–33. IEEE (2006)
6. Cole, P.H., Ranasinghe, D.C.: Networked RFID Systems and Lightweight Cryptography: Raising Barriers to Product Counterfeiting, 1st edn. Springer, Berlin Heidelberg (2008)
7. Duc, D.N., Kim, K.: Securing HB^+ against GRS man-in-the-middle attack. In: Institute of Electronics, Information and Communication Engineers, Symposium on Cryptography and Information Security (2007)
8. Feldhofer, M., Wolkerstorfer, J., Rijmen, V.: AES implementation on a grain of sand. IEE Proc.: Inf. Secur. $152(1)$, 13–20 (2005)
9. Feldhofer, M., Dominikus, S., Wolkerstorfer, J.: Strong authentication for RFID systems using the AES algorithm. In: Joye, M., Quisquater, J.-J. (eds.) CHES 2004. LNCS, vol. 3156, pp. 357–370. Springer, Heidelberg (2004)
10. Frumkin, D., Shamir, A.: Untrusted-HB: Security vulnerabilities of Trusted-HB. Cryptology ePrint Archive, Report 2009/044 (2009)
11. Gaspar, L., Leurent, G., Standaert, F.-X.: Hardware implementation and side-channel analysis of lapin. In: Benaloh, J. (ed.) CT-RSA 2014. LNCS, vol. 8366, pp. 206–226. Springer, Heidelberg (2014)
12. Gilbert, H., Robshaw, M., Sibert, H.: Active attack against HB^+: A provably secure lightweight authentication protocol. Electron. Lett. $41(21)$, 1169–1170 (2005)
13. Gilbert, H., Robshaw, M., Seurin, Y.: Good variants of HB^+ are hard to find. In: Tsudik, G. (ed.) FC 2008. LNCS, vol. 5143, pp. 156–170. Springer, Heidelberg (2008)
14. Gilbert, H., Robshaw, M., Seurin, Y.: $HB^\#$: Increasing the security and efficiency of HB^+. In: Smart, N.P. (ed.) EUROCRYPT 2008. LNCS, vol. 4965, pp. 361–378. Springer, Heidelberg (2008)
15. Gold, R.: Maximal recursive sequences with 3-valued recursive cross-correlation functions (corresp.). IEEE Trans. Inf. Theory $14(1)$, 154–156 (1968)
16. Hammouri, G., Sunar, B.: PUF-HB: A tamper-resilient HB based authentication protocol. In: Bellovin, S.M., Gennaro, R., Keromytis, A.D., Yung, M. (eds.) ACNS 2008. LNCS, vol. 5037, pp. 346–365. Springer, Heidelberg (2008)
17. Heyse, S., Kiltz, E., Lyubashevsky, V., Paar, C., Pietrzak, K.: Lapin: An efficient authentication protocol based on Ring-LPN. In: Canteaut, A. (ed.) FSE 2012. LNCS, vol. 7549, pp. 346–365. Springer, Heidelberg (2012)
18. Hopper, N.J., Blum, M.: Secure human identification protocols. In: Boyd, C. (ed.) ASIACRYPT 2001. LNCS, vol. 2248, pp. 52–66. Springer, Heidelberg (2001)

19. Juels, A.: RFID security and privacy: A research survey. IEEE J. Sel. A. Commun. **24**(2), 381–394 (2006)
20. Juels, A., Weis, S.A.: Authenticating pervasive devices with human protocols. In: Shoup, V. (ed.) CRYPTO 2005. LNCS, vol. 3621, pp. 293–308. Springer, Heidelberg (2005)
21. Katz, J., Shin, J.S.: Parallel and concurrent security of the HB and HB$^+$ protocols. In: Vaudenay, S. (ed.) EUROCRYPT 2006. LNCS, vol. 4004, pp. 73–87. Springer, Heidelberg (2006)
22. Katz, J., Shin, J.S., Smith, A.: Parallel and concurrent security of the HB and HB$^+$ protocols. J. Cryptol. **23**(3), 402–421 (2010)
23. Kiltz, E., Pietrzak, K., Cash, D., Jain, A., Venturi, D.: Efficient authentication from hard learning problems. In: Paterson, K.G. (ed.) EUROCRYPT 2011. LNCS, vol. 6632, pp. 7–26. Springer, Heidelberg (2011)
24. Krawczyk, H.: LFSR-based hashing and authentication. In: Desmedt, Y.G. (ed.) CRYPTO 1994. LNCS, vol. 839, pp. 129–139. Springer, Heidelberg (1994)
25. Leng, X., Mayes, K., Markantonakis, K.: HB-MP$^+$ protocol: An improvement on the HB-MP protocol. In: 2008 IEEE International Conference on RFID, pp. 118–124. IEEE (2008)
26. Levieil, É., Fouque, P.-A.: An improved LPN algorithm. In: De Prisco, R., Yung, M. (eds.) SCN 2006. LNCS, vol. 4116, pp. 348–359. Springer, Heidelberg (2006)
27. Madhavan, M., Thangaraj, A., Sankarasubramanian, Y., Viswanathan, K.: NLHB: A non-linear Hopper-Blum protocol. In: 2010 IEEE International Symposium on Information Theory Proceedings (ISIT), pp. 2498–2502. IEEE (2010)
28. Martin, H., Millán, E.S., Entrena, L., Castro, J.C.H., Peris-Lopez, P.: AKARI-X: A pseudorandom number generator for secure lightweight systems. In: IOLTS, pp. 228–233 (2011)
29. Melià-Seguí, J., Garcia-Alfaro, J., Herrera-Joancomartí, J.: J3Gen: A PRNG for low-cost passive RFID. Sensors **13**(3), 3816–3830 (2013)
30. Munilla, J., Peinado, A.: HB-MP: A further step in the HB-family of lightweight authentication protocols. Comput. Netw. **51**(9), 2262–2267 (2007)
31. Ouafi, K., Overbeck, R., Vaudenay, S.: On the security of HB$^\#$ against a man-in-the-middle attack. In: Pieprzyk, J. (ed.) ASIACRYPT 2008. LNCS, vol. 5350, pp. 108–124. Springer, Heidelberg (2008)
32. Peris-Lopez, P., Hernandez-Castro, J.C., Estevez-Tapiador, J.M., Ribagorda, A.: LAMED - A PRNG for EPC Class-1 generation-2 RFID specification. Comput. Stand. Interfaces **31**(1), 88–97 (2009)
33. Pietrzak, K.: Subspace LWE, Manuscript. http://homepages.cwi.nl/~pietrzak/publications/SLWE.pdf
34. Piramuthu, S., TU, Y.-J.: Modified HB authentication protocol. In: WEWoRC, pp. 41–44 (2007)
35. Poschmann, A.: Lightweight cryptography: Cryptographic engineering for a pervasive world (2009)
36. Poschmann, A., Moradi, A., Khoo, K., Lim, C., Wang, H., Ling, S.: Side-channel resistant crypto for less than 2,300 GE. J. Cryptol. **24**(2), 322–345 (2011)
37. Ranasinghe, D.C., Engels, D.W., Cole, P.H.: Low-cost RFID systems: Confronting security and privacy. In: Auto-ID Labs Research Workshop, Portal (2005)
38. Repec, C.A.: Regulatory status for using RFID in the EPC Gen 2 band (860 to 960 MHz) of the UHF spectrum (2013). http://www.gs1.org/docs/epcglobal/UHF_Regulations.pdf

39. Rizomiliotis, P., Gritzalis, S.: GHB$^{\#}$: A provably secure *HB*-like lightweight authentication protocol. In: Bao, F., Samarati, P., Zhou, J. (eds.) ACNS 2012. LNCS, vol. 7341, pp. 489–506. Springer, Heidelberg (2012)

40. Rizomiliotis, P.: *HB* − *MAC*: Improving the *Random* − HB$^{\#}$ authentication protocol. In: Fischer-Hübner, S., Lambrinoudakis, C., Pernul, G. (eds.) TrustBus 2009. LNCS, vol. 5695, pp. 159–168. Springer, Heidelberg (2009)

41. Rolfes, C., Poschmann, A., Leander, G., Paar, C.: Ultra-lightweight implementations for smart devices – Security for 1000 gate equivalents. In: Grimaud, G., Standaert, F.-X. (eds.) CARDIS 2008. LNCS, vol. 5189, pp. 89–103. Springer, Heidelberg (2008)

42. Saarinen, M.-J.O., Engels, D.W.: A do-it-all-cipher for RFID: Design requirements (extended abstract). IACR Cryptology ePrint Archive, 2012, p. 317 (2012) (informal publication)

43. Song, X., Kobara, K., Imafuku, K., Imai, H.: HB^{b} protocol for lightweight authentication; Its information theoretic indistinguishability against MITM attack watching reader's response. In: 2012 International Symposium on Information Theory and its Applications (ISITA), pp. 536–540. IEEE (2012)

44. Susini, J., Chabanne, H., Urien, P.: RFID and the Internet of Things, p. 304. ISTE - Wiley, London (2011)

45. Tokunaga, C., Blaauw, D., Mudge, T.: True random number generator with a metastability-based quality control. In: Solid-State Circuits Conference, 2007, ISSCC 2007. Digest of Technical Papers. IEEE International, pp. 404–611, Feb 2007

46. Wu, W., Zhang, L.: LBlock: A lightweight block cipher. In: Lopez, J., Tsudik, G. (eds.) ACNS 2011. LNCS, vol. 6715, pp. 327–344. Springer, Heidelberg (2011)

High-Speed Dating Privacy-Preserving Attribute Matching for RFID

Lejla Batina[1]([⊠]), Jens Hermans[2], Jaap-Henk Hoepman[1], and Anna Krasnova[1]

[1] Digital Security Group, Radboud University, Heyendaalseweg 135,
6525 AJ Nijmegen, The Netherlands
{lejla,jhh}@cs.ru.nl
anna@mechanical-mind.org
[2] KU Leuven and IMinds, Kasteelpark Arenberg 10,
3001 Heverlee, Belgium
jens.hermans@esat.kuleuven.be

Abstract. This paper presents a new approach for RFID tag *attribute matching* problem. Unlike previous approaches, most notably the T-Match protocol, presented in [9], we do not need a central database server or any connectivity between readers. Furthermore, we do not need expensive homomorphic encryption or multiparty computation and we extend attribute matching to multiple attributes per tag; a feature that broadens the range of possible applications of the protocol. We achieve this increased flexibility and decreased complexity by moving some relatively cheap cryptographic computations to the tags. Specifically, one of the protocols presented in this paper only needs a (lightweight) hash function implemented on the tags. Two other protocols additionally need asymmetric encryption, which is feasible on more powerful tags that support elliptic-curve scalar multiplication.

Keywords: Attribute matching · RFID · Privacy · Unforgeabilitiy · Unlinkability

1 Introduction

RFID technology is predominantly used for identification and authentication of items and persons. In a typical setup the tag has some key which it uses in an identification or authentication protocol with the reader. Attribute-matching protocols on the other hand focus on determining whether two or more tags have a set of attributes that match a specific relationship. By using an attribute matching protocol one can also authenticate tags by simply matching it with a tag known to be genuine. Provided both tags share an attribute (or key) they will pass the validation.

Anna Krasnova – This research was conducted within the Privacy and Identity Lab (PI.lab, http://www.pilab.nl) and funded by SIDN.nl (http://www.sidn.nl/). Permanent ID of this document: bdc1cee0d2de9dab7248278472d954a5. Date: 2014.08.18.

© Springer International Publishing Switzerland 2014
N. Saxena and A.-R. Sadeghi (Eds.): RFIDSec 2014, LNCS 8651, pp. 19–35, 2014.
DOI: 10.1007/978-3-319-13066-8_2

As an important application for tag authentication by matching we envision preventing counterfeit products. A producer can provide a reference tag to the verifier, containing the same key as the genuine products. By matching product tags with the reference one can detect counterfeits, without the key ever leaving the tags which can be protected on hardware level. Such an approach has major advantages compared to classical authentication protocols. Symmetric key authentication protocols are very efficient but require storing the secret key on the reader. Authentication by matching combines this efficiency with a typical property of asymmetric protocols that do not require secret (private) keys on the verifier.

To illustrate our protocols we will use the example of a *speed-dating* party (or rather, with the protocols presented in this paper, a *high-speed-dating* party). The typical setup of a *speed-dating* party is that singles try to find a partner through many short meetings with many people. The goal of these short conversations is to find out whether the two people share interests and want to engage in a longer conversation or a date. *High-speed dating* replaces these short matchmaking conversations by scanning RFID tags as follows: The organizer of the party has collected all relevant attributes (hobbies, city of residence, kids and pets preferences, etc.) of all participants in advance. Every participant receives an RFID tag which stores his or her attributes. When two persons want to decide whether it is worth starting a conversation, they just have their tags scanned simultaneously by a reader, and the reader determines whether these persons have overlapping interests and wishes. Thus, the task of a reader is to detect the fact that two tags have matches in their interests, and output the number of these matches. No false positives are desirable, since false positive will steal time of participants. The obvious target group for such a party are "nerds and geeks", who typically have very serious concerns about their privacy. They do not want a reader or another person to learn anything about them, except for the fact whether they share interests with another person or not. Also, tags' unlinkability should be preserved, so nobody can trace tags. Last but not least, no attributes stored on tags shall be disclosed. This application may not sound like the most serious scenario, but it illustrates very well what the protocol does and what properties we expect from the protocol.

This paper presents three private-attribute-matching protocols (or *speed-dating protocols*). The first protocol uses only symmetric cryptography, the second only asymmetric cryptography, and the last a combination of both. None of the protocols requires readers to be connected to a central database; they are furthermore not required to have specific knowledge about the tags. The first two protocols provide matching for one attribute per tag. The symmetric protocol provides speed and efficiency at the cost of a lower privacy protection level. The asymmetric ones provides better privacy at the cost of a single asymmetric encryption step. The hybrid encryption protocol still uses a single encryption step with asymmetric encryption, and several with symmetric one, in order to support tags with several attributes. All protocols provide provable security against false positives and provable privacy protection.

The remainder of this paper is organized as follows. Section 2 presents the model of the system and the adversarial games. Section 3 introduces the lightweight symmetric protocol. Section 4 introduces the two remaining protocols using asymmetric primitives. Related work is discussed in Sect. 5.

2   Model and Notations

Let T be the set of all tags in the system. Each tag $t_i \in T$, $i \in \{1, 2, \ldots, n\}$ is supplied with attributes. Each attribute is a human-readable string of arbitrary length, the set of all attributes in the system is denoted as $C = \{a_1, \ldots, a_p\}$. Let the security parameter be λ, and the number of attributes and tags be polynomially bounded in λ. Each attribute in the system is related to a secret key stored on a tag in the following way. An issuer starts with an attribute set C. To setup the system S, the tag issuer generates a set of *keys* $K = \{k_1, \ldots, k_p\}$, which are each associated with an attribute. Each key k_j for $j \in \{1, \ldots, p\}$ is a λ-bit string.

Each tag stores a subset of K of cardinality at most m, where $1 \leq m \leq p$. For two tags t_i and t_j, which share an attribute a_i, the corresponding key for a_i is thus stored on both tags. For simplicity, further in the text we use the term keys and attributes interchangeably.

The goal of the protocol is to determine the number of attributes on two tags that match. Let the state S_i denote the set of attributes stored on a tag t_i. Note, that if tags t_i and t_j have the very same attributes assigned to them, their states are equal $S_i \equiv S_j$. This state is assigned by the issuer during the setup phase: a function $Setup(\lambda)$ is used to assign state S_i to a tag t_i, with $i \in \{1, 2, ..., n\}$, and generates keys for readers (if necessary). All secret values are generated taking the security parameter λ into account. Later, during the protocol run, a reader R simultaneously scans two tags t_i and t_j to obtain the result of the function $Match : T \times T \rightarrow \mathbf{N}$. This function computes the cardinality of the intersection of the states of two tags: $Match(t_i, t_j) = |S_i \cap S_j|$. Some applications do not require $Match$ to compute the cardinality of $S_i \cap S_j$, but only need to know whether this intersection is empty or not. For those applications we use $Match : T \times T \rightarrow \{0, 1\}$.

The function $Match$ must fulfill the following properties:

1. *Correctness:* In the absence of adversaries the output is correct.
2. *Unforgeability:* False positives are impossible, that is an adversary is unable to convince a reader that tags match on more attributes than they actually are.
3. *Unlinkability:* Neither a reader, nor an external adversary is able to decide, whether in two protocol runs the same tags participated twice or not.
4. *Confidentiality:* After a protocol run nobody can learn any of the attributes (corresponding keys) stored on a tag, unless possessing a valid key for an attribute. The amount of attributes stored on tags is computationally hard to derive from a protocol run, unless possessing all keys in the system.

The protocols presented in this paper do not protect against false negatives. Thus, they are useful for applications that do not require to prevent false negatives. To summarize, the system has the following functions:

1. $Setup(\lambda)$: is used to generate a private key or a public/private key pair for a reader (if specified by the protocol) based on the security parameter λ. It assigns a state S_i to all tags $t_i \in T$. The state includes the set of secret keys $k_{i1}, k_{i2}, ..., k_{im}$ assigned to the tag and the publicly known information (e.g. public keys of readers).
2. $Match(t_i, t_j)$: Is a protocol carried out by two tags t_i and t_j, and a reader R. The protocol is initiated by the reader. As a result of the protocol, the reader obtains the cardinality of the intersection of S_i and S_j.

2.1   Adversary Model

The security of our protocols relies on the secrecy of the keys stored on tags. We thus make the common assumption that those keys are stored in a secure way, and that computations involving those keys are implemented in a way that does not leak information about the keys (for example, through side channels). The adversary controls all the communication, pretends to be one of the valid tags, but does not perform relay attacks using a tag outside the proximity of the reader. A reader is assumed to behave according to the protocol. Thus, it is considered "honest but curious".

The type of an adversary A is specified by the actions he can perform. Let π be a protocol execution entity. The oracles below define the whole set of possible actions. An adversary gets an access to a subset if oracles depending on his type. Oracles distinguish between the left and the right message denoted as m_{left}, m_{right}. This notion is needed to distinguish communication with tag of the left and right side. The oracles are:

- $Launch(m_{\text{left}}, m_{\text{right}}) \rightarrow \pi, m$: when this oracle is called, the reader starts a new protocol execution π by sending out the message m. The whole execution of the protocol can then be performed using oracles $SendReader$ and $SendTag$. These two oracles can be used to simulate the $Execute$ oracle from the model defined by Juels and Weis [16]
- $SendReader(m_{\text{left}}, m_{\text{right}}, \pi) \rightarrow (m'_{\text{left}}, m'_{\text{right}})$: sends a message m to a reader from the left side (right side or both) in the context of protocol execution π. The output of the oracle is a response of the reader m' sent in any of the directions according to the description of the protocol.
- $SendTag(m, t_i) \rightarrow m'$: sends a message m to a tag t_i. The output of the oracle is a response of the tag m'.
- $Result(\pi) \rightarrow x$: outputs the result of function $Match$ after the protocol execution π.
- $Corrupt(t_i) \rightarrow s_i$: returns the internal state of the tag, allowing an adversary to learn all secret keys stored on this tag.

The model and the privacy game presented in this section are inspired by work of Juels and Weis [16], Vaudenay [19] and Hermans et al. [14]. Unfortunately, all these models were designed with the classes of protocols in mind that are different from our protocol. All the models consider the scenario of communication between a reader and a single tag. We therefore adopt the classification by Vaudenay and modify the Juels and Weis game for unlinkability to fit the needs of matching protocols.

The classification by Vaudenay is faceted in two dimensions. An attacker who does not have access to the *Result* oracle is called *NARROW*. An attacker who does is called *WIDE*. An attacker who cannot corrupt tags is called *WEAK*. An attacker who is not allowed to perform any protocol interactions after he corrupted one tag is called *FORWARD*. An attacker without any restrictions regarding corruption of tags is called *STRONG*.

2.2   Unforgeability

The goal of an adversary is to convince a reader that the number of matching attributes is larger than it actually is. We call a protocol *unforgeable* if it resists this attack. Let S be a system and A be an adversary.
Unforgeability is defined as the following game $\mathbf{Exp}_{S,A}^{forge}(\lambda)$:

Setup: $Setup(\lambda)$ is used to initialize all readers and tags.
Learning: The adversary may perform calls to the available oracles on the given set of tags T. The set of available oracles depends on the adversary type. The strongest adversary gets access to: *Launch, SendReader, SendTag, Corrupt*. Let the union of the sets of all corrupted tags be C_t.
Challenge:
1. The adversary chooses a tag t_i, to which he did not call a *Corrupt* oracle.
2. The tag t_i is removed from the set T. The challenger returns t_i to the adversary.
3. The adversary is not allowed to modify any of the messages sent to or from the tag t_i. The adversary is simulating a tag t_j on the other side.

Result: The experiment outputs true if the reader outputs a value lager than $|S_i \cap (S_j \cup C_t)|$.
   The advantage of adversary of winning the game is defined as:

$$Adv_{S,A}^{forge}(\lambda) = Pr[\mathbf{Exp}_{S,A}^{forge}(\lambda) = true]$$

We call the system unforgeable if a maximal advantage of all polynomial time adversaries is negligible in the security parameter λ. During the challenge phase an adversary can only passively eavesdrop messages exchanged between the challenge tag and a reader. The adversary has to simulate the other tag, which will be matched by the reader with the challenge tag.

The model above considers tag corruption by taking into account that the keys extracted from corrupted tags will trivially allow the adversary to increase the match count output. For the protocols presented in this paper only WEAK adversaries are considered for unforgeability, and hence $C_t = \emptyset$.

2.3 Unlinkability

The goal of the attacker A is to distinguish tags, thus breaking their unlinkability. In case an attacker is able to obtain the result of the protocol run, an attack on unlinkability becomes trivial as pointed out in [9]. It is sufficient to have one tag participate in two protocol runs with potentially different tags. By comparing the result (i.e. cardinality of the intersection) one can determine if that tag was matched against different tags or not. That implies that the *Result* oracle cannot be used by an attacker. The match protocol by its nature is giving away information about tags, namely the relationships between them. There are two approaches for designing the speed dating protocol to tackle this problem. One is to make sure that the protocol itself is not providing any evidence of the relationships between tags, except for the output of the reader. The other is to provide only a *Minimal* level of protection. In this minimal model an attacker is unable to recognize the same tag he was observing before, once he initiates a protocol with only this tag. To illustrate, assume an attacker was collecting interactions among tags on the speed dating party. After the party is over, he suddenly sees a person wearing an RFID tag from this party. An attacker triggers a protocol, having no other valid tag at hand. He should be unable to learn the identity of the tag even having all the old protocol run transcripts at hand.

Unlinkability of an attacker A in the system S is defined as the following game $\mathbf{Exp}_{S,A}^{link}(\lambda)$:

Setup: $Setup(1^\lambda)$ is used to initialize all readers and tags.
Learning: The adversary may perform calls to the available oracles on the given set of tags T. The set of available oracles depends on the adversary type: *Launch*, *SendReader*, *SendTag*, *Corrupt*.
Challenge:

1. The adversary chooses two tags t_i and t_j, to which he did not call a *Corrupt* oracle.
2. The challenger assigns $t_0^* = t_i$ and $t_1^* = t_j$. Both tags are removed from the set T.
3. Let $b \in_R \{0,1\}$. The challenger returns t_b^* to the adversary.
4. The adversary is allowed to perform calls to the oracles: *Launch*, *SendReader*, *SendTag*, having tag t_b^* on one of the sides and any of the tags from the set T on the other.
5. The adversary outputs a guess bit b'.

Result: The experiment outputs true if the adversary correctly outputs $b' = b$.

Minimal privacy is achieved if an attacker during challenge phase gets only one tag t_b^* to communicate with and he has to simulate a tag on the other side. This game modification is used only against a *WEAK* adversary, if the adversary has an access to the *Result* oracle. Otherwise an attacker could simulate all the tags he corrupted during the learning phase. Thus there would be no difference between two games, since an attacker could use all the broken tags to let them communicate with the challenge tag. This would allow an attacker to use the knowledge of topology of tag's relationships to win the game.

The advantage of adversary of winning the game is defined as:

$$Adv_{S,A}^{link}(\lambda) = |Pr[\mathbf{Exp}_{S,A}^{link}(\lambda) = true] - \frac{1}{2}|$$

We call the system unlinkable if the maximal advantage of all polynomial time adversaries is negligible in the security parameter λ.

2.4 Cryptographic Primitives

One of the important primitives used in speed-dating protocols is a pseudo-random function (PRF), which cannot efficiently be distinguished from a truly random function. In the game definition of a PRF, an adversary submits inputs to the PRF challenger. The challenger replies with either an output of the PRF, or an output of a truly random function. The adversary wins if he has a non-negligible advantage to distinguish these two possible outputs. Let a secure pseudo-random function be denoted as $Fun_k(\cdot)$, where k is a key of the PRF function.

Note that we can efficiently construct a PRF from a hash function through the Merkle-Damgård iteration [18] as described, for example, in [7, Sect. 6]. This approach is particularly interesting for speed-dating protocols, since two of the three versions are using hash function anyway. In a similar way, one can construct a PRF using keyed modes of lightweight sponge-based hash functions like Quark [2] to construct a PRF function. A crytographic hash function is denoted as $H(\cdot)$ further in the text.

It was proven by Bellare et al. [3,4] that any PRF is a secure message authentication code (MAC). This property is essential for our protocols. Let us introduce *secure MACs* in a form of brief game description, for details see [12]. During the MAC-unforgeability game, an adversary queries the challenger with distinct messages and obtains MACs for them. He can also submit several message-tag pairs to the verification oracle. An adversary wins if he succeeds with a non-negligible advantage in outputting a valid message-tag pair not previously requested from the challenger.

Both encryption schemes used in the speed-dating protocol are required to have the *IND-CPA* property. Let a symmetric encryption scheme be denoted as $symENC = (G', E', D')$ and an asymmetric encryption scheme as $pkENC = (G, E, D)$. Let us briefly sketch the game for this property. During the learning phase an adversary gets to query an encryption oracle, which answers an adversary with ciphertexts of received plaintext messages. During the challenge phase the adversary submits several pairs of distinct non-repeating messages (m_0, m_1). Depending on the initial decision, the challenger answers with a cihpertext of one of the messages, either m_0 or m_1. The adversary succeeds if he has a non-negligible advantage to distinguish these two possible outputs.

3   One-Key Symmetric Speed Dating

The protocol presented in this section prevents false positives and provides minimal privacy. False positives occur when a tag does not possess any attribute matching with attributes on the other tag. And yet it manages to make a *Match* function output that tags have a match. Minimal privacy is the privacy protection achieved against an adversary that can read output of the protocol runs and thus build a topology of tag's relationships. The protocol only requires a few calls to a (lightweight) hash functions.

3.1   Single Attribute per Tag

We start with the setting that each user has a single attribute. Assume tags named (for convenience) by their owners, namely Alice and Bob. Tags Alice and Bob possess respectively keys $k_A, k_B \in K$. These keys are representing attributes of tags. A reader scans both tags to figure out whether their attributes match or not. Figure 1 depicts the protocol.

The general idea of the protocol is the following:

1. *Commit phase.* Tags generate random numbers and exchange commitments with each other. These commitments later on help a reader to identify replies of tags and prevent cheating. The exchange is happening with the help of the reader.
2. *Check phase.* Tags create pseudo-random values from the challenges by feeding them to a PRF function *Fun*. These values are exchanged with the help of a reader. Tags perform a check of the values generated by the other tag using their secret keys. After this phase tags know whether they have an equal key or not.

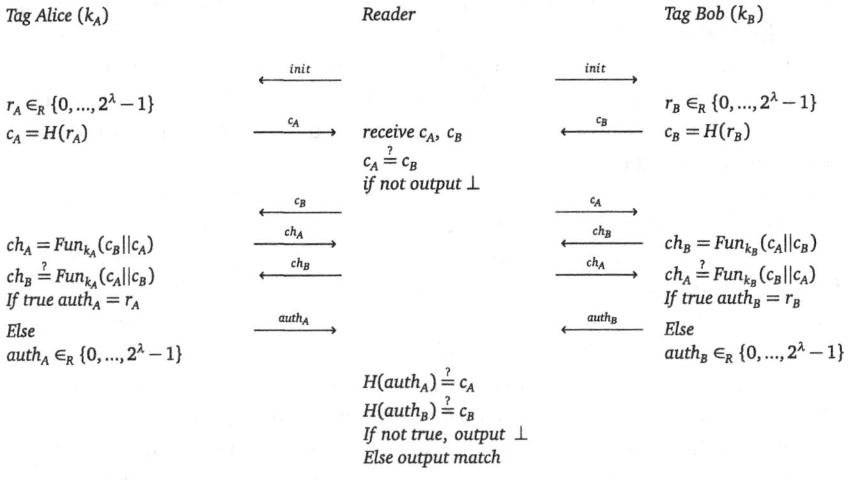

Tag Alice (k_A)		Reader		Tag Bob (k_B)

$\xleftarrow{\quad init \quad}$ $\qquad\qquad$ $\xrightarrow{\quad init \quad}$

$r_A \in_R \{0, ..., 2^\lambda - 1\}$ $\qquad\qquad\qquad\qquad\qquad\qquad$ $r_B \in_R \{0, ..., 2^\lambda - 1\}$

$c_A = H(r_A)$ $\quad\xrightarrow{\;c_A\;}$ receive c_A, c_B $\quad\xleftarrow{\;c_B\;}$ $c_B = H(r_B)$

$c_A \stackrel{?}{=} c_B$

if not output $\perp$

$\xleftarrow{\;c_B\;}$ $\qquad\qquad$ $\xrightarrow{\;c_A\;}$

$ch_A = Fun_{k_A}(c_B || c_A)$ $\quad\xrightarrow{\;ch_A\;}$ $\qquad\qquad$ $\xrightarrow{\;ch_B\;}$ $ch_B = Fun_{k_B}(c_A || c_B)$

$ch_B \stackrel{?}{=} Fun_{k_A}(c_A || c_B)$ $\quad\xleftarrow{\;ch_B\;}$ $\qquad\qquad$ $\xleftarrow{\;ch_A\;}$ $ch_A \stackrel{?}{=} Fun_{k_B}(c_B || c_A)$

If true $auth_A = r_A$ $\qquad\qquad\qquad\qquad\qquad\qquad$ If true $auth_B = r_B$

Else $\quad\xrightarrow{\;auth_A\;}$ $\qquad\qquad$ $\xleftarrow{\;auth_B\;}$ Else

$auth_A \in_R \{0, ..., 2^\lambda - 1\}$ $\qquad\qquad\qquad\qquad\qquad$ $auth_B \in_R \{0, ..., 2^\lambda - 1\}$

$H(auth_A) \stackrel{?}{=} c_A$

$H(auth_B) \stackrel{?}{=} c_B$

If not true, output $\perp$

Else output match

Fig. 1. One-key symmetric speed dating protocol

3. *Match phase.* If there is a match, tags open their commitments towards the reader, which determines the result of the protocol.

Commit phase

1. The tags generate random values and calculate commitments to these values. Alice generates: $r_A \in_R \{0, ..., 2^\lambda - 1\}$, $c_A = H(r_A)$. Bob generates: $r_B \in_R \{0, ..., 2^\lambda - 1\}$, $c_B = H(r_B)$.
2. The tags send the commitments c_A, c_B to a reader.
3. The reader checks if $c_A = c_B$. If so, the protocol run is terminated with output $\bot$. The reader forwards c_B to Alice and c_A to Bob.
4. Each tag concatenates the commitments and puts the value it generated on the last position. Alice, for example, obtains $c_B||c_A$.
5. Each tag computes the PRF function *Fun* using their group keys and send it to the reader. Alice computes: $ch_A = Fun_{k_A}(c_B||c_A)$. Bob computes: $ch_B = Fun_{k_B}(c_A||c_B)$.
6. The reader forwards ch_A to Bob, ch_B to Alice.

Check phase

1. Each tag checks the received commit value. Alice checks $ch_B \stackrel{?}{=} Fun_{k_A}(c_A||c_B)$. Bob checks $ch_A \stackrel{?}{=} Fun_{k_B}(c_B||c_A)$.
2. If the equality holds, Alice computes: $auth_A = r_A$. Else, she sends the response with $auth_A$ filled with a random value. Similarly, Bob computes: $auth_B = r_B$ if equality holds. Else, he sends the response with $auth_B$ filled with a random value.
3. The tags send $auth_A$ and $auth_B$ to the reader.

Match phase

1. The reader checks that $H(auth_A) \stackrel{?}{=} c_A$ and $H(auth_B) \stackrel{?}{=} c_B$. If any of these two values are false, the reader outputs $\bot$, otherwise it outputs a match.

Theorem 1. *If Fun is a PRF, then $Adv_{S,A}^{forge}(\lambda)$ of a WEAK adversary, that runs in polynomial time, to win the unforgeability game is negligible in the random oracle model.*

Proof. Since the protocol is symmetrical, we consider the protocol from the perspective of tag Alice without loss of generality. Since any PRF is a secure MAC [3,4], we can consider *Fun* to be a secure MAC function. Assume an adversary A can break the protocol unforgeability. We show that there exists an adversary A', that can then win the MAC unforgeability game using adversary A as an oracle.

The hash function is modeled as a random oracle RO. The adversary A' is interacting with a MAC game challenger possessing a key k_{ch}. Adversary A' is simulating the unforgeability game for an adversary A by answering all requests an adversary A makes to oracles with a small exception. One particular tag t_i (or more) however is simulated with a help of the MAC challenger. This tag possesses a key k_{ch}. Let us call the corresponding attribute a_{ch}. This tags is simulated to A by A' in the following way:

1. First *SendTag*: A' outputs $c_A = RO(r_A)$ according to the protocol.
2. Second *SendTag*: A' provides $c_B||c_A$ as an input to the MAC challenger, and returns it's output as ch_A.
3. Third *SendTag*: A' validates the input value ch_b. If ch_b was generated by the MAC challenger, then A' knows the values should match (this can be double-checked with the help of the MAC verification oracle). Otherwise A' directly knows what the result should be, as he is simulating the rest of the tags in the system. A' returns an output, as specified by the protocol.

During the learning phase of the adversary A, A' gets to see different tuples of messages and corresponding tags: $m = (c_A||c_B), t = MAC_{k_i}(c_A||c_B)$, MAC value generated by a challenger. Since r_A and hence c_A is selected randomly, there will be no repeating values with overwhelming probability. Additionally, since H is a cryptographic hash function, A cannot win the unforgeability game by finding preimages of commitments c_A with overwhelming probability.

Assume A selects a tag with key k_{ch} as challenge tag. Assume the challenge tag is Bob and the adversary takes the role of Alice. Note that communication between the reader and the challenge tag is performed directly by the challenger. If A wins the unforgeability game, it has to produce a valid ch_A (otherwise r_B will not be sent to the reader and hence validation will fail). This ch_A will be the MAC of an input $c_A||c_B$ that was not used previously in the game, since c_B is fresh. Hence, ch_A can be forwarded to the MAC challenger to win the MAC unforgeability game.

The probability that the adversary selects the tag t_i is at least $\frac{1}{n}$. If the non-negligible advantage of A to win the game is ϵ, and the cardinality of the set of tags is n, then the advantage of A' is $\geq \frac{\epsilon}{n}$. This value is non-negligible, since n is polynomially bounded in a security parameter λ (see Sect. 2).

Theorem 2. *If Fun is a PRF, then $Adv_{S,A}^{link}(\lambda)$ of a WEAK adversary, that runs in polynomial time, to win the minimal unlinkability game is negligible in the random oracle model.*

Proof. Since the protocol is symmetrical, we consider the protocol from the perspective of tag Alice without loss of generality. We are going to show that an attacker is unable to distinguish any of the challenge tags from a simulator that is returning random values, and, thus, is unable to distinguish challenge tags themselves.

The hash function is modeled as a random oracle RO. We now simulate the *SendTag* oracle as follows to an adversary, explaining each step of the protocol:

1. A tag generates fresh pseudo-random values r_A and returns $RO(r_A)$.
2. Upon receiving c_B, the simulated tag returns a random value as ch_A.

3. Upon receiving ch_B, the simulated tag outputs a random value. Since the adversary is playing the minimal game, there is no other valid tag to create the proper ch_B value. Next, an attacker cannot forge a value output by Fun, as proven by Theorem 1. Thus, ch_B can never be accepted as valid.

The above simulated tag is indistinguishable from a real tag. First, the random ch_A is indistinguishable from $Fun_{k_A}(c_A \| c_B)$ since Fun is a PRF, r_A is selected randomly and c_A is never repeated as an output of RO. Second, when replying to ch_B we can rely on the soundness of the protocol, as proven by Theorem 1. This ensures that it is impossible for an adversary to forge ch_B. So either it was sent by a tag (and hence a match will be found) or it was forged and should be rejected by the tag. Finally, since the game is minimal, an attacker does not have any possibility to distinguish between the real tag and the simulator by matching them with other tags and comparing the output.

Assume the challenge bit $b = 0$. Tag t_0 is indistinguishable from a simulated tag. The same argument applies to challenge bit $b = 1$. Hence, an attacker cannot distinguish between two tags.

4   Match Protocol for Asymmetric Encryption

The protocols presented in this section prevent false positives and provide a higher privacy level under the following requirement. An adversary must be unable to obtain the output of the protocol runs and, thus, build a topology of tag's relationships. The cost of the higher privacy level is the usage of public-key encryption.

4.1   One-Key Asymmetric Speed Dating Protocol

The advantage of the protocol in this section is that it protects confidentiality of the exchanged messages. Thanks to that, when an adversary corrupts tags and obtains their secret keys, it will not help him to succeed in identifying tags. This also implies that any external observer is unable to learn the result of the protocol from the exchanged messages. Also, it is easily expandable to handle the case of tags storing multiple attributes.

As in the previous section, assume each user can possess a single attribute. Tag Alice and Bob posses respectively group keys k_A, $k_B \in K$. In the protocol, an asymmetric encryption system $pkENC$ is used. A reader holds a public-private key pair (pk, sk), all tags are supplied with the public key pk of a reader.

This version of the protocol can be obtained from the symmetric one (Sect. 3) in two steps. The first step is encrypting messages sent between a reader and each tag. To ensure encryptions differ, tags append the random number they generate to the Fun value before encrypting. The second is to provide the same inputs to the Fun function on both tags, since there is no need to produce different outputs of the PRF function. The reason is that messages appended with unique randomness are sent encrypted. This way the protocol is protected

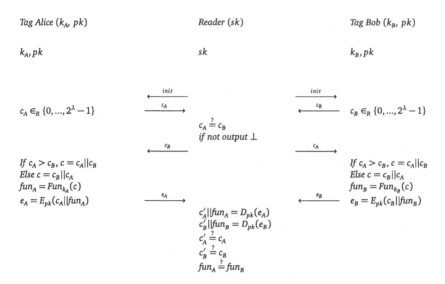

Fig. 2. One-key asymmetric speed dating protocol

from trivial replay attacks, and the need for commitments c_A, c_B and their openings is eliminated. Figure 2 illustrates the protocol.

Speed dating protocol:

1. Tags generate random values and send c_A, c_B to the reader. Alice generates: $c_A \in_R \{0, ..., 2^\lambda - 1\}$. Bob generates: $c_B \in_R \{0, ..., 2^\lambda - 1\}$
2. Reader checks if $c_A = c_B$, then protocol run is terminated with output $\perp$. Otherwise it exchanges random numbers between tags.
3. Tags sort random numbers. Assume, that $c_A > c_B$. Alice learns she has to put c_A in the beginning. Bob learns he has to append c_B to the end.
4. Tags compute *Fun* values using their group keys. Alice computes: $fun_A = Fun_{k_A}(c_A||c_B)$. Bob computes: $fun_B = Fun_{k_B}(c_A||c_B)$
5. Tags send *Fun* values $E_{pk}(c_A||fun_A)$ and $E_{pk}(c_B||fun_B)$ over secure channel.
6. Reader decrypts received values using his secret key sk.
7. Reader checks if there are appended c_A and c_B in the decrypted messages.
8. Reader checks if $fun_A \stackrel{?}{=} fun_B$. If true reader outputs *Match*. Otherwise it outputs $\perp$.

Theorem 3. *If Fun is a PRF, then $Adv_{S,A}^{forge}(\lambda)$ of a WEAK adversary, that runs in polynomial time, to win the unforgeability game is negligible in the random oracle model.*

The proof is omitted because of space limitations, and as it is very similar to the proof of the Theorem 1.

Theorem 4. *If the encryption scheme pkENC is IND-CPA secure, then $Adv_{S,A}^{link}(\lambda)$ of a (non-minimal) NARROW-STRONG adversary, that runs in polynomial time, to win the unlinkability game is negligible in the random oracle model.*

Proof. Since the protocol is symmetrical, we consider the protocol from perspective of tag Alice without loss of generality. The goal of the proof is to show that if an adversary A can break unlinkability of the protocol, the adversary A' can win IND-CPA game. The adversary A' interacts with the IND-CPA game challenger, possessing a key pair (pk, sk). The adversary A' simulates the unlinkability game for an adversary A by answering all requests A makes to oracles. The reader key pair in the simulation is the key pair of the IND-CPA game challenger.

During the learning phase A' queries the encryption oracle to obtain $E_{pk}(fun_A)$, which he then forwards to A. During the challenge phase A' creates messages for both challenge tags fun_{A0} and fun_{A1}. A' then submits both messages to the IND-CPA challenger. The received ciphertext $E_{pk}(fun_{Ab})$ is forwarded to A. If A can break unlinkability of the protocol, A' will be able to distinguish which message was encrypted.

A NARROW-STRONG adversary cannot get the result of the protocol run, but he can corrupt tags. Corrupting tags will provide an adversary with secret keys of tags. However, it does not help him in distinguishing tags and their output. This holds for the simple reason, all the information related to tags is transferred encrypted using the asymmetric IND-CPA encryption scheme *Enc*. This implies, encrypted messages do not provide an adversary any useful information.

Theorem 5. *If Fun is a PRF, then $Adv_{S,A}^{link}(\lambda)$ of a polynomial-time adversary that possesses the private key of a valid reader to win the minimal unlinkability game is negligible in the random oracle model.*

The proof is omitted because of space limitations, and as it is very similar to the proof of Theorem 2.

4.2   Many-Keys Asymmetric Speed Dating Protocol

Assume each user can possess at most m attributes. Tag Alice and Bob posses respectively group keys $s_A = \{k_A[i] \in K \cup \{\bot\}|i \in \{1, \ldots, m\}\}$, $s_B = \{k_B[i] \in K|i \in \{1, \ldots, m\}\}$. All tags are supplied with the public key pk and all readers possess the private key sk.

This protocol can be obtained from the one-key version by changing from using only asymmetric encryption scheme to using a hybrid one. An asymmetric encryption is used to securely transfer key material. A hash function is applied to it as a key derivation function. The result is used as a key for a semantically secure encryption system.

The next change is due to the necessity to hide the amount of attributes a tag has. Tags are generating $f_A[i]$ and $f_B[i]$ values using their keys, $i \in \{1, \ldots, m\}$. Whenever a tag has less then m attributes, the f values are filled with randomness. Tags perform random permutations on f values before they are sent to a reader. This is done in order to conceal the order of attributes, otherwise this could expose sensitive information about tags to the reader.

Upon obtaining and decrypting all of the $f_A[i]$ and $f_B[i]$ values from two tags, a reader starts by sorting both sets descending. After that a reader can easily

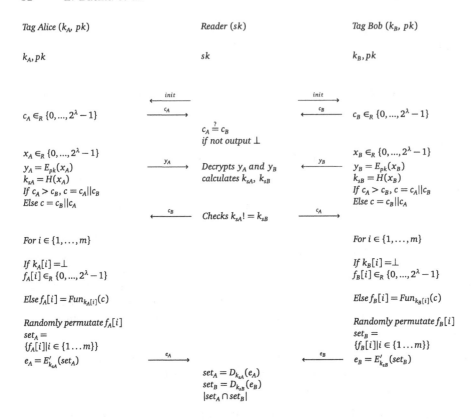

Fig. 3. Many-keys asymmetric speed dating protocol

compute an intersection of two sets Int and outputs its cardinality $|Int|$. Figure 3 depicts the protocol.

Theorem 6. *If Fun is a PRF and H is a cryptographic hash function, then $Adv_{S,A}^{forge}(\lambda)$ of a WEAK adversary, that runs in polynomial time, to win the unforgeability game is negligible in the random oracle model.*

The proof is omitted because of space limitations as it is very similar to the proof of Theorem 1.

Theorem 7. *If the encryption schemes pkENC and symENC used are IND-CPA secure, and H is a cryptographic hash function, then $Adv_{S,A}^{link}(\lambda)$ of a NARROW-STRONG adversary, that runs in polynomial time, to win the unlinkability game is negligible in the random oracle model.*

The proof is omitted because of space limitations.

Theorem 8. *If Fun is a PRF, then $Adv_{S,A}^{link}(\lambda)$ of a polynomial-time adversary that possesses the private key of a valid reader to win the minimal unlinkability game is negligible in the random oracle model.*

The proof is omitted because of space limitations.

5 Related Work

In 2012, Elkhiyaoui, Blass, and Molva presented a protocol that allows an RFID reader to determine whether two tags store some attributes that jointly fulfill a boolean constraint, without violating the privacy of the tags [9]. They motivate their protocol by considering the transportation of chemicals where safety regulations prohibit the joint transportation of chemicals that might react with each other. By equipping each container with a tag and scanning for certain boolean constraint describing reactive combinations the reader can check if the transportation is safe. Elkhiyaoui *et al.* also focus extensively on privacy of their protocol, although this is problematic for their specific application: legal regulations for the transport of dangerous goods require a clear labeling which voids any of the privacy a tag might offer [10].

The speed-dating protocols described in this paper achieve the same goal with a different trade-offs between privacy and efficiency. Tags in our protocol are more costly, since they require to be able to perform calculations. The cost of calculations on tags is fairly low when symmetric encryption is used. Asymmetric encryption on tags is more expensive, but feasible to be implemented in both secure and efficient way, as numerous studies demonstrate in theory and practice [5,11,13,17]. As observed by other researches, asymmetric primitives will provide more secure systems [8,19]. Currently, many studies proposed protocols for which asymmetric encryption schemes are essential, [1,6,8] to mention a few. One of these protocols named "Yoking-Proofs" [15] is similar to speed-dating in the sense that it also considers two simultaneously scanned tags. What is different is the goal of the protocol: they provide a prove of the fact that two particular tags have been scanned simultaneously.

The advantage of using more costly tags is that the infrastructure of readers for our speed-dating protocols is more flexible and robust, because readers do not have to be connected to a central database. Additionally, unlike in the T-Match protocol presented in [9], readers do not need to perform any homomorphic encryption operations, or expensive multi-party computations.

The protocol described in Sect. 4.2 furthermore extends the protocol model to allow multiple attributes per tag. This makes speed-dating a suitable solution for a broader set of applications.

6 Conclusion

Three protocols to privately match attributes on RFID tags were presented in this paper. None of them requires a centralized system with readers constantly connected to a central database. Neither do readers require any knowledge about attributes stored on tags. This makes the system flexible and easy to use for several parties. The first protocol protects privacy of users by only utilizing symmetric encryption, which makes it extremely lightweight. This comes at a cost of a slightly lower protection level, than the one provided by the other two protocols. Just one step of asymmetric encryption that is required by both of them, quite noticeably changes anonymity protection.

There is a restriction in all of the presented protocols. All possible applications are limited to the ones, which are sensitive to false positives. That is, the protocol protects against matching tags with no matching attributes. These applications should not be sensitive to false negatives. The interesting future work is to see how protocol can be improved to add detection of false negatives.

Acknowledgements. We would like to express our very great appreciation to Andreas Hülsing for his valuable support on this project. His constructive suggestions and willingness to spend his time so generously is very much appreciated. We would also like to thank Ari Juels for very fruitful discussions.

References

1. Alpár, G., Batina, L., Lueks, W.: Designated attribute-based proofs for RFID applications. In: Hoepman, J.-H., Verbauwhede, I. (eds.) RFIDSec 2012. LNCS, vol. 7739, pp. 59–75. Springer, Heidelberg (2013)
2. Aumasson, J.-P., Henzen, L., Meier, W., Naya-Plasencia, M.: Quark: a lightweight hash. J. Cryptology **26**(2), 313–339 (2013)
3. Bellare, M., Goldreich, O., Mityagin, A.: The power of verification queries in message authentication and authenticated encryption. Cryptology ePrint Archive, Report 2004/309 (2004). http://eprint.iacr.org/2004/309/
4. Bellare, M., Kilian, J., Rogaway, P.: The security of the cipher block chaining message authentication code. J. Comput. Syst. Sci. **61**(3), 362–399 (2000)
5. Braun, M., Hess, E., Meyer, B.: Using elliptic curves on RFID tags. IJCSNS Int. J. Comput. Sci. Netw. Secur. **8**(2), 1–9 (2008)
6. Bringer, J., Chabanne, H., Icart, T.: Cryptanalysis of EC-RAC, a RFID identification protocol. In: Franklin, M.K., Hui, L.C.K., Wong, D.S. (eds.) CANS 2008. LNCS, vol. 5339, pp. 149–161. Springer, Heidelberg (2008)
7. Buchmann, J., Dahmen, E., Hülsing, A.: XMSS - a practical forward secure signature scheme based on minimal security assumptions. In: Yang, B.-Y. (ed.) PQCrypto 2011. LNCS, vol. 7071, pp. 117–129. Springer, Heidelberg (2011)
8. van Deursen, T., Radomirović, S.: Insider attacks and privacy of RFID protocols. In: Petkova-Nikova, S., Pashalidis, A., Pernul, G. (eds.) EuroPKI 2011. LNCS, vol. 7163, pp. 91–105. Springer, Heidelberg (2012)
9. Elkhiyaoui, K., Blass, E.-O., Molva, R.: T-MATCH: privacy-preserving item matching for storage-only RFID tags. In: Hoepman, J.-H., Verbauwhede, I. (eds.) RFIDSec 2012. LNCS, vol. 7739, pp. 76–95. Springer, Heidelberg (2013)
10. Council of the European Union European Parliament. Regulation (EC) No 1272/2008 of the European Parliament and of the Council of 16 December 2008 on classification, labelling and packaging of substances and mixtures, amending and repealing Directives 67/548/EEC and 1999/45/EC, and amending Regulation (EC) No 1907/2006 (2008). http://new.eur-lex.europa.eu/legal-content/EN/TXT/PDF/?uri=CELEX:32008R1272&rid=3
11. Fürbass, F., Wolkerstorfer, J.: ECC processor with low die size for RFID applications. In: IEEE International Symposium on Circuits and Systems, ISCAS 2007, pp. 1835–1838 (2007)
12. Goldwasser, S., Bellare, M.: Lecture notes on cryptography (2008). http://cseweb.ucsd.edu/users/mihir/papers/gb.pdf

13. Hein, D., Wolkerstorfer, J., Felber, N.: ECC is ready for RFID – a proof in silicon. In: Avanzi, R.M., Keliher, L., Sica, F. (eds.) SAC 2008. LNCS, vol. 5381, pp. 401–413. Springer, Heidelberg (2009)
14. Hermans, J., Pashalidis, A., Vercauteren, F., Preneel, B.: A new RFID privacy model. In: Atluri, V., Diaz, C. (eds.) ESORICS 2011. LNCS, vol. 6879, pp. 568–587. Springer, Heidelberg (2011)
15. Juels, A.: "yoking-proofs" for RFID tags. In: Proceedings of the Second IEEE Annual Conference on Pervasive Computing and Communications Workshops 2004, pp. 138–143 (2004)
16. Juels, A., Weis, S.A.: Defining strong privacy for RFID. In: Fifth Annual IEEE International Conference on Pervasive Computing and Communications Workshops, PerCom Workshops '07, pp. 342–347 (2007). http://www.emc.com/ emc-plus/rsa-labs/staff/bios/ajuels/publications/rfid_privacy/rfidprivacy.pdf
17. Lee, Y.K., Sakiyama, K., Batina, L., Verbauwhede, I.: Elliptic-curve-based security processor for RFID. IEEE Trans. Comput. 57(11), 1514–1527 (2008)
18. Merkle, R.C.: One way hash functions and DES. In: Brassard, G. (ed.) CRYPTO 1989. LNCS, vol. 435, pp. 428–446. Springer, Heidelberg (1990)
19. Vaudenay, S.: On privacy models for RFID. In: Kurosawa, K. (ed.) ASIACRYPT 2007. LNCS, vol. 4833, pp. 68–87. Springer, Heidelberg (2007)

Massively Parallel Identification
of Privacy-Preserving Vehicle RFID Tags

Rui Figueiredo, André Zúquete$^{(\boxtimes)}$, and Tomás Oliveira e Silva

DETI/IEETA/Univ. de Aveiro, Campus Univ. de Santiago,
3810-193 Aveiro, Portugal
andre.zuquete@ua.pt

Abstract. This article proposes a massively parallel identification sche-me of vehicle RFID tags. These tags use a pseudo-random identifier, which is the output of a hash function fed by a fixed secret key that uniquely identifies the tag and by two random challenges that change on each tag activation. The use of random challenges makes it extremely difficult for someone not knowing the secret key of a tag to track its multiple activations. For someone knowing all valid keys, finding out the key that generated a specific tag response requires a time-consuming exhaustive search, if the number of valid keys is large. This can be performed in a very efficient way on a general purpose graphics processing unit. Our simulations show that on a very demanding scenario a single Tesla S1070 system can identify in near real-time the tags generated by 100 single-lane highway RFID readers.

1 Introduction

Traditional authentication protocols involve the exchange of two elements: (i) an identity claimed by the entity being authenticated and (ii) a proof that the claim is true. Thus, in authentication scenarios where authentication protocols are subject to eavesdropping, consecutive authentications using the same identity claim potentiate unwanted tracking activities, therefore undermining the privacy of the entity being authenticated. Among the many solutions that could be considered to tackle this problem, one of them consists on the suppression of the identity claim. However, this forces the authenticator to check whether or not the identity proof is correct for one (and only one) of the identities it knows about, which naturally involves an exhaustive search.

This paper addresses this topic in the context of RFID-based identification and GPU-based massively parallel computation. Assuming that we could have a very large population of RFID tags subject to authentication, and that those tags would never disclose directly their identity, could we identify (and authenticate) them from variable identity proofs in small enough time delays with a single, mid-range GPU device?

For addressing a demanding, though realistic and privacy-demanding sce-nario, we considered the RFID identification of vehicles, which is used nowadays

© Springer International Publishing Switzerland 2014
N. Saxena and A.-R. Sadeghi (Eds.): RFIDSec 2014, LNCS 8651, pp. 36–53, 2014.
DOI: 10.1007/978-3-319-13066-8_3

in many countries for highway toll collection or parking payments. For the vehicle population we considered a rough estimate of the number of highway vehicles in the United States (250 million). For the massively parallel identity search we used a slightly outdated device: an NVidia Tesla S1070[1] system.

1.1 RFID-Based Identification

An RFID tag [1] is a device that is activated by a nearby contact-less reader by means of radio signals. It has at least one identifier that is conveyed to the reader at the appropriate time. RFID tags can have different identifiers for different communication levels, e.g., one for link-level communications and another one for application-level communications.

Many RFID tags have a single, constant, unique link-level identifier. When a tag of this kind is attached to some item one can link the RFID identifier to that item. On the other hand, unauthorized readers that could have access to these identifiers could perform clandestine, passive tracking and inventorying actions [2]. Notably, some tags, such as the ones used in electronic passports, use random link-level identifiers in order to prevent passports and their owners from being tracked just by gathering that identifier [3, §A1.16]. In this case, the RFID link-level identifier is used only for initiating an application-level dialog with the tag, and not for direct identification of the passport owner.

This article assumes that an RFID tag can be identified by means of a deterministic, pseudo-random identifier (PRId). As far as the authors are aware, such identifiers do not exist in real implementations but were already discussed in the literature (cf. Sect. 2).

In our work the PRId is deterministically generated from a secret key (stored in the tag) combined with random values (challenges or nonces), and stays constant while the tag is active. The identifier is generated after the first contact by a reader upon entering its energy field. For an external observer the tag identifier will look as a purely random number, thus not conveying any useful information regarding the object it is attached to. Someone possessing the key of the tag (and the challenges) can check whether or not the computed PRId is the correct one (i.e. was generated with that key).

1.2 Untraceable Vehicle Identification

RFID tags are being progressively used to identify many types of objects, such as vehicles on highways. Using an RFID tag with a constant identifier for each vehicles creates a security problem, as it enables, for example, tracking vehicle movements by unauthorized entities and execution of arbitrary actions initiated by the proximity of a particular vehicle (e.g., triggering a bomb explosion).

On the other hand, the exploitation of protocols enabling the authentication of authorized readers, in order to prevent unauthorized tracking initiatives,

---

[1] Gracefully provided by NVidia, under its Academic Partnership Program.

increases the deployment cost and security risk of legitimate vehicle identification infrastructures. Not surprisingly, the EN 15509 standard [4], that regulates the utilization of vehicle RFID tags (called On-Board Units, OBUs) in electronic toll collection systems [5], considers that security level 1, the one that requires authentication of the reader (called a Road Side Unit, RSU), is optional. We will come back to this topic latter on, in Sect. 3.2.

Therefore, we considered another type of identification strategy for non-traceable OBU tags, namely one using a pseudo-random generation process. The identifier is produced, using a cryptographic one-way function, from a unique OBU secret key and random challenges. Someone knowing the challenges and the secret keys of all OBU tags can also generate the same identifier, thus is able to match the identifier with a key in a reasonably short time using massively parallel computation. On the other hand, with a large enough key space, it should be unfeasible for everybody else to find the key used by an OBU. Consequently, unauthorized OBU reader could not obtain the identity of each and every OBU.

1.3 Contribution

This article presents a massively parallel approach to identify RFID tags capable of generating a cryptographically-verifiable PRId. Given a pair of challenges used to compute an identifier, and a large set of known tag keys, we want to find the key used to compute the identifier presented by a tag as fast as possible. This enables us to link in near real-time a PRId, through a key, to some entity (account, person, material object, etc.):

$$\textbf{pseudo-random}\atop\textbf{OBU identifier} \xrightarrow[\text{parallel search}]{\text{exhaustive}} \textbf{key} \xrightarrow[\text{lookup}]{\text{list}} \textbf{OBU account}$$

For the computation of each PRId we used 128-bit keys, two 64-bit challenges, one generated by the RSU and the other by the tag, and the MD5 digest function [6]. By using 128-bit keys we discourage any attempt to perform a brute-force attack, i.e., an exhaustive key search considering all possible key values. By using two 64-bit random challenges we reduce to nearly zero the probability of getting twice the same identifier out of a specific tag, even in the presence of a rogue RSU that always generates the same challenge. Finally, we used a digest function, namely MD5, because it is a fast non-invertible function.

MD5 has known security problems with collisions [7–9], but in our case that is not an issue. These problems could in theory enable an attacker to run personification attacks, but in practice it cannot be done because 128 bits (50 %) of the hashed content (the key) is unknown to the attacker, and another 64 bits (25 %) is chosen by the interlocutor (the RFID reader), and not by the attacker. We will come back to this topic in Sect. 3.3.

Irrespective of the hash function used, collisions are potentially problematic for another reason, viz., the possibility of having a PRId that is not unique, i.e., that could have been generated by more than one valid key for the same random challenges. In our case the probability of that happening is very small; for 2^{32} valid keys it should be about 2^{-96}.

As a side-effect, our cryptographically-based pseudo-random identifier generation paradigm prevents an OBU from being cloned, as long as we are able to keep the secrecy of the key deployed in each OBU. Nevertheless, the compromise of an OBU's key is not a problem for all other OBU tags, since they all have different and (preferably) random keys. This side effect was already identified in previous works (e.g. [10]).

Our computational solution was designed for a parallel processing device, namely an NVidia Tesla S1070 system. This device has 4 graphics processing units capable of doing general-purpose computations (GPGPUs), with 240 cores and 4 GiB of memory each. Although more recent and faster GPGPUs are now available, the 16 GiB of memory at our disposal on the S1070 system allowed us to perform experiments with up to one billion (10^9) valid keys.

We developed and optimized a program capable of performing key searches given tag activation data. We performed experiments with large vehicle populations suitable to be tracked centrally by a unique entity. According to a report from the United States Bureau of Transportation Statistics [11], there were about 254 million highway vehicles in the United States in 2009. Consequently, our experiments used mainly 100 and 250 million valid keys. A scalability experiment with one billion keys was also performed. Although it may be argued that these numbers are too large (for example, why would the car tag systems in California and Florida be compatible?), by demonstrating that key searches of this magnitude are feasible with slightly outdated computing resources makes their deployment with a smaller number of valid keys more justifiable.

2 Related Work

S. Weis *et al.* [12] were the first to propose a mechanism for randomizing a tag identifier to avoid its traceability. They proposed a computation of the identifier from a secret value and a random nonce generated by the tag. Both the nonce and the derived identifier are conveyed to the reader, which must then search among all known tag keys to find a match. In our work we introduce another random value, generated by the reader, and we evaluate the search cost in a massively parallel computing device. In [12] the authors claim that (sic) "*this mode is feasible for owners of a relatively small number of tags*"; other authors follow this line of thinking, namely [13] states that (sic) "*this protocol can be extremely inefficient when the number of possible IDs [...] is large*". With our work we show that it is both feasible and efficient for a not so small (hundreds of millions) population of vehicles' tags, held by a single toll collection company.

This exact exhaustive search, that we demonstrate being feasible even for demanding scenarios, was considered too demanding by several other authors, who developed alternative approaches.

M. Ohkubo *et al.* [14], G. Avoine and P. Oechslin [15], T. Dimitriou [10] and D. Henrici and P. Muller [16] developed alternative approaches where the tag key changes each time it is used to produce an identifier. The new key is (i) an hash of the former [14,15], (ii) a successor of the former, computed in some suitable and secure way [10], or (iii) triggered hash chains [16], further enhanced in [17]. However, these approaches raise critical synchronization issues between tags and identification applications and often require the authentication of readers to avoid unwanted key updates in tags.

D. Molnar and D. Wagner [18], D. Molnar *et al.* [19] and T. Dimitriou [20] proposed the use of a tree search structure where each branch has a particular key. A small set of branch keys is uploaded to each tag and they use their branch keys to transform two concatenated random nonces, one generated by the tag and the other by the reader. The identification application uses only the keys on each tree level and on a particular tree branch to identify a tag (with a unique sequence of branch keys). This proposal may in theory speed-up the identification of tags but increases the computation within tags (requires many key encryptions) and increases the length of the tag replies. Furthermore, it complicates the utilization of tags with random keys, as they must be carefully initiated, one by one, with a unique set of branching keys. Our approach goes in the opposite direction, as we rely on tags with randomly created keys and on heavy computational power of the identification application in order to keep a reduced computing capability on tags and small message contents.

The interested reader can find many other proposals for protecting the privacy of tags (see, for instance, the reviews by A. Juels [2], by M. Lehtonen *et al.* [21] or by M. Langheinrich [22]). We found no evidence of works exploring massively parallel computation for finding the key of a tag among a large set of known keys. Furthermore, many protocols assume that the tag "travels" along many ownership domains (i.e., identifies an object that may have many owners during its lifetime), something that raises security issues related with forward untraceability [23]. We do not have this problem, since we assume that vehicles' identification tags and the related key validators are constant over time.

3   Tag Identification Protocol

The tag identification protocol runs conceptually as follows (see Fig. 1). First, both the tag and the reader generate random challenges, C_T and C_R, respectively. The reader communicates its challenge to the tag, which uses both challenges and its key K_T to compute an identifier with the MD5 message digest function as follows:

$$PRId = MD5(K_T, C_T, C_R).$$

The tag then sends its challenge and the identifier to the reader, which sends the identifier and both challenges to a central location where the exhaustive identification procedure will take place. The identification application will search through all the known keys, corresponding to valid tags, to find out the one that generated the identifier from the two challenges used. This exhaustive search algorithm is similar to a password guessing attack using a dictionary.

Note that the exploitation of a central identification facility simplifies the protection of the tag keys against involuntary disclosure, as they only exist in one single location. Namely, we don't need to deploy part or the whole key set

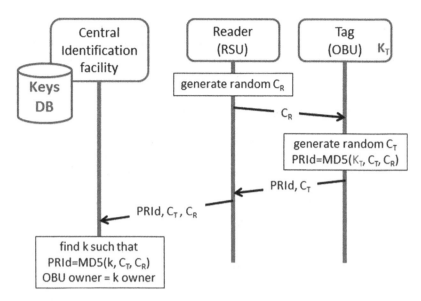

Fig. 1. Tag identification protocol: conceptual computations and message exchanges.

in tag readers, therefore tag readers don't need to use specific hardware devices, such as SAM modules, to protect secrets.

As already stated, for our tests we used a very demanding set of dimensions for challenges and keys: two 64-bit challenges (C_T and C_R) and 128-bit keys and identifiers (K_T and PRId). The identifier PRId is the exact output of MD5 (128 bits), while the data that we provide as input to MD5 is only half of its input block size (which is 512 bits). This means that MD5 will run only one iteration to compute the identifier from K_T, C_T, and C_R.

3.1 Possible Implementation

This protocol can be implemented as an extension to the existing RFID standards for vehicle identification, namely the widely used EN 12795 standard [24], that regulates link-layer communications between an RSU and an OBU. An RSU uses a down-link window to periodically broadcast a Beacon Status Table, which could be used to convey the challenge C_R to nearby OBU tags. An OBU responds in an up-link window, and its first response is a Vehicle Status Table (VST).

The OBU Manufacturer ID (4 bytes), conveyed in the VST, and the Manufacturer Serial Number (MSN, 6 bytes), present in information elements conveyed later to the RSU, form a unique 10-byte OBU identifier. In our case, a pseudo MSN could convey part of C_T, and the rest of C_T, together with the ID computed from C_R and C_T, could be both conveyed in the VST, or latter in information elements queried by the RSU.

The computation of the ID, which can only happen after receiving C_R, may prevent the OBU from sending the VST in the available up-link windows that immediately follow a down-link window, but the standard already includes mechanisms for dealing with late responses.

3.2 EN 15509 Authentication Protocols

The EN 15509 standard [4] defines two security levels for the interaction between and RSU and an OBU: level 0 (mandatory) and level 1 (optional).

In security level 0, an OBU must authenticate to the RSU, i.e., it must prove to the RSU that it is legitimate. This is accomplished with secret shared keys known both by the RSU and the OBU. Each OBU can carry up to 8 different authentication keys per application (i.e., service provided, such as toll collection). Each authentication key is generated from a proper master key and from some OBU attributes, allowing the same OBU application to be managed by 8 different stakeholders (e.g. different toll collecting companies), each with its own master key. Values generated by an OBU to authenticate its responses (4-byte authenticators) can be immediately checked by the RSU (online) or latter by central, validation applications (offline). Online validation forces an RSU to have access to computations with master keys, which implies the possession of a Secure Access Module (SAM) for storing them.

In security level 1, an OBU authenticates an RSU. The authentication must take place online and uses an access credential key derived from a master key. This access key is stored by the OBU and must be computed by the RSU to interact with each OBU. For this purpose, an RSU must use a SAM for holding access master keys, and uses a one-byte diversifier value provided by the OBU (in the VST):

$$\text{Access Key} = f(\text{Master Key}, \text{OBU diversifier}).$$

Only the security level 1 mechanism prevents an OBU from being tracked by unauthorized readers. The identification of the OBU is provided in two steps: during the initial handshake protocol, when an OBU responds with a VST (containing the Manufacturer ID), and latter, when queried by the RSU for information elements, with the MSN. Security level 1 prevents unauthorized readers from getting the MSN, thus effectively prevents them from getting four of the six bytes of the OBU unique identifier.

OBU tags can also be tracked by monitoring some fields with unique values, other than tag identifiers, present in information elements conveyed to an RSU. For instance, for the Electronic Fee Collection application, the RSU asks for an attribute called *PaymentMeans*, which includes a 12-digit (6-byte) individual account number. Security level 1 also protects against tracking this attribute, and other similar ones with uniqueness properties (e.g., license plates).

Comparing level 0 security with our approach, our PRId can be used to authenticate responses, and the PRId can be used to identify the OBU owner (with a massive search along all known OBU keys). To do so we could store our unique OBU key, which was chosen (once and for all) in a purely random way and not derived from any master key, on the space currently reserved for OBU authentication keys. We could also have a different key per stakeholder. Note, however, that OBU authentication keys currently have only 8 bytes, while we used 16-byte keys.

Comparing level 1 security with our approach, we do not need to authenticate the RSU as long as the information conveyed by an OBU does not contain any information suitable for tracking a car. By changing the way an OBU is identified from a fixed set of 6 bytes to a pseudo-random 16-byte identifier, we did the first step. Other steps may be required, depending on the information presented by the OBU. For instance, the individual account number of the *PaymentMeans* attribute may be used to convey part of the pseudo-random ID, and the effective individual account number may be linked to the OBU key by the OBU authentication service.

In conclusion, using our PRId strategy for an OBU does not prevent level 0 security to be explored, it is just explored in a slightly different way, and we can also achieve a security level equal to level 1 without requiring the distribution of master keys in all RSU installations. Consequently, the whole system can become much more robust against security breaches and cheaper to deploy: an OBU only needs to have a unique, random key per stakeholder, and no master keys are required anywhere. Therefore, an RSU does not need to have master keys nor SAM modules to store them.

3.3   MD5 Collision Issues

Digest functions with collision issues, such as MD5, allow people to find pairs of different pre-images that, once hashed, generate the same digest. However, this cannot be used to weaken the security of our proposal.

Our PRId-based identification system could be misused if an attacker could provide, for a given C_R value, a C_T and an ID suitable to be matched by a given key. However, without knowing any keys other than its own, a tag has to resort to a random key to get a match with any of the existing keys. The success probability would be $N/2^{128}$, where N is the total number of assigned keys.

Using collisions, an attacker could try to reuse an ID eavesdropped from another tag to get a match with the same key of that tag. But in this case, on each dialog with a reader he must choose a proper C_T that, together with C_R (that he does not control) and the key (that he does not know), generates the same ID. We cannot firmly state that this is not at all possible, but without knowing the key (50 % of the MD5 input) we find it very unlikely to succeed.

In any case, the goal of this paper is not to provide a security mechanism to prevent the impersonation of RFIDs (which is of course much easier when they are constant). Our goal is to provide privacy to RFID owners, and this is not endangered by the collision issues of MD5.

Last but not least, we could have used, say, SHA-1 instead of MD5, but we did not for two reasons: first, the 160-bit output of SHA-1 is excessive for our problem, and would represent extra computations on the (slow) RFID tags;

second, preliminary performance evaluations of SHA-1 and MD5 in our NVidia devices showed that SHA-1 is 2.35 times slower that MD5, because it has nearly twice the number of instructions. Current super-scalar CPUs, with their SIMD instructions, are able to blur this performance difference, but current GPGPUs cannot do so.

3.4 Privacy Concerns

In [25] G. Avoine *et al.* analyse the privacy of several RFID authentication protocols and demonstrate that the protocol described in [12], which is similar to ours, does not provide *forward privacy*. Forward privacy means that, after the disclosure of a tag's key (e.g. upon its corruption by an attacker), both past and future authentication dialogs performed by such tag can be linked, therefore undermining the privacy property inherent to the former unlinkability of several authentication protocol runs.

In [25] it is also said that a protocol like ours is insecure against a *timeful adversary*, which is and adversary that has access to the time it takes to find a tag's key among all known keys. In our case the search time is only available to the central facility that performs the exhaustive search, therefore we can assume that such an attacker could have as well access to the exact tag key. Therefore, this vulnerability is somehow similar to the potential disclosure of tags' keys by the authenticator, which should never happen.

It was not our goal for this article to propose a method for providing the best possible privacy to tag owners. Instead, our goal was to show the feasibility of exhaustive searches of tags' keys when a protocol such as ours (that removes all direct and obvious tag identifiers from tag authentication dialogs) is used. On the other hand, the exact implementation of our protocol could circumvent the privacy issues previously referred. In other hands, if tags could not be corrupted to reveal their keys and if the central facility could protect properly its tags' keys, then both issues related with forward privacy and timeful attacks could be successfully tackled.

4 The NVidia Tesla S1070 System and the CUDA Programming Environment

The NVidia Tesla S1070 rack-mounted system is composed of four independent devices (GPGPUs). These devices are grouped in two pairs, each pair sharing a PCIe x16 connection to the host computer. Each device has 30 so-called Stream Multiprocessors (SM), 4 GiB of dedicated memory, and a clock frequency of 1.44 GHz. Each SM has 8 processing cores, 16384 32-bit general purpose registers, and 16 kB of shared memory.

NVidia GPGPUs are best programmed using CUDA [26,27]. Each CUDA parallel sub-program, called a kernel, is composed of a user-specified number of threads, each of which running exactly the same code (not necessarily at the same time). The threads are grouped in blocks and each block is assigned to one SM.

When there are enough hardware resources, up to 8 blocks can be running in a single SM. Threads of the same block can use simultaneously (part of) the shared memory of each SM; it is also possible to synchronize them. Threads of different blocks cannot be synchronized easily, and can only communicate via (slow) global memory, or via (even slower) mapped host memory.

The threads of each block are grouped in so-called warps, which are groups of 32 threads. All threads of a warp are executed simultaneously Each SM queues the warps that can be run. To hide the long latency of memory accesses, many warps should be assigned to each SM, i.e., the number of threads per block times the number of blocks that can be assigned to a SM should be large.

Each thread receives two sets of coordinates: one to specify its coordinates within a block, and another to specify the coordinates of the block (one talks about a grid of blocks); both can be uni-, bi-, or tri-dimensional. By properly choosing the block and grid dimensions the programmer can subdivide the entire computational work among all SMs of the GPGPU.

Each thread can load, and in some cases store, data in several address spaces: constant memory, shared memory, texture memory, and global memory; host memory can be mapped on the global memory space. On the Tesla S1070 devices only the constant and texture memory accesses are cached. Given the nature of our problem, our kernels use only a small amount of constant memory and a large amount of global memory. Each (aligned) global memory read access, triggered by the threads of a single warp, can read 32, 64, or 128 bytes in a single transaction. For peak efficiency, all the bytes read should be consumed by one of the threads of the warp. The situation is similar for writes. In our case, since the MD5 algorithm performs a significant amount of computation for each key (which has 16 bytes), it is possible and convenient to store the four 32-bit words of each key in consecutive memory positions without degrading performance.

5   Search Algorithms

The key search activities are conducted by a GPGPU kernel that has access to all assigned keys. Briefly, searches are performed as follows:

1. The set of keys is copied from the host to an array in device memory.
2. Both the challenges and the MD5 message digest computed by the RFID tag are stored into device constant memory. The termination flag is set to zero (in global memory, if only one device is being used).
3. The search kernel is launched on the device. If a match is found, the termination flag is set to one and the key (or its position) is stored in a predefined area of device global memory.
4. When the kernel terminates, the host program collects the search results.

For several key searches, steps 2 to 4 are performed, always using the keys installed (only once) on the device in step 1. The set of keys only needs to be updated when new keys are assigned or deassigned (perhaps on a daily basis),

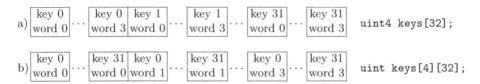

Fig. 2. Two possible memory layouts for a group of 32 keys: (a) linear order, (b) transposed order. Memory addresses increase from the left to the right.

or key reordering actions are performed on the host. For 250 million keys step 1 requires less than ten seconds; if millions of searches are subsequently performed, this overhead is irrelevant.

5.1 Kernel Termination After a Match

Terminating an exhaustive search when a match is found is fundamental to release the GPGPU so that it could be used by another search kernel. Unfortunately, the CUDA API does not include any function to terminate a running kernel. The kernel is terminated only when all its threads terminate.

Terminating the threads of the same block is easy and fast. One only needs to test a completion flag stored in shared memory. Terminating the threads launched in a given device is also easy, but slower. One only needs to test a completion flag stored in the global memory (of that device). Terminating the threads of kernels launched on several devices is more difficult, but still possible. For each device there is a completion flag stored in a write-through area of host memory and memory-mapped on device global memory. Once the key is found, the corresponding completion flag is set. Using a pooling loop on the host (in CUDA versions greater or equal to 4.0 it is possible to control several devices from a single processor thread), the completion flag is set for the other devices, so that all threads of all kernels (one kernel per device) know it is time to terminate the kernel. In Appendix A we show the skeleton of the code for doing the described kernel termination policy.

5.2 Layout of the Keys in Device Memory

To make the best use of the large available memory bandwidth to global memory of a GPGPU, all the data fetched on each memory load should be used. To this end, two memory layouts for the keys were compared (cf. Fig. 2): the obvious one (top), in which a key is stored in 4 consecutive 4-byte words, and a transposed one (bottom), in which 32 consecutive keys are stored in 128 consecutive words, so that the first word of the 32 keys are stored consecutively in memory.

Profiling tests showed that these two memory layouts provide almost equal performance, if the `uint4` data type is used to load the keys in the first layout. The first one reached a global memory read throughput of 10.99 GiB/s and the second one reached 10.83 GiB/s. It must be noted that these results were obtained on a "production" kernel, i.e., one that computed the MD5 message digest after each key is read from memory. Given that the theoretical maximum memory throughput per device of the Tesla S1070 is several times larger than the values we obtained (102 GiB/s [28]), as expected our kernels are clearly compute bound (and not memory bound).

It is interesting to observe that on the Tesla S1070 testing the termination flag in all threads, despite requiring a large amount of memory reads, does not result in any measurable performance loss, and allows the kernel to be stopped almost immediately after a match is found, thus preventing an unnecessary computation of a possibly large number of keys.

5.3 Work Done by a Kernel

In the first kernel we developed each thread is responsible for checking a single key. One-dimensional blocks of threads and a bi-dimensional grid were used to distribute the work among all stream multiprocessors of a single S1070 device. It turned out that a block size of 128 was optimal. Due to coordinate range limitations, a bi-dimensional grid was necessary to be able to do experiments with up to 250 million keys (this number of keys used up almost all memory available of each device). For coding convenience, one of the grid dimensions was fixed and the other was adjusted so that the total number of threads deployed was the smallest integer not smaller than the number of keys. Since in general there were more threads than keys, it was necessary to add a test in the kernel code to deactivate the extra threads. An alternative, which provided slightly better performance, consisted in padding the key data with a (repeated) unassigned key until the number of keys matched the number of threads; this required a small amount of memory but made the test not necessary.

The original MD5 code [6] was optimized to take into account the specificity of the data we need to digest. Since the length of the input bits is lower than the MD5 block size, which is 512 bits, only one iteration per key is required, and so the loop responsible for going over all the 512 bit blocks of the input message is not necessary. Furthermore, padding and appending the message length uses constant data, which can be hard-coded.

Performance tests with sets of 100 and 250 million keys (cf. Table 1) revealed that when there is a match with the key at index 0, the execution time in the device is far from zero. Furthermore, this deviation from zero increases linearly with the total number of keys. This is due to the overhead of launching the threads and testing the termination flag.

To address this problem we devised a second search kernel, where the number of threads is fixed and matched to the number of stream multiprocessors of the device (it turned out that 512 threads per SM was optimal). Every thread tests a subset of the array of keys, using a stride equal to the total number of threads (thus, the number of keys tested by each thread is equal to the total number of keys divided by the total number of threads). This kernel introduces some overhead (loop management) but virtually eliminates the larger overhead of launching much more threads. This strategy made also possible, using the

Table 1. Execution times (in ms) of the two CUDA kernels

Key position	$N = 10^8$ keys		$N = 2.5 \times 10^8$ keys	
	1st kernel	2nd kernel	1st kernel	2nd kernel
0	21.39	0.07	53.38	0.07
$0.1\,N$	36.41	16.94	90.93	42.23
$0.2\,N$	51.43	33.79	128.48	84.44
$0.3\,N$	66.45	50.68	166.03	126.58
$0.4\,N$	81.46	67.53	203.57	168.78
$0.5\,N$	96.48	84.40	241.12	210.99
$0.6\,N$	111.50	101.26	278.66	253.11
$0.7\,N$	126.52	118.17	316.21	295.34
$0.8\,N$	141.54	135.03	353.76	337.51
$0.9\,N$	156.56	151.89	391.30	379.79
$N - 1$	171.54	168.73	428.83	421.85

method described in Subsect. 5.1, to launch the search kernel in the four devices of the Tesla S1070 (with the key set split equally among the devices). Table 1 presents timing results for the two kernels, for sets with 100 and 250 million keys, using a single device and the first kernel termination strategy described in Subsect. 5.1. It turns out that the second kernel is always faster than the first kernel, despite taking more time to test one key.

The second kernel times were almost unchanged when the second termination strategy was used and when it was deployed (almost) simultaneously on the four devices, using the same number of keys per device. Thus, keeping the total number of keys constant, using four devices results in a speed-up of four.

Let N be the number of keys and let i, with $0 \leq i < N$ be the position of a given key. From the data of Table 1, it can be inferred that the search time, in nanoseconds, to find a given key is very well approximated by $0.214N + 1.502i$ for the first kernel, and by $47500 + 1.687i$ for the second kernel. For comparison, the search time of an optimized one-thread CPU only version, using SIMD instructions, is $57.319i$ on a single core of a 3.07 GHz Core i7 950 Intel processor. From these results it follows that using the second kernel results in a speed-up of about 34 with respect to a CPU-only implementation (the comparison is between one CUDA device and one CPU core).

We also tested our kernel code on a Fermi GPGPU (GeForce GTX480, with has 480 cores). It was necessary to disable the Level 1 memory cache of the SMs in order to make the change of the completion flag visible to all SMs. This did not have a significant effect on the performance of the kernel, because there is no data reuse. It turned out that for our kernels the Fermi GPGPU was about twice as fast as one device of the Tesla GPGPU. This was expected for a compute bound kernel, because the Fermi has twice the number of cores of each device of the Tesla, and they have similar clock frequencies.

5.4   Search Time Improvements

The order of the keys affects the average time it takes to search for one of them. Let key number k, stored in position i_k have a relative occurrence frequency equal to f_k; in practice, one can keep track of the number of times each key was activated, possibly using a sliding time window, and infer the relative frequency of occurrence from that. Let the search time for a key in position i_k be given by $A + Bi_k$, with constants A and B depending on the search kernel used and on the total number of keys N. The average search time is thus given by $T = \sum_{k=0}^{N-1} f_k(A + Bi_k) = A + BI$, where $I = \sum_{k=0}^{N-1} f_k i_k$ is the weighted average key position. The average search time is minimized when I is minimized, which, if $i_k = k$, happens when $f_{k+1} \leq f_k$ for $k = 0, \ldots, N-2$, i.e., when the more frequent keys appear first. Let $\mathrm{pos}(f_k)$ be the position of f_k when all relative frequencies are sorted in decreasing order. The smallest average weighted key position is then given by $I_{\mathrm{opt}} = \sum_{k=0}^{N-1} f_k \, \mathrm{pos}(f_k)$. On the other hand, if the keys are in random order, the expected weighted average key position is $I_{\mathrm{rand}} = \sum_{k=0}^{N-1} f_k \, E[i_k] = \frac{N-1}{2}$, where $E[\cdot]$ denotes mathematical expectation. These results suggest the following figure of merit for a particular key order:

$$M = \frac{I_{\mathrm{rand}}}{I} = \frac{N-1}{2 \sum_{k=0}^{N-1} f_k i_k}.$$

Clearly, $1 \leq M \leq M_{\mathrm{opt}}$, where

$$M_{\mathrm{opt}} = \frac{N-1}{2 \sum_{k=0}^{N-1} f_k \, \mathrm{pos}(f_k)}.$$

M_{opt} is the speed-up, with respect to a random key order, one can expect by using the optimal key order (assuming that A is zero, or close to zero, as happens in our best search kernels).

Table 2 presents the value of M_{opt} for several possible relative frequency profiles; in all cases $i_k = k$, $A = 0$, and N is large. In the last two columns, the free parameter a was chosen such that the relative frequency of the key in position bN is one half the relative frequency of the first key. For $b = 0.1$, the expected speed-up is about 3.5 for the exponential profile and about 7.4 for the half-normal profile; smaller values of b give even larger speed-ups.

We experimented with kernels that modified the key order every time a key was found, moving it closer to the beginning of the array of keys. As expected, over time the average search time approached $A + BI_{\mathrm{opt}}$. For a pre-specified relative frequency profile, starting from a random key order, this required many key activations, on the order of $100N$. Given that this number of key activations is expected to occur over a period of many days, and given that the key array should be updated at least on a daily basis, this idea was abandoned in favor of a host-based key reordering strategy: every time a new key array has to be installed, it is sorted first. This activity can be done offline, so the time it takes (less than a minute for one billion valid keys) is irrelevant.

Table 2. Expected search speed-up for some relative frequency profiles

profile	polynomial	exponential	half-normal
	0 N	0 bN N	0 bN N
f_k	$\dfrac{(N-k)^a}{\sum_{n=1}^{N} n^a}$	$\dfrac{(1-a)a^k}{1-a^N}$	$\approx \dfrac{2a}{\pi} e^{-(ak)^2/\pi}$
conditions	$a \geq 0$	$a^{bN} = \dfrac{1}{2}, \, 0 < b < 1$	$e^{-(abN)^2/\pi} = \tfrac{1}{2}, \, 0 < b \ll 1$
$\lim\limits_{N\to\infty} M_{opt}$	$\dfrac{a+2}{2}$	$\dfrac{\log 2}{2b - 2\log 2/(2^{1/b}-1)}$	$\approx \dfrac{\sqrt{\pi}\log 2}{2b}$

5.5   A Realistic Demanding Scenario

Given the above results, for 100 million valid keys and for an exponential distribution with $b = 0.1$, a single Tesla S1070 system (all four devices in parallel) can perform, on average, about $4 \times 3.5/(1.687 \times 50 \times 10^6 \times 10^{-9}) \approx 166$ key searches per second. Assuming an average vehicle speed of 90 km/h, i.e., 25 m/s, and an average distance between vehicles' front wheels of 15 m, a single Tesla S1070 system can manage in near real time about 100 single-lane toll stations (under heavy traffic rolling conditions).

On highway systems on which tolls are collected on a per-link basis, such as those now in use in our home country (Portugal), it would be possible to use a key cache (per toll station) to explore the expected spatial and temporal locality of key activations, thereby increasing the number of single-lane toll stations managed by a single Tesla S1070 system even further. The cache would function in the obvious manner: before performing a search in the entire valid key data set, a much smaller, and faster, search would be performed on the keys stored in the cache; only if that failed would the full search be performed. It would be necessary to use actual traffic data or data extracted from traffic flow simulation software to find out the best cache sizes for a given highway system.

6   Conclusions

In this paper we have studied the identification of vehicle RFID tags with pseudo-random identifiers with massively parallel computation. We conceived a very simple challenge-response protocol capable of producing 128-bit pseudo-random identifiers from 128-bit secret keys, compatible with RFID standards such as EN 12795 and EN 15509. On a demanding scenario we demonstrated that a single Tesla S1070 system could be responsible for at least 100 single-lane toll-collecting stations.

Our pseudo-random RFID tags can also be used in other scenarios where privacy-preserving identification is desirable, such as, for example, access-control to buildings.

There is a very small probability that two (or more) tags generate the same response for some (unlucky) pseudo-random nonces. That may happen irrespective of the hash function used. Further research is needed to address this problem.

Acknowledgements. This work was funded by FCT (Foundation for Science and Technology), in the context of the project PEst-OE/EEI/UI0127/2014. The S1070 Tesla was gracefully provided by NVidia, under its Academic Partnership Program. The access to the Fermi device was gracefully provided by Prof. F. Vístulo de Abreu and B. Faria, from the Physics Department of the University of Aveiro, Portugal.

A   Code Skeletons for Kernel Termination After a Match

Figure 3 illustrates how to terminate a kernel on a single device (top) or on multiple devices (bottom) after a match; ... denotes omitted irrelevant code.

```
__global__ void search(volatile int *found,...)
{ // for a single device
    if(*found != 0)
        return;
    ...
    if(key_matches) {
        *found = 1;
        return;
    }
    ...
}
```

```
volatile __shared__ int l_found; // per block

__global__ void search(volatile int *found,...)
{ // for multiple devices
    if(threadIdx.x == 0)
        l_found = 0;
    __syncthreads();
    ...
    for(int n = 0;...;n += 32) {
        if(threadIdx.x == n % n_threads_per_block)
            l_found = *found;
        if(l_found != 0)
            return;
        ...
        if(key_matches)
        {
            l_found = *found = 1;
            return;
        }
        ...
    }
    ...
}
```

Fig. 3. CUDA code skeletons for terminating a running kernel.

On the latter case, our solution is only effective if the test is done inside a loop (in our case, this corresponds to each thread checking many keys). Given that accessing memory-mapped host memory from the device is very slow (the transaction is over the PCIe bus), on each round only one thread of each block does the access, and stores the value read in fast shared memory. To keep things balanced, the thread doing this slow access is changed as the computation progresses (an increment of 32 corresponds to a jump to the next warp).

References

1. Lahiri, S.: RFID Sourcebook. IBM Press, Upper Saddle River (2005)
2. Juels, A.: RFID security and privacy: a research survey. IEEE J. Sel. Areas Commun. **24**(2), 381–394 (2006)
3. International Civil Aviation Organization: Machine Readable Travel Documents, Part 3: Machine Readable Official Travel Documents, Volume 2: Specifications for Electronically Enabled MRtds with Biometric Identification Capability (2008)
4. BSI: Road transport and traffic telematics - Electronic fee collection - Interoperability application profile for DSRC. BS EN 15509:2007 (2007). ISBN 978-0-580-50884-4
5. European Commission, Directorate-General for Mobility and Transport: The European Electronic Toll Service (EETS): Guide For the Application of the Directive on the Interoperability of Electronic Road Toll Systems (2011). ISBN 978-92-79-18637-0, doi:10.2833/6832, http://ec.europa.eu/transport/publications/doc/2011-eets-european-electronic-toll-service_en.pdf
6. Rivest, R.: The MD5 Message-Digest Algorithm. RFC 1321 (1992)
7. Wang, X., Feng, D., Lai, X., Yu, H.: Collisions for Hash Functions MD4, MD5, HAVAL-128 and RIPEMD. Cryptology ePrint Archive, Report 2004/199 (2004)
8. Klima, V.: Finding MD5 Collisions - a Toy For a Notebook. Cryptology ePrint Archive, Report 2005/075 (2005). http://eprint.iacr.org/2005/075
9. Klima, V.: Tunnels in Hash Functions: MD5 Collisions Within a Minute. Cryptology ePrint Archive, Report 2006/105 (2006). http://eprint.iacr.org/2006/105
10. Dimitriou, T.: A Lightweight RFID protocol to protect against traceability and cloning attacks. In: 1st IEEE/CreateNet International Conference on Security and Privacy for Emerging Areas in Communication Networks (SecureComm 2005), Athens, Greece (2005)
11. Bureau of Transportation Statistics (BTS): Table 1–11: Number of U.S. Aircraft, Vehicles, Vessels, and Other Conveyances. http://www.bts.gov/publications/national_transportation_statistics/html/table_01_11.html
12. Weis, S.A., Sarma, S.E., Rivest, R.L., Engels, D.W.: Security and privacy aspects of low-cost radio frequency identification systems. In: 1st International Conference on Security in Pervasive Computing (SPC 2003), Boppard, Germany (2003)
13. Liu, A.X., Bailey, L.A.: PAP: a privacy and authentication protocol for passive RFID tags. Comput. Commun. **32**(7), 1194–1199 (2009)
14. Ohkubo, M., Suzuki, K., Kinoshita, S.: Cryptographic approach to privacy-friendly tags. In: RFID Privacy Workshop, MIT (2003)
15. Avoine, G., Oechslin, P.: A scalable and provably secure hash based RFID Protocol. In: 2nd IEEE International Workshop on Pervasive Computing and Communication Security (PerSec 2005), Kauai Island, Hawaii, USA (2005)

16. Henrici, D., Muller, P.: Providing security and privacy in RFID systems using triggered hash chains. In: Proceedings of the 6th Annual IEEE International Conference on Pervasive Computing and Communications (PerCom'08), Hong Kong (2008)

17. Lim, T.L., Li, T., Gu, T.: Secure RFID identification and authentication with triggered hash chain variants. In: 14th IEEE International Conference on Parallel and Distributed Systems (ICPADS'08), Melbourne, Victoria, Australia (2008)

18. Molnar, D., Wagner, D.: Privacy and security in library RFID: issues, practices, and architectures. In: Proceedings of the 11th ACM Conference on Computer and Communications Security (CCS 2004), Washington, DC, USA (2004)

19. Molnar, D., Soppera, A., Wagner, D.: A Scalable, delegatable pseudonym protocol enabling ownership transfer of RFID tags. In: Preneel, B., Tavares, S. (eds.) SAC 2005. LNCS, vol. 3897, pp. 276–290. Springer, Heidelberg (2006)

20. Dimitriou, T.: A secure and efficient RFID protocol that could make big brother (partially) obsolete. In: Proceedings of the 4th Annual IEEE International Conference on Pervasive Computing and Communications (PerCom'06), Pisa, Italy (2006)

21. Lehtonen, M., Staake, T., Michahelles, F., Fleisch, E.: From identification to authentication - a review of RFID product authentication techniques. In: Workshop on RFID Security (RFIDSec 06), Graz, Austria (2006)

22. Langheinrich, M.: A survey of RFID privacy approaches. Pers. Ubiquit. Comput. **13**(6), 413–421 (2009)

23. Lim, C.H., Kwon, T.: Strong and robust RFID authentication enabling perfect ownership transfer. In: Ning, P., Qing, S., Li, N. (eds.) ICICS 2006. LNCS, vol. 4307, pp. 1–20. Springer, Heidelberg (2006)

24. BSI: Road transport and traffic telematics - Dedicated short range communication (DSRC) - DSRC data link layer - Medium access and logical link control. BS EN 12795 (2003). ISBN 0-580-41964-9

25. Avoine, G., Coisel, I., Martin, T.: Time measurement threatens privacy-friendly RFID authentication protocols. In: Ors Yalcin, S.B. (ed.) RFIDSec 2010. LNCS, vol. 6370, pp. 138–157. Springer, Heidelberg (2010)

26. Sanders, J., Kandrot, E.: CUDA by Example: An Introduction to General-Purpose GPU Programming. Addison-Wesley, Reading (2010)

27. Kirk, D.B., Hwu, W.-M.W.: Programming Massively Parallel Processors: A Hands-on Approach. Morgan Kaufmann, Burlington (2010)

28. NVidia: NVidia Tesla 1U Computing System. http://www.nvidia.com/docs/IO/43395/NV_DS_Tesla_S1070_US_Jun08_NV_LR_Final.pdf

PIONEER—a Prototype for the Internet of Things Based on an Extendable EPC Gen2 RFID Tag

Hannes Gross[1]([⊠]), Erich Wenger[1], Honorio Martín[2], and Michael Hutter[1]

[1] Institute for Applied Information Processing and Communications (IAIK),
Graz University of Technology, Inffeldgasse 16a, 8010 Graz, Austria
{Hannes.Gross,Erich.Wenger,Michael.Hutter}@iaik.tugraz.at
[2] Department of Electronic Technology, Carlos III University of Madrid,
28911 Leganés, Spain
hmartin@ing.uc3m.es

Abstract. The Internet of Things (IoT) envisions an autonomous network between everyday objects to create real-life services. This enables new applications that necessarily require a high level of security and privacy. In this paper, we present PIONEER—a Prototype for the Internet of Things based on an Extendable EPC Gen2 RFID tag. It is the first prototype that integrates the Internet Protocol Security suite (IPsec) into the new EPC Gen2 Version 2 standard. Furthermore, it integrates all mandatory cryptographic primitives to support IPsec on an RFID tag, i.e., AES-128 for encryption/decryption, 192-bit Elliptic Curve Diffie Hellman (ECDH) for key agreement, and a True Random Number Generator (TRNG). To keep the flexibility high, we further integrated an 8-bit microcontroller that implements the new security features of the EPC Gen2 standard in C code. The entire design was synthesized for a 130 nm CMOS process technology. It requires about 52 kGEs including all necessary components to establish a secure IPsec tunnel between the RFID tag and a client on the Internet. The prototype is fully compliant with already existing Internet and RFID standards and allows first cost estimations for a practical realization of high-security IoT applications.

Keywords: Radio frequency identification · UHF tags · Security · IPsec

1 Introduction

The term "Internet of Things" goes back to the early days of the Auto-ID Labs—formerly Auto-ID Center—, and its co-founder Kevin Ashton [4] who was the first to use this term in context of logistics. The Auto-ID Center was founded at the Massachusetts Institute of Technology to work on the first version of the Electronic Product Code (EPC) standard. Therefore, the vision of the Internet of Things (IoT) is historically strongly related to the EPC standard. Later on, Ashton defined the idea behind the IoT more generally as to be not just "a bar code

© Springer International Publishing Switzerland 2014
N. Saxena and A.-R. Sadeghi (Eds.): RFIDSec 2014, LNCS 8651, pp. 54–73, 2014.
DOI: 10.1007/978-3-319-13066-8_4

on steroids", but to be an autonomous network that allows computers to gather information about things in the real world. In 2000, Sarma, Brock, and Ashton [48] envisioned their ideas for a "single open architecture system for networking physical objects" to be used instead of "multiple smaller scale alternatives". The situation today shows that the latter approach is dominating the IoT world at the moment. There are many different realizations of unrelated networks of things, e.g., used in logistics, in supermarkets, for home automation, for smart parking, et cetera. One reason for this situation might be that restricted networks are far easier to handle for companies than open networks—not only in terms of security considerations. This is comparable to the beginning of the Internet, when there were Internet service providers offering services restricted to their own network. However, the services that were open for the whole Internet were far more successful in the long term (e.g., email, messaging, or file sharing service).

EPC Gen2 Version 1 tags are not yet prepared to provide reliable, confidential, and authentic services in an open accessible network, because they lack the required cryptographic functionality. With the introduction of the EPC Gen2 Version 2 standard [16] released at the end of 2013, the first attempt towards standardized security on EPC tags has been performed. This represents an important step towards the realization of an open and secure Internet of Things.

Our contribution. In this paper, we first evaluate the integration of the Internet Protocol Security suite (IPsec) into the new EPC Gen2 Version 2 standard. As an outcome, we present a complete prototype system that supports all mandatory features to establish a secure tunnel between RFID tags and clients on the Internet. To keep the resource requirements low, we decided to implement the minimal set of necessary—but standardized—cryptographic primitives, i.e., AES-128, ECDH over the NIST P-192 curve, and a TRNG. Moreover, we integrated a very flexible 8-bit microcontroller into our design to be able to implement different Internet of Things applications. We call our prototype PIONEER because it is based on an extendable EPC Gen2 RFID-tag platform that features a reconfigurable Spartan-3 FPGA.

Within this work, we aim for presenting a fully working prototype including all necessary functionalities that are required for a secure Internet of Things. We base our investigations on standardized algorithms and protocols in order to facilitate the evaluation of existing system integration. Note that we do not claim for an efficient or yet practical implementation but rather provide first results of a prototyping system to estimate the costs for high-security IoT applications.

Our results interestingly show the feasibility of a running IPsec stack on an EPC Gen2 tag. With our prototype, we are successfully able to demonstrate the establishment of secure end-to-end connections between tags and clients in the Internet *without* needing to trust readers or nodes between the tag and the client. Due to the high area requirements of around 52 kGEs, we consider implementation of mid-to-high cost IoT applications that require particular security features.

Outline. The remainder of the work is organized as follows. At first, the scientific work related to this paper is discussed in Sect. 2. The cryptographic algorithms and the security features used in the EPC Gen2 Version 2 and the IPsec protocols are then considered in Sects. 3 and 4 respectively. Afterwards, Sect. 5 discusses the integration of IPsec into the EPC Gen2 standard as a cryptographic suite in detail. As a practical contribution we present our prototype design of an IPsec enabled EPC Gen2 tag in Sect. 6, and discuss the implementation results in Sect. 7. Finally, conclusions are drawn in Sect. 8.

2   Related Work

The EPC standard has opened a broad field of research topics covering different kinds of security aspects, privacy-preserving protocols [20,51], hardware designs for tags [17,31,47], the practical realization of the IoT [8,13,21], and even the social and political impact of it [34]. Other works focus on increasing the tamper resistance of EPC Gen2 tags to prevent cloning or skimming, like the papers from Noman et al. [38] and Lehtonen et al. [32]. A lot of research has also been done on security and light-weight authentication schemes suitable for low-cost EPC Gen2 tags [39,40,56]. Most of these published light-weight protocols are considered insecure or are already broken [5,46]. The integration of public key cryptography is also part of ongoing research for passive RFID tags. Besides the typical constraints, e.g., a very restrictive power budgets, limited computational power, and a small chip size of an RFID tag design, it was stated by Arbit et al. [3] that reader devices limit the suitability of such protocols trough inefficient implementation of the EPC standard functionality.

Many of the security aspects mentioned above are also covered in the new EPC Gen2 Version 2 standard, introducing so-called cryptographic suites. Engels et al. [15] were the first to evaluate different security aspects of the new EPC Gen2 Version 2 standard in 2013—even before the standard was ratified. Their work focuses on eavesdropping, snooping, relay, and man-in-the-middle attacks, with special regard to timing constraints. Two different cryptographic suites for the Advanced Encryption Standard were considered, and it was stated that the new EPC standard introduces new vulnerabilities against different attacks. The main weakness of the new standard comes with the enhanced complexity of the security commands which allow longer tag-response delays (cf. *In-process tag reply* [16], on page 38). Hinz et al. [22] showed their implementation of the RAMON cryptographic suite. This suite uses the Rabin-Montgomery (RAMON) public-key scheme to authenticate tags against the readers. The authentication mechanism consists of a challenge-response step, with optional verification of the Tag ID by using a public-key infrastructure. It is also stated that the scheme allows only tag authentication. Hence, further security features like reader authentication or secured communication, require additional cryptographic primitives.

Yao-Chung et al. [8] showed in 2008 how different RFID networks can be connected using IPv6 technology by introducing so-called RFIPv6 gateways as network bridges. In this scenario, the tag information is collected by the readers, and stored on servers connected via the RFIPv6 gateways to other RFID networks. In 2010, Dominikus et al. [12] suggested using Mobile IPv6 functionality to connect low-cost EPC tags with the Internet. Therefore, the tag needs to carry an IPv6 home address that uniquely identifies the tag on the Internet. When the tag is outside its home network, the associated "home agent" works as a proxy, and receives packets addressed to the tag's home address. The packet is then forwarded to the tag's current IPv6 care-of-address, which is a temporary leased address identifying the tag in its currently located subnet. Furthermore, it is suggested to use IPsec to establish a secure end-to-end communication between a tag and a "corresponding node" on the Internet. A more detailed description of the communication between the tag, the reader, and the corresponding node to establish an IPsec channel was given in [13].

Further related research is done by the IETF's 6LoWPAN working group on making IPv6 technology more suitable to use with Wireless Personal Area Networks (WPAN). WPAN nodes are part of the IoT and are energy constrained devices that often use batteries and active communication to communicate over higher distances than, e.g., passive UHF RFID tags. In order to save energy, so-called header compression mechanisms are used to reduce the communication overhead costs. Raza et al. [43] presented one approach to integrate these mechanisms into the IPsec protocol's packets. However, the 6LoWPAN extensions are not yet widely used and are therefore out of scope for this paper.

3   EPC Gen2 Version 2 and Its Security Concepts

The Electronic Product Code (EPC) Generation 2 Version 2.0.0 standard [16] was ratified in November 2013, and offers the first comprehensive approach to integrate standardized security into the UHF RFID tag standard. The majority of changes target the User memory management, and the tag's security features. The standard itself defines no cryptographic operations or primitives, but it defines the command frames that encapsulate the payloads specified in so-called cryptographic suites. Cryptographic suites can either be assigned by the ISO/IEC 29167 standard, GS1, or by the tag manufacturer itself. The EPC Gen2 security commands include an 8-bit cryptographic suite identifier (CSI) that selects a cryptographic suite for the interpretation of the included payload. A cryptographic suite is usually defined over a particular cryptographic primitive (e.g., the Advanced Encryption Standard [11], PRESENT-80 [7], et cetera.), and contains the description of different security services.

In Fig. 1 the different phases typically transited during a communication procedure are illustrated. On the top, the tag states defined by the EPC Gen2 standard are shown that are linked to the communication phases defined in the middle of the figure. The related security commands are listed below. As long as the tag is not killed, the tag enters the "Select" phase right after a reader field is detected. During this phase, tags are selected by a reader—according to criteria defined by the Select commands (*Select* or *Challenge*)—that will participate in the next inventory round. The *Challenge* command allows to trigger the

Fig. 1. Tag phases with according EPC Gen2 tag states (on top) and associated security commands

computation of a cryptographic response, in order to determine the authenticity of a tag. Furthermore, it is ensured that only tags will participate in the subsequent inventory round, that possesses the ability to handle security commands defined in the selected cryptographic suite. A tag that supports the *Challenge* command with the given parameters computes a response, stores it into the so-called *ResponseBuffer*, and informs the reader device about the presence of a response by setting one bit (C flag) in the Protocol Control (PC) word. The response is read by the reader device during the "Access" phase.

The "Inventory" phase has not been extended by any commands, but additional information is transmitted at the end of this phase, like the *Challenge* command's response or the Extended PC word (XPC). If the XPC is supported by the tag, it informs the reader about special abilities of the tag. In the subsequent "Access" phase, a wide range of optional security commands are supported. The *Authenticate* command is used to identify the reader or the tag to the other communication partner by means of a cryptographic function. It can also be applied as a secure substitution of the *Access* command, that is used in previous EPC Gen2 standards to transfer from the "Access" phase into the "Secured Access" phase, and to grant associated privileges. With the *AuthComm* command, a command is encapsulated by an integrity-protected command frame. Contrary to the *SecureComm* command (which offers confidentiality and usually also integrity) the encapsulated command is transmitted as plain text, and only the integrity of the message is ensured by, e.g., using a message authentication code (MAC). Since cryptographic operations are usually more time consuming than the strict timing of the standard allows, so-called *In-Process* tag replies have been introduced. This reply type sets the timeout value for a consecutive tag reply up to 20 milliseconds, and can be sent multiple times to give the tag enough time to finish its computations.

The rest of the security commands (*KeyUpdate*, *TagPrivilege*, *Authenticated Kill*) are of less relevance for this paper, and for the sake of brevity not discussed in the remaining work. In the next subsection, the currently available information to the ISO/IEC 29167 cryptographic suites is briefly discussed.

3.1   Cryptographic Suites of the ISO/IEC 29167 Standard

While the EPC Gen2 Version 2 protocol is already released, the standardization process of the cryptographic suites is still in progress. At the moment, the only information publicly available at the ISO web page [26] are the names of the cryptographic suites to be published in future (see Table 1).

However, in the work of Engels et al. [15], two Advanced Encryption Standard (AES [11]) based cryptographic suites are considered, using the Cipher Block Chaining mode (AES-CBC), and the Output Feedback mode (AES-OFB [14]). Furthermore, two mutual authentication schemes relying on these cryptographic suites are introduced, and a security evaluation is performed considering different passive and active attacks. Other listed symmetric-key suites use the lightweight block cipher PRESENT-80 [7], or the stream cipher Grain-128A [1] that also supports message authentication codes (MAC). The XOR suite most likely uses an ultra lightweight approach, based on one or more XOR operations as primary cryptographic primitive (cf. Vernam cipher or one-time pad in Menezes et al. [35], on page 21).

Table 1. Currently listed cryptographic suites for EPC Gen2 Version 2 (see ISO [26] for the most recent list of cryptographic suites)

ISO/IEC 29167	Cryptographic suite	Description
... Part 10	AES-128	Block cipher (128-bit) with 128 bit key length
... Part 11	PRESENT-80	Block cipher (64-bit) with 80 bit key length
... Part 12	ECC-DH	ECC based Diffie-Hellman key agreement
... Part 13	Grain-128A	Stream cipher, 128-bit key, optional MAC
... Part 14	AES-OFB	Output feedback mode (OFB) for AES
... Part 15	XOR	Vernam cipher or one-time pad
... Part 16	ECDSA-ECDH	ECC-DH and digital signature algorithms
... Part 17	cryptoGPS	Low-cost public-key cryptography (coupons)
... Part 19	RAMON	Rabin-Montgomery based cryptography

From the public-key perspective, there are currently two Elliptic Curve Cryptography (ECC) based suites listed mentioning Diffie-Hellman key agreement (ECDH [2]), and the Elliptic Curve Digital Signature Algorithm (ECDSA [28]). Another suite uses the cryptoGPS [19] algorithm either based on RSA [44] or ECC. This is a resource-aware alternative to the ECDH suite. For the key agreement, the tags do not need to calculate expensive operations like the ECC point multiplication, because they can be done in advance, and only the result—in form of coupons—is stored on the tags. Hinz, Finkenzeller, and Sysen [22] published a paper that gives some insight into the RAMON cryptographic suite (Rabin-Montgomery public-key encryption scheme [36,41]). They show how tag authentication can be implemented conforming to the EPC Gen2 Version 2 standard, and how the keys are managed.

4 Internet Protocol Security (IPsec)

IPsec [30] is a protocol suite that generates a confidential and integrity protected connection between two Internet peers over an unsecured data channel (also known as virtual private network connection). The IPsec protocol can be subdivided into the security association (SA) negotiation phase—where the properties of the established secured channel are declared—and a subsequent working phase. The IPsec works on the Internet layer of the TCP/IP protocol stack. Thus it is fully transparent for applications that use the secured communication channel.

Phase 1: Internet Key Exchange Protocol Version 2 (IKEv2). An Internet peer can host multiple IPsec secured connections to multiple peers. Therefore, so-called security associations (SA) are used to manage the connection parameters (used cryptographic algorithms, negotiated keys, et cetera.) for different negotiated IP and Port ranges. The first SA between two peers is created by exchanging an *IKE_SA_INIT*, and a subsequent *IKE_AUTH* request and response pair using the UDP protocol (see [29]). The initial *IKE_SA_INIT* message exchange provides the negotiation of the cryptographic algorithms, and the Diffie-Hellman key agreement in plain text. Hence, the subsequent *IKE_AUTH* messages are already encrypted and integrity protected according to the terms of the mutual agreement. The identity of the hosts is then ensured either by using pre-shared keying or certificates, and the authenticity of the exchanged messages is proven to the opposite communication partner. Furthermore, another SA is derived (Child SA) that is associated either to the *Authentication Header* protocol or the *Encapsulation Security Payload* protocol.

4.1 Phase 2: Authentication Header and Encapsulation Security Payload

Once a secure connection has been established via IKEv2, outgoing IP packets that match the negotiated IP and Port ranges are either wrapped into an Authentication Header (AH), or an Encapsulation Security Payload (ESP). AH provides integrity and authenticity protection of the enclosed IP packets without encryption of the data. ESP also offers confidentiality protection by encrypting the encapsulated packet. On the other side of the communication channel, the packets are automatically decrypted—if the packet contains an ESP—, unwrapped, and checked before they are processed any further.

4.2 Cryptographic Algorithms Used by IPsec

IPsec defines different types of cryptographic algorithms, which are also called Transforms in the context of IKEv2. Table 2 summarizes the currently available algorithms for each of the Transform types. The first category defined are encryption algorithms that are used for IKEv2 (*IKE_AUTH*) and ESP to protect the confidentiality of the exchanged messages. Pseudo-random functions (PRFs) are

Table 2. IKEv2 transforms and according algorithms (see IANA [25])

Algorithm name	Transform types			
	Encryption	PRF	Integrity	Diffie-Hellmann
Advanced Encryption Standard (AES [11])	✓	✓	✓	
Blowfish	✓			
CAST	✓			
Camellia	✓			
Data Encryption Standard (DES)	✓		✓	
Int. Data Encryption Algorithm (IDEA)	✓			
Message-Digest Algorithm 5 (MD5)		✓	✓	
Modular Exponential Groups (MODP)				✓
Elliptic Curve Groups modulo a Prime (ECP [33])				✓
Secure Hash Algorithm (SHA1, SHA2)		✓	✓	
Tiger		✓		

used to derive the initial keying material for the other Transforms, and to derive new keying material when a Child SA is created. The key seed for the key derivation is calculated from the Diffie-Hellman exchange in the *IKE_SA_INIT* step. To protect the integrity of the payloads, and in order to authenticate the involved peers, integrity algorithms are used to create irreversible message authentication codes (MAC).

5   Integrating IPsec Functionality into EPC Gen2

The prime motivation for implementing IPsec on an EPC Gen2 Class 1 tag is to enable tags—and the things they are attached to—to become secure and independent participants on the Internet of Things. The tags then no longer depend on the trustworthiness of the readers, because a secure communication channel is established between the tag and another participant on the Internet of Things. Also the service a tag provides is no longer limited to the functionality a reader provides. In the suggested system, the functionality of a reader is primarily to work as a router, and forward IP packets from and to the tags. This enables a secure connection to any device on the Internet.

5.1   IPsec as Cryptographic Suite for EPC Gen2

In order to implement IPsec with IKEv2, at least one of each Transform class listed in Table 2 needs to be implemented. When compared to Table 1, it can be seen that the only algorithms currently proposed for both the EPC Gen2 cryptographic suites and the IPsec protocol, are the Advanced Encryption Standard (AES), and the Diffie-Hellman key exchange over an Elliptic Curve (ECP/ECC-DH). However, with these two cryptographic primitives, all required Transforms can be realized. Even though not all modes of operation defined in the cryptographic suites are currently publicly available, the presence of the cryptographic primitives, e.g. as cryptographic co-processors, allows implementation of all modes needed with reasonable effort.

The communication between any active participant (initiator) on the Internet of Things, and a particular EPC Gen2 tag is illustrated in Fig. 2. At first a *IKE_SA_INIT* message—encapsulated in an IP/UDP packet—is sent by an initiator and routed to the tag ①. The reader receives the packet, and sends a *Challenge* command to the tag containing the *IKE_SA_INIT* message. This message consists of a Diffie-Hellman value (ECC point), the initiator nonce, and one or more proposals for the cryptographic algorithms to be used for the next step. If one proposal is acceptable to the tag it begins to create the initial Security Association (SA). Therefore, the tag calculates its own Diffie-Hellman value, creates another nonce, and derives the key material from the Diffie-Hellman shared secret and the nonces. The key material for the initial SA consists of seven keys. The first derived key is used to create new key material for future Child SAs. Additionally, for each communication direction a key for encryption and decryption is generated, as well as a key for integrity protection, and another key for authentication purposes.

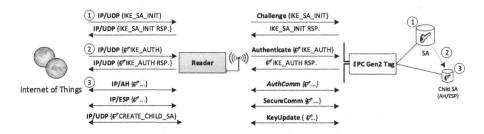

Fig. 2. Communication scenario for IPsec enabled EPC Gen2 tags

Similar to the *IKE_SA_INIT*, the tag's response contains the accepted SA proposal, the calculated Diffie-Hellman value, and the generated nonce. Once the response has been created and stored in the *ResponseBuffer*, the tag calculates the so-called *AUTH* value, which is used for authentication of the tag. The *AUTH* value is calculated by signing the whole *IKE_SA_INIT* response, the initiator nonce, and a unique identifier (e.g., the tag's IPv6 address), by applying the selected signing algorithm. The output is a signature that is transferred in the *IKE_AUTH* step. In the upcoming inventory round, the reader recognizes that the tag has finished the processing of the *Challenge* command by preselecting only tags that store a message in the *ResponseBuffer*. After the tag was successfully inventoried, the reader either received the *IKE_SA_INIT* response together with the tag's EPC after the tag was "acknowledged" during the inventory, or the *ResponseBuffer* is read by using the *ReadBuffer* command in the "Access" phase (see Fig. 1). The reader then encapsulates the gathered response in an IP/UDP frame and sends it back to the initiator. On the initiator side, similar calculations are performed as for the tag, resulting in the same SA.

For the next step ②, the SA is used to encrypt the *IKE_AUTH* payloads, and to protect the integrity of the message by concatenating a message authentication code (MAC) calculated over the whole message. With the *IKE_AUTH* message, the initiator reveals its identity, and proves its genuineness either via a pre-shared secret (PSK), or a certificate that is used to generate a signature. This message type perfectly fits into an EPC Gen2 Version 2 *Authenticate* command, because the initiator authenticates itself against the tag, and vice versa. The rest of the message consists of a proposal for the Child SA that is created for the AH or ESP message exchange, and the Traffic Selectors. If the tag is able to verify the identity of the initiator and accepts the other parameters, it transits from the "Access" phase to the "Secured Access" phase. The response of the tag consists of the same payloads as the *IKE_AUTH* request, but carries the identity of the tag, its *AUTH* value calculated in the *Challenge* step, and confirms the proposed parameters for the Child SA and the Traffic Selectors. In step ③, the Child SA on both sides was successfully established, and the communication between initiator and tag is protected. Figure 2 shows the counterparts of the EPC Gen2 standard's *AuthComm* and *SecureComm*, which are the IP extension headers AH and ESP. On top of these extensions headers any application protocol can be implemented, without taking care of the underlying security mechanisms. Since, the lifetime of keys for a secured communication should be limited to guarantee the security of the communication channel, the IKEv2 *CREATE_CHILD_SA* message can be used for rekeying an already existing SA. The EPC Gen2 pendant for the *CREATE_CHILD_SA* message is the *KeyUpdate* that generates new key material for existing SAs.

6   Implementation of an IPsec-enabled Tag Prototype

In order to prove the feasibility of the protocol stated in Sect. 5, a "Prototype for the Internet of Things based on an extendable EPC Gen2 RFID tag" (*PIONEER*) has been implemented. The *PIONEER* tag consists of a printed circuit board, with a dipole antenna, an analog EPC Gen2 Front-end for modulation and demodulation of the electromagnetic signals, and an Xilinx Spartan-3A FPGA. All digital components are placed on the FPGA. For low-level encoding/decoding of the information signals, a dedicated hardware module is used which is connected to the I/O bus of an 8-bit microcontroller (designed by E. Wenger et al. [54]) implemented in software (C code), including the proposed IPsec cryptographic suite with its cryptographic library. All cryptographic functions are based on an already existing AES (designed by M. Feldhofer et al. [18]) and the ECC co-processors. To generate nonces that fulfill the necessary security requirements for unpredictability, a true random number generator has been implemented and connected to the microcontroller. A system overview containing the most important hardware and software modules of the tag is shown in Fig. 3. In the following, the modules and their interactions are described in more detail.

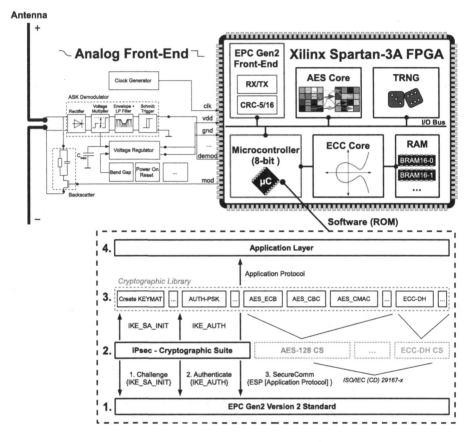

Fig. 3. System overview of the PIONEER tag containing the analog and digital components, as well as the four layers of the software architecture

6.1   The EPC Gen2 Front-end and Microcontroller

For reader-to-tag communication, the ASK (amplitude-shift keying) modulated electromagnetic reader signal is first obtained by the antenna (see Fig. 3). Then the signal is filtered, amplified, and finally demodulated in the *analog font-end*. At the output of the *analog font-end* the Xilinx Spartan-3A FPGA is fed by a clean digitalized data signal. Moreover, the clock and reset signals, the power supply, and a data input signal for the tag-to-reader communication are also provided by the *analog font-end*. The next processing stage is the decoding of the PIE (pulse-interval encoding) encoded data signal in the *EPC Gen2 Front-end* module. In parallel, the CRC (cyclic redundancy checksum) is calculated, and checked for the entire reader command. The *EPC Gen2 Front-end* collects a maximum of eight bits of input data, before an interrupt is triggered that signals the *microcontroller* once data is ready to be picked up. In the interrupt service routine, the *microcontroller* fetches the received reader command by reading the data from the 8-bit I/O bus, and then processes it according to the EPC Gen2 Version 2 standard.

The back channel of the communication works similarly. At the beginning of the transmission, the *microcontroller* writes the first 8-bit chunk of the reply to the *EPC Gen2 Front-end*. The *EPC Gen2 Front-end* then signals the *microcontroller* per interrupt as soon as the next data part can be transmitted. According to the modulation settings of the last received *Query* command, the *EPC Gen2 Front-end* generates an FM0 (bi-phase space) or Miller encoded data signal. The encoded data signal is forwarded to the *analog font-end*, where this signal controls the transistor of the backscatter network that connects or disconnects a load impedance connected to the antenna.

Software Implementation. The firmware of the PIONEER tag is entirely written in C code, and can be subdivided into four layers (see Fig. 3). On the first layer, all the EPC Gen2 Version 2 functionality is implemented that is marked mandatory in the standard. On top of this layer there is the cryptographic suite (CS) layer consisting of the proposed IPsec CS. The AES-128 and ECC-DH CS are shown grayed in Fig. 3, because they are not actually implemented—since the standards have not yet been released—, but it is assumed here that a subset of the future CS functionality is already implemented as a side product of the IPsec CS. All IPsec related reader commands are handled on this layer. The required cryptographic functionality, e.g. derivation of the keys, hashing, encryption and decryption, et cetera., are implemented in the cryptographic library beyond. This layer also provides the software interface to the AES and ECC cryptographic co-processors, and is used in most of the other library functions. After the creation of the secure communication channel, incoming ESP packets are first handled (integrity checked, authenticated, and decrypted) in the IPsec CS. Afterwards, the payload of the ESP packet is transferred into the application layer. The inverse path through the software layers is taken for outgoing ESP packets. All IPsec functionality works completely transparently for the application layer. The implemented top-level example application of the *PIONEER* tag waits for an incoming IP/UDP packet, checks the validity of the packet, and prepends a string to the received UDP payload data before it is returned as a valid ESP packet. With this example application we have been able to create an IPsec channel between the tag and a computer in our network that uses the open source implementation of IPsec "strongSwan" [50].

6.2 The ECC Core

The requirements for the ECC module of the PIONEER tag are a small chip area, low power consumption, and that it delivers a runtime that is sufficient for interactive protocols. To reach all those goals, a rigorous hardware-software co-design approach has been taken. The timing-critical finite-field arithmetic is built into a so-called drop-in ECC module [53], while the point arithmetic is done in software. To safe area, the ECC module does not come with a dedicated memory, but instead reuses the CPU's data memory. Therefore, the drop-in module is placed between the CPU and the memory. However, the drop-in ECC module does not hinder the CPU to access the data memory, as the drop-in module has a built in light-weight arbiter that always prioritizes the CPU.

Our software and hardware is specially optimized for the NIST P-192 [37] elliptic curve. The scalar multiplication algorithm uses the Montgomery-ladder formulas as proposed by Hutter *et al.* [24], multiple point validation checks, and randomized projective coordinates [10] to counter some of the most powerful power-analysis attacks. In order to prevent timing attacks, the scalar multiplication is computed in constant time. Therefore all finite-field addition, subtraction, multiplication and inversion algorithms are also executed in constant time. The inversion algorithm is based on Itoh and Tsuji's [27] trick which minimizes the number of multiplications during inversion.

The ECC drop-in module for PIONEER is based on the drop-in module by Unterluggauer and Wenger [52]. While their drop-in module is designed to do efficient Montgomery multiplications, the drop-in module for PIONEER is optimized for the NIST P-192 prime $p = 2^{192} - 2^{64} - 1$. Additionally, to ensure a performant point multiplication, the RAM has to be modified. While the interface to the CPU is a traditional 8-bit wide bus, the data memory has a 32-bit interface (with a byte-wise write-enable feature). The drop-in ECC module is responsible for mapping the CPU's 8-bit addresses to 32-bit RAM addresses. With a 32-bit interface between the ECC module and the RAM, it was possible to keep the ECC module without dedicated memory and to achieve a practical performance.

The combined hardware-software co-design approach enables a fast runtime of a scalar multiplication in around 695 000 cycles. This runtime is especially impressive considering that a comparable AVR processor would require 15 million cycles to compute the scalar multiplication on its own (cf. [55]). Even at a clock rate of mere 4 MHz, PIONEER is able to compute a scalar multiplication within 178.63 ms.

6.3   True Random Number Generator (TRNG)

The implemented TRNG was presented by Cherkaoui et al. in [9]. This TRNG was designed following the recommendation of AIS-31 [49]. The entropy per bit can be determined by using the provided stochastic model. This TRNG consist of a Self-Timed Ring (STR) that generates multiple jittery clock signals which are sampled using the same clock. An XOR-tree is used to hash all the sampled signals in one bit. If at least one of the STR signals is sampled in the jitter zone the output will be random. The statistical test of NIST [45] has been applied to 100 traces of 10^6 bits. The TRNG output passes this test successfully. In addition, the TRNG has been evaluated using different core voltages and for different temperatures (from 35 °C to 85 °C), obtaining good results in terms of randomness.

7   Implementation Results

The hardware implementation mainly consists of five modules—the microcontroller's program memory and RAM not included. The left part of Table 3 shows the resource utilization of these modules for the used Xilinx Spartan-3A FPGA split into the number of consumed flip-flops (FFs), the number of used look-up tables (LUTs), and the number of occupied Block RAM instances (BRAM). The microcontroller is by far the most area consuming module of the design with 389 FFs and 2 517 LUTs. For the cryptographic cores, 329 FFs and 710 LUTs for the AES core, and 229 FFs and 1 164 LUTs for the ECC core are required. The least hardware consuming modules are the EPC Gen2 Font-end with 178 FFs and 427 LUTs, and the TRNG with 90 FFs and 254 LUTs. The program memory and the microcontroller's RAM are both mapped into 16 and 4 dedicated Block RAMs respectively.

Table 3. Area requirement of the digital components for the Xilinx Spartan-3A FPGA, and the results for an 130 nm ASIC design flow

Hardware modules	FPGA resource utiliz.			ASIC area	
	[FFs]	[LUTs]	[BRAM]	[GEs]	[%]
AES Core	329	710	–	3 678	7.08
ECC Core	229	1 164	–	6 577	12.67
EPC Gen2 Front-end	178	427	–	2 253	4.34
Microcontroller	389	2 517	–	7 906	15.23
ROM	–	–	16	19 161	36.91
RAM	–	–	4	11 339	21.84
TRNG	90	254	–	1 000	1.93
Total	1 215	5 072	20	51 914	

On the right side of Table 3, the post-synthesis area results for an UMC L130E Low Leakage CMOS cell library from Faraday for 4 MHz clock frequency, and 1.2 V power supply are listed. The area metric for the application-specific integrated circuit (ASIC) design flow results are the gate equivalents (GE, $1\,GE \approx 5.12\,qm^2$ for the 130 nm UMC cell library) of the modules. For the calculation of the RAM and ROM area requirements, dedicated UMC *Sync. High Density Single Port SRAM*, and *Via-1 ROM* macros are used. The TRNG of the FPGA design could not be synthesized for an ASIC design flow—because it uses FPGA specific functionality. Hence, the area requirement of the TRNG has been estimated on the basis of following related work. Holleman et al. [23] uses a floating-gate memory cell for their *DC-nulling* TRNG that consumes about 564 GE for a 0.35 μm process (AMS C35B4C3). Another TRNG was published by Ben-Romdhane et al. [6] which is a metastability based *open-loop delay chain* design, and needs about 300 gates in a 65 nm CMOS process from STMicroelectronics. The upper bound for the TRNG size estimation of 1 kGE comes from Ranasinghe et al. [42]. They presented a TRNG which utilizes a PUF (physically unclonable function) with challenges that create unstable (random) responses. Thus, the resulting overall area requirement for the digital part of the PIONEER tag is about 52 kGE or 0.266 mm^2 for the UMC 130 nm process. The design was synthesized with the Cadence Encounter RTL Compiler Version v08.10-s28_1, and place and route was done using Cadence NanoRoute v08.10-s155.

In Table 4, the size of the tags program memory parts are listed according to the software layers in Fig. 3. The whole implementation takes about 18.3 kilobytes of ROM. The biggest part of the program memory is consumed by the mandatory EPC Gen2 Version 2 functionality with 6.83 kilobytes. For the IPsec cryptographic suite 5.76 kilobytes ROM were needed. The cryptographic library is subdivided into three parts. The AES subpart consists of the encryption and decryption functionality, and the CBC mode (cipher block chaining). All other IPsec specific functionality like key material derivation and the PRF function (cf. AES_XCBC) are summed up in the IPsec subpart. If it is assumed that the AES and ECC subparts are already implemented as cryptographic suites, the additional implementation costs for the IPsec functionality are about 6.7 kilobytes. The smallest part of the ROM is the example application with 1.43 kilobytes only.

Table 4. Size and partitioning of the program memory in bytes and percent

Software layer	ROM Size	
	[bytes]	[%]
1. EPC Gen2 Version 2	6 828	37.31
2. IPsec CS	5 762	31.49
3. Cryptographic Library	4 280	23.39
- AES	738	4.03
- ECC	2 608	14.25
- IPsec	934	5.11
4. Application	1 426	7.79
Total	18 296	

In order to prove the correctness of the IPsec implementation, a laboratory setup was built that simulates the communication scenario shown in Fig. 2. For the left communication partner (interrogator), a virtual machine running Linux Kernel 3.10.7 with the open source IPsec implementation strongSwan 5.1.0 is used. The network packets generated by the interrogator are then captured by a Java application that extracts the IPsec payloads of the network packets and forwards them via an UHF reader device to the PIONEER tag, and vice versa. To determine the timing of the protocol in detail, the handling of the EPC Gen2 commands encapsulating IPsec messages was also simulated using Cadence

NCsim. The biggest amount of time with 410.95 ms is consumed by process-ing the initial Challenge (IKE_SA_INIT) command, because the Diffie-Hellman key exchange involves two point multiplications. Therefore, almost 87 % of the processing time is spent on calculating the elliptic curve points. The derivation of the keying material and the calculation of the authentication and integrity check values consume another 11.94 ms (about 12 %). For the handling of the Authenticate (IKE_AUTH) command 15.76 ms are required. Most of the time (94.7 %) is spent on performing AES operations for decrypting the message, integrity and authenticity checking, deriving keying material for the ESP Child SA, and calculating the response. When optimum timing for the reader to tag communication is considered with 640 kbps uplink frequency and 128 kbps down-link frequency, the inventory procedures takes at least 1.2 ms. The IKE_SA_INIT exchange takes about 13.98 ms, and the IKE_AUTH message exchange consumes almost 17.38 ms communication time. Considering both communication effort and processing effort on tag side, it takes at least 459.25 ms until an IPsec chan-nel is established, when the interrogator to reader communication is not taken into account. The results show that almost 92.9 % of the time is spent on process-ing the messages and only 7.1 % is required for communication.

After the IPsec tunnel is established, the interrogator sends an UDP data-gram encapsulated into a protected ESP packet to the PIONEER tag. The tag decrypts the payload of the received packet and checks the authenticity of the sender. Eventually, the tag creates a reply and sends it back to the interrogator. Since, the ESP packet uses AES with 128-bit (16 bytes) block size, the time for sending and receiving ESP packets depends on the number of 16-byte blocks (n_b) that are transmitted. The up-link and down-link speed can therefore be expressed as a linear function with a fixed intercept value and an n_b dependent slope para-meter. The reader to tag communication thus consumes $5.6 + 1.99 * n_b$ ms, and in the other communication direction it takes $4.2 + 1.19 * n_b$ ms to transmit one ESP packet—including sending and processing efforts.

8   Conclusions

In this paper, we presented an RFID-tag prototyping platform that integrates IPsec into the new EPC Gen2 Version 2 standard. The obtained results can help to estimate the costs for practical implementations that aim an open and secure Internet of Things where EPC tags play a central role. The cryptographic primitives suggested for the EPC Gen2 Version 2 cryptographic suites—in the ISO/IEC 29167 standard—provide strong symmetric and asymmetric cryptog-raphy. Additionally, the EPC Gen2 security functionality partially overlaps with the IPsec protocol which is used to create a secure communication channel over the Internet. We have also shown that by merging the IPsec and EPC Gen2 functionality, RFID tags can be enabled to work as independent nodes on the Internet without the need for trusted readers. Our theoretical considerations have been proven by an FPGA based tag prototype, with which we were able to establish an IPsec tunnel between the tag prototype and a computer inside our local network. We support the meaning of Sarma et al. [48], who believe in an Internet of Things based on a single and open architecture as the key to a successful system. Moreover, we believe that the potential impact is even higher, if already established protocols and standardized security is used to create the Internet of Things.

Acknowledgements. This work has been supported by the Austrian Science Fund (FWF) under the grant number TRP251-N23 (Realizing a Secure Internet of Things - ReSIT) and the FFG research program SeCoS (project number 836628).

References

1. Agren, M., Hell, M., Johansson, T., Meier, W.: Grain-128a: a new version of grain-128 with optional authentication. Int. J. Wire. Mob. Comput. **5**(1), 48–59 (2011)
2. ANSI. Public Key Cryptography for the Financial Services Industry - Key Agreement and Key Transport Using Elliptic Curve Cryptography. Accredited Standards Committee X9 (2001) (Incorporated)
3. Arbit, A., Oren, Y., Wool, A.: Toward practical public key anti-counterfeiting for low-cost EPC tags. In: RFID, pp. 184–191. IEEE, April 2011
4. Ashton, K.: That 'Internet of Things' Thing (2009). http://www.rfidjournal.com/articles/view?4986. Accessed 18 Feb 2014
5. Avoine, G., Carpent, X.: Yet another ultralightweight authentication protocol that is broken. In: Hoepman, J.-H., Verbauwhede, I. (eds.) RFIDSec 2012. LNCS, vol. 7739, pp. 20–30. Springer, Heidelberg (2013)
6. Ben-Romdhane, M., Graba, T., Danger, J.-L., Mathieu, Y.: Design methodology of an ASIC TRNG based on an open-loop delay chain. In: IEEE International Workshops on New Circuits and Systems Conference (NEWCAS), pp. 1–4, June 2013
7. Bogdanov, A., Knudsen, L.R., Leander, G., Paar, C., Poschmann, A., Robshaw, M.J.B., Seurin, Y., Vikkelsoe, C.: PRESENT: an ultra-lightweight block cipher. In: Paillier, P., Verbauwhede, I. (eds.) CHES 2007. LNCS, vol. 4727, pp. 450–466. Springer, Heidelberg (2007)
8. Chang, Y.-C., Chen, J.-L., Lin, Y.-S., Wang, S.M.: RFIPv6 - a novel IPv6-EPC bridge mechanism. In: International Conference on Consumer Electronics - ICCE, pp. 1–2 (2008)
9. Cherkaoui, A., Fischer, V., Fesquet, L., Aubert, A.: A very high speed true random number generator with entropy assessment. In: Bertoni, G., Coron, J.-S. (eds.) CHES 2013. LNCS, vol. 8086, pp. 179–196. Springer, Heidelberg (2013)
10. Coron, J.-S.: Resistance against differential power analysis for elliptic curve cryptosystems. In: Koç, Ç.K., Paar, C. (eds.) CHES 1999. LNCS, vol. 1717, pp. 292–302. Springer, Heidelberg (1999)
11. Daemen, J., Rijmen, V.: The block cipher Rijndael. In: Schneier, B., Quisquater, J.-J. (eds.) CARDIS 1998. LNCS, vol. 1820, pp. 277–284. Springer, Heidelberg (2000)
12. Dominikus, S., Aigner, M., Kraxberger, S.: Passive RFID technology for the internet of things. In: International Conference for Internet Technology and Secured Transactions (ICITST), pp. 1–8 (2010)

13. Dominikus, S., Kraxberger, S.: Secure Communication with RFID tags in the Internet of Things. Secur. Commun. Netw., n/a–n/a (2011). http://onlinelibrary.wiley.com/doi/10.1002/sec.398/abstract
14. Dworkin, M.: Recommendation for Block Cipher Modes of Operation: Methods and Techniques. NIST (2001)
15. Engels, D., Kang, Y.S., Wang, J.: On security with the new Gen2 RFID security framework. In: 2013 IEEE International Conference on RFID (RFID), pp. 144–151 (2013)
16. EPCglobal. EPC Radio-Frequency Identity Protocols Generation-2 UHF RFID Specification for RFID Air Interface Protocol for Communication at 860 MHz - 960 MHz Version 2.0.0 Ratified, November 2013. http://www.gs1.org
17. Ertl, J., Plos, T., Feldhofer, M., Felber, N., Henzen, L.: A security-enhanced UHF RFID tag chip. In: Euromicro Conference on Digital System Design (DSD), pp. 705–712 (2013)
18. Feldhofer, M., Wolkerstorfer, J., Rijmen, V.: AES implementation on a grain of sand. IEEE Proc. Inf. Secur. **152**(1), 13–20 (2005)
19. Girault, M., Poupard, G., Stern, J., Girault, M., Poupard, G., Stern, J.: On the fly authentication and signature schemes based on groups of unknown order. J. cryptology **19**, 463–487 (2006)
20. Ha, J., Moon, S., Zhou, J., Ha, J.: A new formal proof model for RFID location privacy. In: Jajodia, S., Lopez, J. (eds.) ESORICS 2008. LNCS, vol. 5283, pp. 267–281. Springer, Heidelberg (2008)
21. Hada, H., Mitsugi, J.: EPC based internet of things architecture. In: IEEE International Conference on RFID-Technologies and Applications (RFID-TA), pp. 527–532 (2011)
22. Hinz, W., Finkenzeller, K., Seysen, M.: Secure UHF tags with strong cryptography - development of ISO/IEC 18000–63 compatible secure RFID tags and presentation of first results. In: SENSORNETS, pp. 5–13 (2013)
23. Holleman, J., Otis, B., Bridges, S., Mitros, A., Diorio, C.: A 2.92 uW hardware random number generator. In: European Solid-State Circuits Conference, pp. 134–137 (2006)
24. Hutter, M., Joye, M., Sierra, Y.: Memory-constrained implementations of elliptic curve cryptography in Co-Z coordinate representation. In: Nitaj, A., Pointcheval, D. (eds.) AFRICACRYPT 2011. LNCS, vol. 6737, pp. 170–187. Springer, Heidelberg (2011)
25. IANA - Internet Assigned Numbers Authority. Referenced 2014 at http://www.iana.org/assignments/ikev2-parameters/ikev2-parameters.xhtml
26. ISO - International Organization for Standardization. Referenced 2014 at http://www.iso.org/
27. Itoh, T., Tsujii, S.: Effective recursive algorithm for computing multiplicative inverses in $GF(2^m)$. Electron. Lett. **24**(6), 334–335 (1988)
28. Johnson, D., Menezes, A., Vanstone, S.: The elliptic curve digital signature algorithm (ECDSA). Int. J. Inf. Secur. **1**(1), 36–63 (2001)
29. Kaufman, C., Hoffman, P., Nir, Y., Eronen, P.: Internet Key Exchange Protocol Version 2 (IKEv2). RFC 5996 (Proposed Standard), Sept 2010. Updated by RFCs 5998, 6989
30. Kent, S., Seo, K.: Security Architecture for the Internet Protocol. RFC 4301 (Proposed Standard), Dec 2005. Updated by RFC 6040
31. Lee, J.-W., Phan, N.D., Vo, D.H.-T., Duong, V.-H.: A fully integrated EPC Gen-2 UHF-band passive tag IC using an efficient power management technique. IEEE Trans. Industr. Electron. **61**(6), 2922–2932 (2014)

32. Lehtonen, M., Ostojic, D., Ilic, A., Michahelles, F.: Securing RFID systems by detecting tag cloning. In: Tokuda, H., Beigl, M., Friday, A., Brush, A.J.B., Tobe, Y. (eds.) Pervasive 2009. LNCS, vol. 5538, pp. 291–308. Springer, Heidelberg (2009)
33. Lepinski, M., Kent, S.: Additional Diffie-Hellman Groups for Use with IETF Standards. RFC 5114 (Informational), Jan 2008
34. Mattern, F., Floerkemeier, C.: From the internet of computers to the internet of things. In: Sachs, K., Petrov, I., Guerrero, P. (eds.) Buchmann Festschrift. LNCS, vol. 6462, pp. 242–259. Springer, Heidelberg (2010)
35. Menezes, A.J., Vanstone, S.A., Oorschot, P.C.V.: Handbook of Applied Cryptography, 1st edn. CRC Press Inc., Boca Raton (1996)
36. Montgomery, P.L.: Modular multiplication without trial division. Math. Comput. **44**(170), 519–521 (1985)
37. National Institute of Standards and Technology (NIST). FIPS-186-3: Digital Signature Standard (DSS) (2009). http://www.itl.nist.gov/fipspubs/
38. Noman, A., Rahman, M., Adams, C.: Improving security and usability of low cost RFID tags. In: International Conference on Privacy, Security and Trust (PST), pp. 134–141 (2011)
39. Pang, L., He, L., Pei, Q., Wang, Y.: Secure and efficient mutual authentication protocol for RFID conforming to the EPC C-1 G-2 standard. In: Wireless Communications and Networking Conference (WCNC), pp. 1870–1875 (2013)
40. Peris-Lopez, P., Lim, T.-L., Li, T.: Providing stronger authentication at a low cost to RFID tags operating under the EPCglobal framework. In: IEEE/IFIP International Conference on Embedded and Ubiquitous Computing, vol. 2, pp. 159–166 (2008)
41. Rabin, M.O.: Digitalized Signatures and Public-Key Functions as Intractable as Factorization. Technical report, Cambridge, MA, USA (1979)
42. Ranasinghe, D.C., Limb, D., Devadas, S., Jamali, B., Zhu, Z., Cole, P. H.: An Efficient Hardware Random Number Generator
43. Raza, S., Duquennoy, S., Chung, T., Yazar, D., Voigt, T., Roedig, U.: Securing communication in 6LoWPAN with compressed IPsec. In: International Conference on Distributed Computing in Sensor Systems (IEEE DCOSS 2011) (2011)
44. Rivest, R.L., Shamir, A., Adleman, L.: A method for obtaining digital signatures and public-key cryptosystems. Commun. ACM **21**(2), 120–126 (1978)
45. Rukhin, A., Soto, J., Nechvatal, J., Smid, M., Barker, E., Leigh, S., Levenson, M., Vangel, M., Banks, D., Heckert, A., Dray, J., Vo, S.: A Statistical Test Suite for Random and Pseudorandom Number Generators for Cryptographic Applications (2001). http://csrc.nist.gov/rng/
46. Safkhani, M., Bagheri, N., Peris-Lopez, P., Mitrokotsa, A., Hernandez-Castro, J.: Weaknesses in Another Gen2-based RFID Authentication Protocol. In: 2012 IEEE International Conference on RFID-Technologies and Applications (RFID-TA), pp. 80–84 (2012)
47. Sample, A., Yeager, D., Powledge, P., Smith, J.: Design of a passively-powered, programmable sensing platform for UHF RFID systems. In: IEEE International Conference on RFID, pp. 149–156, March 2007
48. Sarma, S., Brock, D.L., Ashton, K.: White Paper: The Networked Physical World (2000). http://www.autoidlabs.org/uploads/media/MIT-AUTOID-WH-001.pdf. Accessed 18 Feb 2014
49. Schindler, W., Killmann, W.: Evaluation criteria for true (physical) random number generators used in cryptographic applications. In: Kaliski Jr., B.S., Koç, Ç.K., Paar, C. (eds.) CHES 2002. LNCS, vol. 2523, pp. 431–449. Springer, Heidelberg (2003)

50. strongSwan - the OpenSource IPsec-based VPN Solution. Referenced 2014 at http://www.strongswan.org/
51. Sun, D.-Z., Zhong, J.-D.: A hash-based RFID security protocol for strong privacy protection. IEEE Trans. Consum. Electron. **58**(4), 1246–1252 (2012)
52. Unterluggauer, T., Wenger, E.: Efficient pairings and ECC for embedded systems. In: Batina, L., Robshaw, M. (eds.) CHES 2014. LNCS, vol. 8731, pp. 298–315. Springer, Heidelberg (2014)
53. Wenger, E.: Hardware architectures for MSP430-based wireless sensor nodes performing elliptic curve cryptography. In: Jacobson, M., Locasto, M., Mohassel, P., Safavi-Naini, R. (eds.) ACNS 2013. LNCS, vol. 7954, pp. 290–306. Springer, Heidelberg (2013)
54. Wenger, E., Baier, T., Feichtner, J.: JAAVR: introducing the next generation of security-enabled RFID tags. In: Niar, S. (ed.) Digital System Design, pp. 640–647. IEEE (2012)
55. Wenger, E., Unterluggauer, T., Werner, M.: 8/16/32 shades of elliptic curve cryptography on embedded processors. In: Paul, G., Vaudenay, S. (eds.) INDOCRYPT 2013. LNCS, vol. 8250, pp. 244–261. Springer, Heidelberg (2013)
56. Yi, X., Wang, L., Mao, D., Zhan, Y.: An Gen2 based security authentication protocol for RFID system. Phys. Procedia **24, Part B**, 1385–1391 (2012). (International Conference on Applied Physics and Industrial Engineering 2012)

SeAK: Secure Authentication and Key Generation Protocol Based on Dual Antennas for Wireless Body Area Networks

Chitra Javali[1,2]([⊠]), Girish Revadigar[1,2], Lavy Libman[1,2], and Sanjay Jha[1]

[1] School of Computer Science and Engineering, UNSW, Sydney, Australia
[2] NICTA, Sydney, Australia
{chitraj,girishr,llibman,sanjay}@cse.unsw.edu.au

Abstract. The increasing interest in the usage of wireless body area networks (WBAN) in healthcare and other critical applications underscores the importance of secure communication among the body sensor devices. Associating an unknown device with an existing network without prior knowledge of a secret key poses a major challenge. Existing authentication schemes in WBAN are typically based on received signal strength (RSS). However, RSS techniques using a single antenna are susceptible to environmental factors and are vulnerable to attacks that use variable transmission power. We present SeAK, the first secure light-weight device pairing protocol for WBAN based on RSS obtained by dual-antenna transceivers utilizing spatial diversity. With spatially separated antennas, the RSS values from a nearby device are large and distinct, as opposed to those from a far-away device. SeAK exploits this effect to accomplish authentication and shared secret key generation simultaneously. We have implemented a prototype of SeAK on the Opal sensor platform with a 2.4 GHz compatible RF231 radio. We demonstrate that our protocol is able to achieve a 100 % success acceptance rate, securely authenticate a nearby device and generate a 128-bit secret key in 640 ms, as opposed to 15.9 s in other recent RSS-based schemes (e.g. ASK-BAN).

1 Introduction

In recent years, the medical field has observed a tremendous growth of wireless medical devices ranging from low-power medical radios that harvest body energy [12], to implanted medical devices (IMD) and wearable devices for remote monitoring of patients [25]. The ability of devices such as cardiac defibrillators, pacemakers, pulse-oximeters and glucose monitors to communicate in a wireless medium has opened up new opportunities for more reliable e-healthcare. According to a recent survey, the global market for wearable medical devices was valued at USD 2.0 billion in 2012 and is expected to reach a value of USD 5.8 billion in 2019 [5].

NICTA is funded by the Australian Department of Communications and the Australian Research Council through the ICT Centre of Excellence program.

© Springer International Publishing Switzerland 2014
N. Saxena and A.-R. Sadeghi (Eds.): RFIDSec 2014, LNCS 8651, pp. 74–89, 2014.
DOI: 10.1007/978-3-319-13066-8_5

Though the wireless medium provides numerous advantages, on the flip side there are a number of threats associated with authenticity, confidentiality and integrity of the sensitive health information. As the wireless system is an open access medium, an intruder can pair with the body area network and send false health-related information to the BS which may result in diagnosis errors, tamper the physiological data sensed by other body-worn devices, jam the network by creating interference or inject false commands leading to fatal outcomes.

As per the IEEE 802.15.6 Technical Requirements Document [4], *"Consideration should be given to secure device pairing (or association). Pairing consists of device authentication and key exchange. WBAN devices should successfully complete the secure pairing process before engaging in secure data communication with other WBAN devices"*. The initial trust establishment without any prior stored key from the manufacturer is a challenging aspect of security in WBAN. Employing cryptographic algorithms like Diffie-Hellman to generate shared secret keys is expensive for WBAN devices due to limited memory and computation power. Furthermore, in case of emergency, a third party/hospital authority must be able to communicate with the body-worn device of a patient which holds critical health information with minimal human intervention. The patient might not be able to provide the security information when he/she is unconscious or in critical condition. If the authority is unaware of the cryptographic key or the key is lost, then the problem of gaining access to WBAN becomes more complicated. Additionally, WBAN security must be robust enough to avoid active attacks as well as accidental access/commands from external devices. Access must be provided only to the legitimate external off-body devices such as wireless monitoring devices [2], external device programmers [3] etc. by dynamic authentication.

As the body worn devices have size and power constraints, security mechanisms should not add a high overhead to the devices in terms of hardware or software complexity. Some prior efforts of adapting public key cryptography protocols (e.g., TinyECC) to tiny sensor nodes have been evaluated as complex and memory consuming [27]. In recent years, there has been growing research interest in physical layer security which exploits the unique wireless channel characteristics between two devices. The unique channel characteristics are space and time dependent and decorrelate rapidly after a distance of $1/2$ the wavelength (λ) of the wireless transmission channel [22]. These spatio-temporal characteristics have been exploited for authentication [23] and pairwise session key-generation [7,24] in WBAN.

However, the previously proposed device authentication mechanisms are based on received signal strength (RSS) from a single antenna. It has been shown in recent work that RSS is susceptible to environmental factors and is unreliable as it varies over a period of time even for a static transceiver [11]. In addition, as RSS is a function of the transmission power, an attacker can easily vary the transmitting power to induce high received signal strength and get authenticated as a legitimate device. Thus, the existing authentication procedures for WBAN [23,24] may not be able to distinguish between a malicious node and a legitimate device. Furthermore, the existing work in WBAN address authentication and pair-wise secret key generation separately.

In this paper, we propose a physical-layer based efficient, light-weight, close proximity secure device pairing protocol (SeAK) for WBAN, which performs authentication and shared secret key generation *simultaneously*. Our proposed scheme employs dual-antenna devices, utilizing the spatial diversity of antennas and the property that RSS values on the two antennas tend to be substantially different when the other device is nearby, in contrast to similar RSS values on both antennas obtained from far-away devices. This allows legitimate nearby devices to be distinguished effectively from potential attacker far-away devices.

Although RSS from multiple antennas of a receiver has been exploited in Wi-Fi systems with MIMO capability [9,30], multiple antenna architectures have not been used in WBAN. As the WBANs are being increasingly employed in pervasive healthcare applications, a revolution has already started in the research area of designing specialized devices and smart antennas for WBAN, e.g. tiny and flexible strip antennas, micro-strip antennas, textile antennas, and button antennas [6,8,17]. With the advent of smart wearable devices and antennas, the use of multi-antenna architecture in WBAN devices is expected to be widely employed in the near future. To the best of our knowledge, the work presented in this paper is the first to demonstrate the use of dual-antenna based secure pairing in the context of WBAN.

Our contributions can be summarised as follows:

- We propose an efficient secure pairing protocol for resource constrained devices of WBAN, which uses the spatial diversity of dual-antenna transceivers to perform authentication and secret key generation concurrently, and requires minimal human intervention.
- We validate the proposed approach experimentally and show that it completes the authentication and generation of a 128-bit secret key in 640 ms with a 100 % acceptance success rate, which indicates the suitability of our protocol for practical applications.

The rest of the paper is organized as follows. Section 2 discusses the related work. Section 3 explains our system model and assumptions. Sections 4 and 5 present the SeAK protocol and its implementation. Section 6 presents our experiments and results. In Sect. 7, we discuss the security evaluation of our protocol. We conclude the paper in Sect. 8.

2 Related Work

Extensive research has been carried out on secure device pairing based on wireless channel characteristics [16,20,26,29]. Authenticating a device in close proximity was first proposed in Amigo [26]. Ensemble [16] extended Amigo and proposed a cooperative proximity based authentication, in which the nearby trusted devices analyse the RSS variations between pairing devices to determine legitimacy. In [20], two devices located within a distance of $\lambda/2$ authenticate each other based on the analysis of phase and amplitude measurements of radio frequency (RF) signal from a public RF transmitter. The above mechanism requires multi-band transceivers and hence is not suitable for WBAN. Authors in [29] have proposed a hypothesis testing mechanism for physical layer authentication in which the two communicating parties store the channel responses of initial communications between them and subsequently compare those for the current message to validate a legitimate transmitter.

Ideally, for wearable medical devices, security mechanisms must be simple, light-weight, robust, and should not be dependent on specialized hardware or sensors. RSS based authentication has received little attention in the research community [23,24]. In WBAN, BANA [23] has studied the RSS characteristics of single antenna devices and has proposed an authentication protocol for on-body devices of WBAN. BANA takes about 12 s for authentication and requires frequent packet exchanges between the body-worn devices. An extended version ASK-BAN [24] addresses authentication and key generation separately. ASK-BAN uses two different channel states — static channel for authentication and dynamic channel for key generation, i.e., the subject should not perform any body movement during the authentication process, whereas the key generation mechanism requires body motion. In ASK-BAN, the time taken for authentication and key generation is 12 s and 15.9 s respectively.

RSS has been exploited in prior work [9,30] for security in Wi-Fi systems with MIMO capability. In [9], though authentication is based on channel characteristics, the key exchange protocol is based on the computationally complex Diffie-Hellman mechanism. In [30], key generation is performed with the cooperation of multiple mobile Wi-Fi devices equipped with multiple antennas.

Based on our survey of security protocols for wireless networks and body area networks, we believe that our work is the first secured pairing/association protocol based on physical layer characteristics using antenna diversity for low-data rate, small form-factor devices of WBAN.

3   System Model and Assumptions

3.1   RSS on Single v/s Dual Antenna

RSS has been widely used for localization [13,21] and attack detection [11] in wireless networks. The authors in [28,31] have shown that RSS has an irregular pattern even for a fixed transmitter and receiver. In a typical system consisting of a receiver and transmitter, if the sender sends a radio signal with power P_s, then the received power P_r at the receiver can be expressed as

$$P_r = P_s K / d_r^\alpha \tag{1}$$

where K is a constant, α is the distance power exponent and d_r is the distance between receiver and sender.

Now, if we consider receiver employing two antennas to capture the radio signals then the received power ratio can be calculated from (1) as

$$\frac{P_{r1}}{P_{r2}} = \frac{P_s K/d_1^\alpha}{P_s K/d_2^\alpha} \tag{2}$$

where $d_1 \neq d_2$.

From (2), the received power ratio is dependent only on the two distances, namely, the distance between the sender and receiver antennas A1 (d_1) and A2 (d_2) in contrast to (1), which implies that the received power P_r is dependent on transmission power P_s.

The concept discussed in this section forms the basis for our proposed protocol.

3.2   System Overview

In our system model, we assume there is one CU and one or more wearable sensor devices to be authenticated. The CU and wearable devices are within the communicating range of WBAN ($\approx$3 m) [14]. In our system design, the CU is the only device that requires the additional feature of dual-antenna, and has the potential to authenticate other devices communicating with it by its unique property of antenna diversity. The sensor devices may have one or two antennas. We assume there is no prior association or secret key exchanged between the CU and other devices, and none of the devices are compromised. We also assume that the user or any other person authenticating a legitimate device is honest. We assume the availability of suitable secret key renewal procedures for wearable devices after on-body deployment.

As our focus is on secure device pairing, we are mainly concerned in detecting the masquerade attack in which a non-legitimate node poses as a legitimate node and communicates with the CU. We assume the presence of off-body adversaries only, i.e. the attacker is not present on-body or in the close vicinity of the WBAN, and is located at a distance of at least 1–2 m away from the CU. The adversary may use high or varying transmit power, and attempt to pair with the CU. The adversary lacks the capability of jamming the communication.

Figure 1 depicts our proposed system in which the CU and the device B to be authenticated are placed close to each other. The two antennas A1 and A2 of CU are separated by a distance D cm. The RSS values measured by A1 and A2 will yield a large difference for the nearby device B placed at a distance of d_1 and d_2 from A1 and A2 respectively. In contrast, for a far-away device E, the difference in RSS values measured at A1 and A2 of CU will be small.

4   SeAK Protocol

Our main focus in this paper is to achieve initial trust between an already trusted device CU and a new sensor device. The sensor device has to establish a secure link with the already trusted CU before joining the network (WBAN) and begin

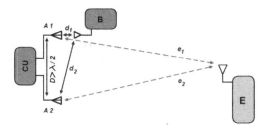

Fig. 1. The CU equipped with two spatially separated antennas A1 and A2 can effectively distinguish between a nearby legitimate device and a far-away attacker based on the RSS indicator difference obtained on its two antennas.

measuring the physiological data. Our proposed SeAK protocol is executed during the device pairing/association to establish a secure channel between the CU and device, by performing authentication and shared secret key generation simultaneously. SeAK protocol is described below.

1. The user holds the device to be authenticated in close proximity at a distance of d cm aligned to any one of the antennas A1 or A2 of CU. The device sends an association request *Assoc Req* to CU. The CU responds with an acknowledgement ACK to notify the start of association process.
2. The CU sends a probe packet *Probe[i]* to the device from antenna A1. In response, the sensor device measures the RSSI of the received packet and transmits a probe response *Probe Resp[i]* to CU. The CU in turn measures the RSS indicator (RSSI). The index value $i = \{1, 2, \ldots N\}$ tracks the number of packets N required for the association procedure.
3. The CU transmits a total of N packets at an interval of t ms by randomly switching between the two antennas A1 and A2. Let $X = \{x_1, x_2, \ldots x_N\}$ and $Y = \{y_1, y_2 \ldots y_N\}$ represent the set of RSSI measured by CU and device. Additionally, in order to evaluate the RSSI difference, CU stores the RSSI obtained at the two antennas A1 and A2 in separate data sets $R1 = \{r1_1, r1_2, \ldots r1_p\}$ and $R2 = \{r2_1, r2_2, \ldots r2_q\}$ respectively.
4. The absolute average RSSI difference RD_{avg} is calculated as $((r1 - r2)_j + (r1 - r2)_{j+1} + \ldots + (r1 - r2)_n)/n$. where $j = \{1, 2, \ldots n\}$ and n represents the minimum of p and q. The notations p and q denote the total number of samples captured by A1 and A2 respectively.
5. CU compares RD_{avg} with the threshold RSSI difference RD_{th} and the device is confirmed as legitimate if RD_{avg} is greater than RD_{th}, else discarded. CU notifies the device about successful authentication by sending an *Assoc Resp[ACCEPT]* message.
6. After successful authentication, both CU and device use the RSSI values stored during probe exchange for generating a shared secret key. The maximum max and minimum min values of RSSI are determined to obtain a mid value as $(max - min)/2$. Each RSSI sample is decoded as either bit 0 or 1 based on whether the sample value is smaller or greater than mid. Due to

spatial separation of the two antennas of CU, the RSSI measured by both the devices when CU employs A1 will be substantially distinct compared to RSSI obtained when CU employs A2. The process of bit extraction is repeated for N samples at both the nodes. Thus, both CU and the device derive an initial shared secret key.

Any packet loss during the probe exchange is handled by retransmissions. Once the CU and device have established a secure channel between them, the device is ready to be worn on-body.

5   Implementation

We have implemented the proof of concept in TinyOS environment. The Opal sensor platform [15], used in testbeds like FlockLab [19] and Twonet [18], was used for CU, and Iris motes were used as the sensor devices to be authenticated and as eavesdroppers. Our protocol can be implemented for commercially available off-the-shelf sensor devices which support dual antenna architecture.

Opal can be configured to work in either single antenna mode or antenna diversity mode. When single antenna mode is enabled, only one default antenna is used for both transmission and reception of packets. In antenna diversity mode, the transceiver radio checks the preamble field of a received frame to select one of the two antennas with the highest radio frequency (RF) signal strength. The scanning of preamble field is repeated for every new frame. The probability that both the antennas experience identical fading and multi-path effects is less when the two antennas are spatially separated to receive independent signals. However, in our system design we require that both the antennas should be able to receive RF signals independently, and also our system must not be dependent on the radio transceiver for the receiver diversity. Hence, we have modified the TinyOS driver and RF231 lower layer stack code to select one of the two antennas from the application layer, for transmission as well as reception of the packets.

For our implementation, the antenna diversity algorithm is disabled for dual-antenna RF230 radio [1] by setting the bit ANT_DIV_EN of ANT_DIV (0x0D) register to 0. The two externally connected 2.4 GHz antennas A1 and A2 are enabled by setting ANT_SEL bit of the same register to 0 and 1 respectively in the TinyOS driver program. At any instant of time only one of the antennas is enabled by the application and the time taken to switch between the two antennas is less than 100 ns [19]. Hence the power consumed by the CU is equivalent to that of a single antenna device.

6   Experiments and Results

6.1   Test Environment

In order to authenticate a legitimate device, there are two main factors to be identified: (i) The optimal displacement between the two antennas of CU to gain a large RSSI difference, (ii) An upper bound distance between CU and device. In order to get uncorrelated signal characteristics, we placed the two receiving antennas of CU 7 cm ($> \lambda/2$) apart and incremented the separation in steps up to 30 cm[1]. We conducted the first set of experiments by placing CU and the device off-body and the second set for on-body. In the following subsections we describe the test set up for off-body and on-body environments.

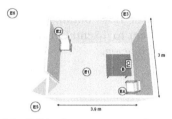  

(a) Off-body set up environment. CU: Control Unit, B: Device, E1-E6: Eavesdroppers

(b) Off-body set up: The device to be authenticated placed close to one of the antennas of CU

(c) CU on-body: Subject wearing CU and holding the device to be paired in close proximity

Fig. 2. Test environment

CU off-body: The experiments were conducted in a room of dimension 3.9 × 3 m^2 as shown in Fig. 2a. Figure 2b shows the off-body set-up where both CU and the device were placed on a table. These experiments were conducted to study the off-body channel characteristics and the ability of authenticating a device when CU is present off-body. Experiments were conducted by placing the device B at different distances d varying from 1 cm to 30 cm with respect to antenna A1 of CU. Evaluation was done by placing the device at various angles, e.g. 0°, 45° and 90° w.r.t A1, and also repeated for the antenna A2.

The tests were conducted for inter-packet intervals t of 250 ms, 100 ms, 50 ms, 10 ms and 5 ms respectively. For the experiments we set the number of packets exchanged between CU and device to be $N = 250$.

CU on-body: In this set-up, CU was placed on the body of a subject as shown in Fig. 2c and the device B to be authenticated was held in close proximity of the CU. The distance between the two receiving antennas D was varied from 10 cm to 30 cm, and for various D the distance d between CU and device was also changed[2]. A similar set of experiments to that of off-body set-up were conducted.

---

[1] For 2.4 GHz, $\lambda = 12.5$ cm

[2] We believe that the use of specialised antennas like micro-strip antennas and button antennas as well as advances in wearable technologies more generally, will allow such levels of spatial diversity in the near future [8,17].

6.2   Results

In this section we evaluate the experimental results obtained for off-body and on-body scenarios. We analyse the set of results obtained when the device was aligned to A1 of CU.

CU off-body: From Fig. 3, one can observe that for $d = 1$ cm, RSSI obtained at A1 is greater than that of A2 and the RSSI obtained at both the antennas decrease as the distance d of the device increases with respect to CU. From Figs. 3a and b it can be observed that the difference in the RSSI obtained at A1 and A2 substantially reduces when d increases from 1 cm to 15 cm. On further increasing d to 30 cm, the RSSI of A1 and A2 almost coincide.

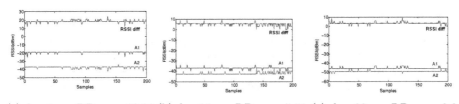

(a) d = 1cm, $RD_{avg} = 18.21$ (b) d = 15cm, $RD_{avg} = 5.51$ (c) d = 30cm, $RD_{avg} = 3.0$

Fig. 3. Results for off-body setup when D = 10 cm

Figure 5a reveals that, as the distance between the 2 antennas D increases, the RSSI difference of A1 and A2 also increases. In contrast, for a fixed D, the RSSI difference decreases as the distance d between the device and CU increases. At $d = 30$ cm for various values of D, the RSSI difference of A1 and A2 is substantially smaller compared to $d = 1$ cm.

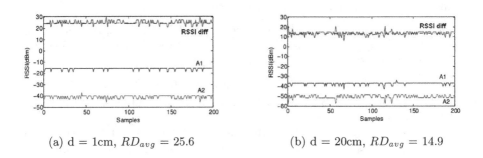

(a) d = 1cm, $RD_{avg} = 25.6$ (b) d = 20cm, $RD_{avg} = 14.9$

Fig. 4. Results for on-body setup when D = 30 cm

CU on-body: Fig. 4 depicts the on-body experimental results for $D = 30$ cm. The graphs reveal that the behaviour of on-body characteristics resemble the off-body ones. There is a comparatively large difference in the RSSI difference of A1 and A2 when the device is very near to CU and 20 cm away from CU. Figure 5b shows the variation of RSSI difference with d and D, which resembles the off-body characteristics.

Comparing the RSSI difference varying with distance d for off-body and on-body experiments from Figs. 5a and 5b respectively, it can be observed that both the set-ups indicate similar characteristics. The results for a few additional configurations are presented in Figs. 7 and 8 in the Appendix.

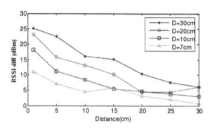 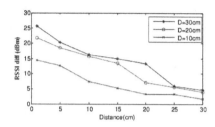

(a) RSSI difference for CU off-body setup

(b) RSSI difference for CU on-body setup

Fig. 5. RSSI difference with respect to distance d for various D

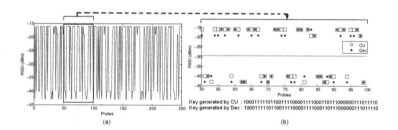

(a)

(b)

Fig. 6. Secret key generation (a) RSSI samples obtained at CU (b) Key generation mechanism

Key Generation: In this section, we illustrate the secret key generation mechanism of our proposed protocol which utilises the RSSI samples measured by the CU and the device during probe exchange. We present the results for one of the on-body set-up with $D = 30$ cm and the device aligned to one antenna at a distance of 1 cm from the CU. Figure 6a depicts the RSSI samples from both antennas at CU. Figure 6b shows a subset of data (samples with index 50 to 100) from Fig. 6a overlapped with the corresponding RSSI samples at the device. From the above figure, we observe that there is a high correlation between the channel characteristics of CU and the device. Though both CU and the device are stationary, the spatial separation between the two antennas of CU result in obtaining distinct RSSI values, approximately equal to $-15\,$dBm and $-44\,$dBm on either side. By assigning 1 bit binary coding, i.e., bit 1 and 0 to the upper and lower block respectively, CU and the device extract 100 % matching keys.

6.3   Impact of Parameter Variation

Variation of D: The two antennas of CU have to be spatially separated so that there is no channel correlation and the characteristics of the received signals differ. From Fig. 5, the RSSI differences obtained for $D = 30\,$cm are much greater than the values obtained for $D = 7\,$cm and $10\,$cm. Hence we select $D > 10\,$cm as an appropriate displacement between A1 and A2 to achieve a large RSSI difference.

Variation of d: Observing Fig. 5 for $d \leq 15\,$cm, the RSSI difference ranges from 25.88 to 5.51 where as for $d > 15\,$cm, the RSSI difference drops dramatically compared to the maximum value for each of the corresponding D. Thus, we set the threshold values RD_{th} for each D as shown in Table 1.

Table 1. RSSI difference threshold (RD_{th}) for $D = 10\,$cm, $20\,$cm and $30\,$cm

D (cm)	RSSI difference threshold (RD_{th})
10	5.51
20	10.17
30	15.07

Effectiveness: To differentiate between a legitimate and a non-legitimate device, several experiments were conducted for $D = 20\,$cm, $30\,$cm and d was varied from $1\,$cm to $40\,$cm. For each set-up we calculated the average value of RSSI difference from the two antennas A1 and A2 and compared with the RD_{th} from Table 1. We computed the acceptance rate of legitimate device and rejection rate of a non-legitimate device by repeating the off-body experiments for 40 different positions aligned with antenna A1 and A2 separately. We observed from our experimental results that $t = 5\,$ms was an appropriate inter-packet interval to determine the legitimacy of a device. Thus, in order to successfully authenticate and generate a shared secret key of 128 bit length our protocol requires $640\,$ms. The success acceptance rate accomplished is 100 % and the rejection rate of a non-legitimate device for $D = 30\,$cm is 100 % which drops to 95 % for $D = 20\,$cm. This variation in RSSI difference from RSSI threshold RD_{th} is due to noise and path loss components.

7   Security Evaluation

In this section we evaluate the robustness of our system against active and passive attacks. An attacker may impose as a legitimate device by sending probe packets to CU and try to pair with CU, to further gain access to the WBAN. We have analysed the possibility of such an attack by placing multiple adversaries at different locations as shown in Fig. 2a. The RSSI difference obtained at CU from different adversaries is shown in Table 2. It can be seen that the RSSI difference is significantly less than the RSSI threshold for any of the values of D from Table 1.

Table 2. RSSI difference obtained by Eve (E1 - E6) at distances of E1 = 270 cm, E2 = 360 cm, E3 = 180 cm, E4 = 100 cm, E5 and E6 > 4 m for $D = 10$ cm

Adversary	E1	E2	E3	E4	E5	E6
RSSI Difference	0.05	1.3	1.5	0.1	0.5	2.3

Additionally, an adversary can achieve high RSSI by either of the following two possible mechanisms:

Varying transmission power attack: To evaluate our proposed protocol against varying transmission power attack, we have placed the attacker "Eve" at 360 cm from the CU. For each $D = 10$ cm, 20 cm and 30 cm, the attacker's transmission power was set at different levels. As seen from Table 3, though the attacker transmits with the highest possible power, the RSSI difference at CU is very small. The RSSI difference for Eve is in the range of 0.0 to 2.4 which is significantly smaller than the RSSI difference threshold RD_{th}.

Table 3. RSSI difference for $d = 360$ cm and varying transmitting power

D (cm)	RSSI difference		
	$Ps = 3\,dBm$	$Ps = 0\,dBm$	$Ps = -17\,dBm$
10	0.0	0.9	1.9
20	0.2	0.03	1.5
30	0.15	0.2	2.4

Beam-forming attack: In this type of attack, the adversary forms a focused beam on the CU to induce an acceptable value of RSSI difference. In order to have a focused beam with narrow-width main lobe, the attacker would require a large antenna array [9]. The presence of such a large antenna would be easily noticeable. In addition, in our system model, the distance between the two receiving antennas is < 40 cm, hence a beam-forming attack would be difficult to achieve.

Robustness of key generation: A passive eavesdropper situated at any other location will not be able to derive the same key as CU/B due to unique spatio-temporal characteristic of the wireless channel [22]. The secret keys generated during secure device pairing have been verified for randomness by performing NIST statistical tests and the results reveal that the keys generated have highest entropy $= 1$. The shared randomness between any two devices is exemplified by the mutual information (MI) [10]. The MI $I(X:Y)$ between CU and B is 0.9896 and that of eavesdroppers placed at different locations ranges from 0.322 to 0.00225. Which is far less than that of CU and B, thereby decreasing the probability of Eve obtaining the same secret key as CU/B. Even if Eve has multiple antennas, the MI of Eve will be further reduced due to multi-path effects and other random factors like noise [30].

8   Conclusion

We have presented a light-weight secure device pairing protocol for WBAN which utilizes the spatial diversity of dual-antenna devices to obtain large and distinct values of RSS on the two antennas from a communicating node placed near one of the antennas. In contrast, a device placed far-away cannot induce such large difference in the measured RSSI. Hence, a nearby legitimate device can be easily distinguished from a far-away attacker. At the same time, the considerably different values of RSS obtained from the two spatially separated antennas are used for shared key generation. Our experimental results demonstrate that the success acceptance rate of a legitimate nearby device is 100 %, and authentication combined with secret key generation can be achieved in 640 ms, which is faster by more than an order of magnitude in authentication and key generation as compared to the most recent related work in WBAN.

A   Off-Body Set-Up

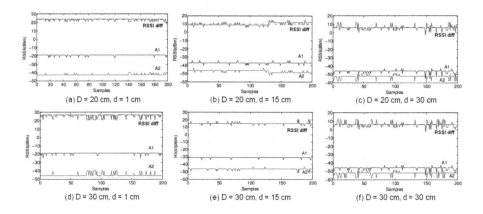

Fig. 7. RSSI variation for various off-body experiments

B   On-Body Set-Up

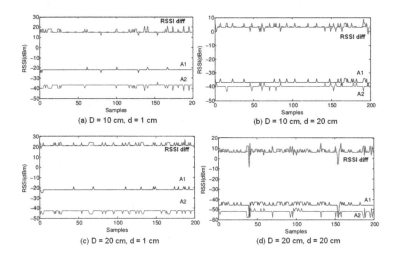

Fig. 8. RSSI variation for various on-body experiments

References

1. AT86RF231/ZU/ZF datasheet. http://www.atmel.com/images/doc8111.pdf. Accessed 31 Jan 2014
2. Glucose monitor. http://www.medtronic.com.au/your-health/diabetes/device/continuous-glucose-monitor/what-is-it/index.html. Accessed 12 Feb 2014
3. InterStim iCon Patient Programmer. https://professional.medtronic.com. Accessed 18 Feb 2014
4. TG6 technical requirements document (TRD) IEEE P802.15-08-0644-09-0006. https://mentor.ieee.org/802.15. Accessed 24 Feb 2014
5. Wearable medical devices market survey. http://www.prnewswire.com/news-releases/wearable-medical-devices-market-is-expected-to-reach-usd-58-billion-globally-in-2019-transparency-market-research-235220471.html. Accessed 18 Feb 2014
6. Wearble Antennas. http://www.pharad.com/wearable-antennas.html. Accessed 5 Feb 2014
7. Ali, S.T., Sivaraman, V., Ostry, D.: Zero reconciliation secret key generation for body-worn health monitoring devices. In: Proceedings of ACM Conference on Security and Privacy in Wireless and Mobile Networks (WiSec) (2012)
8. Batchelor, J., Swaisaenyakorn, S., Miller, J.: Personal and body area network channels between dual band button antennas. In: Proceedings of Asia-Pacific Microwave Conference (APMC) (2009)
9. Cai, L., Zeng, K., Chen, H., Mohapatra, P.: Good neighbor: Ad hoc pairing of nearby wireless devices by multiple antennas. In: Proceedings of Network and Distributed System Security Symposium (NDSS) (2011)
10. Cover, T.M., Thomas, J.A.: Elements of Information Theory. Wiley, New York (1991)

11. Demirbas, M., Song, Y.: An RSSI-based scheme for sybil attack detection in wireless sensor networks. In: Proceedings of International Symposium on World of Wireless, Mobile and Multimedia Networks (WoWMoM) (2006)

12. Gollakota, S., Hassanieh, H., Ransford, B., Katabi, D., Fu, K.: They can hear your heartbeats: non-invasive security for implantable medical devices. In: Proceedings of ACM SIGCOMM (2011)

13. Haeberlen, A., Flannery, E., Ladd, A.M., Rudys, A., Wallach, D.S., Kavraki, L.E.: Practical robust localization over large-scale 802.11 wireless networks. In: Proceedings of ACM MobiCom (2004)

14. Hanlen, L.W., Smith, D., Zhang, J.A., Lewis, D.: Key-sharing via channel randomness in narrowband body area networks: is everyday movement sufficient?. In: Proceedings of International Conference on Body Area Networks (BodyNets) (2009)

15. Jurdak, R., Klues, K., Kusy, B., Richter, C., Langendoen, K., Brünig, M.: Opal: a multi-radio platform for high throughput wireless sensor networks. IEEE Embed. Syst. Lett. **3**(4), 121–124 (2011)

16. Kalamandeen, A., Scannell, A., de Lara, E., Sheth, A., LaMarca, A.: Ensemble: cooperative proximity-based authentication. In: Proceedings of ACM MobiSys (2010)

17. Khaleel, H.R., Al-Rizzo, H.M., Rucker, D.G., Elwi, T.A.: Wearable yagi microstrip antenna for telemedicine applications. In: Proceedings of IEEE Radio and Wireless Symposium (RWS) (2010)

18. Li, Q., Han, D., Gnawali, O., Sommer, P., Kusy, B.: Twonet: large-scale wireless sensor network testbed with dual-radio nodes. In: Proceedings of ACM Conference on Embedded Networked Sensor Systems (SenSys) (2013)

19. Lim, R., Ferrari, F., Zimmerling, M., Walser, C., Sommer, P., Beutel, J.: Flocklab: a testbed for distributed, synchronized tracing and profiling of wireless embedded systems. In: Proceedings of International Conference on Information Processing in Sensor Networks (IPSN) (2013)

20. Mathur, S., Miller, R.D., Varshavsky, A., Trappe, W., Mandayam, N.B.: ProxiMate: proximity-based secure pairing using ambient wireless signals. In: Proceedings of MobiSys (2011)

21. Park, J.G., Curtis, D., Teller, S.J., Ledlie, J.: Implications of device diversity for organic localization. In: Proceedings of IEEE INFOCOM (2011)

22. Rappaport, T.S.: Wireless Communications: Principles and Practice. Prentice Hall, Englewood Cliffs (2001)

23. Shi, L., Li, M., Yu, S., Yuan, J.: BANA: body area network authentication exploiting channel characteristics. In: Proceedings of ACM Conference on Security and Privacy in Wireless and Mobile Networks (WiSec) (2012)

24. Shi, L., Yuan, J., Yu, S., Li, M.: ASK-BAN: authenticated secret key extraction utilizing channel characteristics for body area networks. In: Proceedings of ACM Conference on Security and Privacy in Wireless and Mobile Networks (WiSec) (2013)

25. Shnayder, V., Chen, B.R., Lorincz, K., Jones, T.R.F.F., Welsh, M.: Sensor networks for medical care. In: Proceedings of International Conference on Embedded Networked Sensor Systems (SenSys) (2005)

26. Varshavsky, A., Scannell, A., LaMarca, A., de Lara, E.: Amigo: proximity-based authentication of mobile devices. In: Krumm, J., Abowd, G.D., Seneviratne, A., Strang, T. (eds.) UbiComp 2007. LNCS, vol. 4717, pp. 253–270. Springer, Heidelberg (2007)

27. Wilhelm, M., Martinovic, I., Schmitt, J.B.: Secret keys from entangled sensor motes: Implementation and analysis. In: Proceedings of ACM Conference on Security and Privacy in Wireless and Mobile Networks (WiSec) (2010)
28. Wu, K., Tan, H., Ngan, H., Liu, Y., Ni, L.M.: Chip error pattern analysis in IEEE 802.15.4. IEEE Trans. Mob. Comput. **11**(4), 543–552 (2012)
29. Xiao, L., Greenstein, L.J., Mandayam, N.B., Trappe, W.: Fingerprints in the ether: using the physical layer for wireless authentication. In: Proceedings of IEEE ICC (2007)
30. Zeng, K., Wu, D., Chan, A., Mohapatra, P.: Exploiting multiple-antenna diversity for shared secret key generation in wireless networks. In: Proceedings of IEEE INFOCOM (2010)
31. Zhou, G., He, T., Krishnamurthy, S., Stankovic, J.A.: Impact of radio irregularity on wireless sensor networks. In: Proceedings of ACM MobiSys (2004)

Cryptanalysis of SIMON Variants
with Connections

Javad Alizadeh[1], Hoda A. Alkhzaimi[5]($\boxtimes$), Mohammad Reza Aref[1],
Nasour Bagheri[2], Praveen Gauravaram[3], Abhishek Kumar[4],
Martin M. Lauridsen[5], and Somitra Kumar Sanadhya[4]

[1] Information Systems and Security Lab (ISSL), Electrical Engineering Department,
Sharif University of Technology, Tehran, Iran
alizadja@gmail.com, aref@sharif.edu
[2] Electrical Engineering Department, Shahid Rajaee Teacher Training University,
Tehran, Iran
NBagheri@srttu.edu
[3] Innovation Labs Hyderabad, Tata Consultancy Services Limited,
Hyderabad, India
P.Gauravaram@tcs.com
[4] Indraprastha Institute of Information Technology,
New Delhi, India
{abhishek1101,Somitra}@iiitd.ac.in
[5] Section for Cryptology, DTU Compute, Technical University of Denmark,
Lyngby, Denmark
{hoalk,mmeh}@dtu.dk

Abstract. SIMON is a family of 10 lightweight block ciphers published
by Beaulieu *et al.* from the United States National Security Agency
(NSA). A cipher in this family with K-bit key and N-bit block is called
SIMONN/K. We present several linear characteristics for reduced-round
SIMON32/64 that can be used for a key-recovery attack and extend
them further to attack other variants of SIMON. Moreover, we provide
results of key recovery analysis using several impossible differential characteristics starting from 14 out of 32 rounds for SIMON32/64 to 22 out
of 72 rounds for SIMON128/256. In some cases the presented observations do not directly yield an attack, but provide a basis for further
analysis for the specific SIMON variant. Finally, we exploit a connection
between linear and differential characteristics for SIMON to construct
linear characteristics for different variants of reduced-round SIMON. Our
attacks extend to all variants of SIMON covering more rounds compared
to any known results using linear cryptanalysis. We present a key recovery attack against SIMON128/256 which covers 35 out of 72 rounds with
data complexity 2^{123}. We have implemented our attacks for small scale
variants of SIMON and our experiments confirm the theoretical bias presented in this work.

Keywords: Lightweight · RFID · Feistel · SIMON · Linear cryptanalysis · Impossible differential cryptanalysis · Rotational cryptanalysis ·
Weak keys

© Springer International Publishing Switzerland 2014
N. Saxena and A.-R. Sadeghi (Eds.): RFIDSec 2014, LNCS 8651, pp. 90–107, 2014.
DOI: 10.1007/978-3-319-13066-8_6

1   Introduction

In RFID systems, wireless tags communicate with a reader, and sensitive data is transferred between the two parties. Although the reader may have no constraint on the resources, passive tags are highly constrained in resources and, in some cases, cannot support conventional cryptographic primitives such as the AES, SHA-256 or standard public-key cryptosystems. Tags that are built with resources to possibly accommodate lightweight cryptographic algorithms can be categorized into light-tags, Gen2-tags and Crypto-tags. Light-tags can perform bitwise operations. Certain Gen2-tags can perform 16- or 32-bit operations and have a built-in 16-bit Pseudorandom Number Generator (PRNG) and Cyclic Redundancy Check (CRC) functionality. Finally, Crypto-tags support resource constrained cryptographic algorithms [16].

To meet the rising demand of security primitives for RFID use in industry, the topic of lightweight cryptography and cryptanalysis has received much attention from the cryptographic community in the past years. As a result, various new designs of lightweight block ciphers has been proposed and some were ISO-standardized as CLEFIA [20] and PRESENT [10] in ISO/IEC 29192-2 [13].

SIMON [5] is a new family of lightweight block ciphers designed by Beaulieu *et al.* the NSA. The aim of SIMON is to provide optimal hardware performance for low-power limited gate devices such as RFID devices. The SIMON family has been designed to meet hardware implementation flexibility and support efficient implementations across a wide variety of platforms as well as several implementations on a single platform. The design supports plaintext block sizes of 32, 48, 64, 96 and 128 bits, with up to three key sizes for each block size. SIMONN/K denotes a variant of SIMON that has a block size of N bits and a key size of K bits. There are 10 specified (N, K) pairs, defining the family.

Typically, a Gen2 passive RFID tag allows for an area up to 2000 gate equivalents (GE) to be used for security implementation. SIMON48/96 with 96-bit security requires 763 GE with throughput 15 kbit/s [5], making it a possible candidate for encryption in passive RFID tags. This is supported by Saarinen and Engels in [19]. With this in mind, we stress the importance of employing a security primitive in any scenario or environment only after it has stood the test of rigorous cryptanalytic scrutiny. This work is considered a step into that direction.

Previous Work. Besides the work presented in this paper, Abed *et al.* [1,2] presented analysis of SIMON with various techniques including linear-, differential-, impossible differential- and rectangular attacks. In the direction of differential cryptanalysis, the authors have presented differential attacks on reduced-round versions of all SIMON variants. In the direction of impossible differential analysis, the authors attack 13 out of 32 rounds for SIMON32/64 with data complexity 2^{30} and time complexity $2^{50.1}$, and up to 25 out of 72 rounds for SIMON128/256 with data complexity 2^{119} and time complexity 2^{195}. With regard to linear cryptanalysis, [2] presented key-recovery attacks on variants of SIMON reduced to 11, 14, 16, 20 and 23 rounds for the respective block sizes of 32, 48, 64, 96 and 128 bits respectively.

In [8], Biryukov *et al.* presented a method for searching for differentials in ARX ciphers. The authors apply the method to SIMON and improve the previous differential characteristics to present attacks on 18 out of 32 rounds for SIMON32/64 and up to 26 out of 44 rounds for SIMON64/128.

Contributions. In this paper we analyze the security of SIMON against impossible differential-, linear- and rotational cryptanalytic techniques. In the direction of linear cryptanalysis, we present linear characteristics for different variants of SIMON, that can be used for key recovery attacks on SIMON reduced to 13, 15, 19, 28 and 35 rounds for the respective block sizes of 32, 48, 64, 96 and 128 bits. Furthermore, we show an impossible differential for 10 rounds that we utilize in investigating the possibility of a key recovery attack covering 14 out of 32 rounds of SIMON32/64 and 22 out of 72 rounds of SIMON128/256. Additionally, observations regarding rotational cryptanalysis and differential rotational properties of the SIMON round function and weak key classes are also investigated. Implementation details of these attacks and observations are presented in the appendices. We also show a direct connection between our linear characteristic and the differential characteristic of Abed *et al.* We use this connection to present linear characteristics for different reduced-round SIMON variants to mount key recovery attacks. Finally, we note that this paper combines the results of [3,4] and we refer to those papers for any technical details omitted in this combined version.

Organization. The paper is structured as follows. In Sect. 2 we present a brief description of SIMON. In Sect. 3 we present the idea of linear attacks on SIMON and apply it to SIMON32/64. In Sect. 4 we present the main structure of impossible differential analysis on SIMON variants and discuss the different results obtained. In Sect. 5 we present further observations that have not led directly to attacks, but pose open and interesting research problems for further investigation. Section 6 shows the connection between linear and differential cryptanalysis of SIMON and its application to extend the attacks to other variants of SIMON. Finally, we conclude the paper in Sect. 7 and propose possible future directions of research.

2   Description of the SIMON Family

SIMON has a classical Feistel structure with the round block size of $2n$ bits, where n is the word size. The number of rounds of cipher is denoted by r and depends on the variant of SIMON. For a $2n$-bit string X, we use X_L and X_R to denote the left, respectively right halves, of the string. The output of round r is denoted by $X^r = (X_R^r \parallel X_L^r)$ and the subkey used in round r is denoted by K^r. Given a string X, $(X)_i$ denotes the i-th bit of X. Bitwise circular rotation of string a by b position to the left is denoted by $a \lll b$. Further, $\oplus$ and $\&$ denote bitwise XOR and AND operations respectively.

The function $F : \mathbb{F}_2^n \to \mathbb{F}_2^n$ used in each round of SIMON is non-linear and non-invertible, and is applied to the left half of the state, so the state is updated as

$$X^{r+1} = (F(X_L^r) \oplus X_R^r \oplus K^r \parallel X_L^r). \tag{1}$$

The F function is defined as

$$F(X) = (X \lll 2) \oplus ((X \lll 1) \,\&\, (X \lll 8)).$$

The subkeys are derived from a master key. Depending on the size of the master key, the key schedule of SIMON operates on two, three or four n-bit word registers. Detailed description of SIMON structure and key scheduling can be found in [5].

3   Linear Cryptanalysis of SIMON32/64

Linear cryptanalysis [17] is a well-known cryptanalytic technique that was employed on several block ciphers such as FEAL-4, DES, Serpent and SAFER [12,14,17,21]. Linear cryptanalysis, being a known-plaintext attack, is closer to a realistic attack scenario than e.g. differential cryptanalysis, which commonly requires chosen-plaintext capabilities. We present several approaches to produce linear characteristics for SIMON32/64 and present the best known linear characteristic for 11-round SIMON 32/64 with the bias of 2^{-16}. This characteristic is then extended to 13 rounds with no additional complexity. We have implemented the attack on SIMON32/64 reduced to 11 rounds to demonstrate the validity of our analysis.

In [1], Abed *et al.* present a linear cryptanalysis attack on 11 rounds of SIMON 32/64 with bias 2^{-11}. Indeed, this is the only linear cryptanalysis of SIMON thus far. In comparison with [1], our attacks cover more rounds on any variant of SIMON.

We remark that both our linear attack and the linear attack of [1] are bounded by the data complexity which is far below the complexity of exhaustive key search. Hence, the attack presented for SIMONN/K is also applicable to other variants with the same block length but different key sizes. For example, our attacks on SIMON48/96 would also be applicable to SIMON48/72. Thus, we have linear attacks on the reduced round versions of all 10 variants of SIMON. In the round function of SIMON, the only non-linear operation is the bitwise AND. Note that, given single bits A and B, then $\Pr(A \,\&\, B = 0) = \frac{3}{4}$. Hence, we can extract the following highly biased linear expressions for the F function:

$$\begin{aligned}
&\text{Approximation 1}: \ \Pr\left((F(X))_i = (X)_{i-2}\right) = \tfrac{3}{4}, \\
&\text{Approximation 2}: \ \Pr\left((F(X))_i = (X)_{i-2} \oplus (X)_{i-1}\right) = \tfrac{3}{4}, \\
&\text{Approximation 3}: \ \Pr\left((F(X))_i = (X)_{i-2} \oplus (X)_{i-8}\right) = \tfrac{3}{4}, \\
&\text{Approximation 4}: \ \Pr\left((F(X))_i = (X)_{i-2} \oplus ((X)_{i-1} \oplus (X)_{i-8})\right) = \tfrac{1}{4}.
\end{aligned} \tag{2}$$

In the following, we use P to denote a plaintext. Given the round function (1) and Eq. (2) we can extract the following linear expression for the first round of the SIMON:

$$(P_R)_2 \oplus (P_L)_0 \oplus (X_L^1)_2 = (K^1)_2. \tag{3}$$

Equation (3) holds with probability $\frac{3}{4}$. With the help of the above expression, we can extract a 3-round linear expression as follows (see Fig. 1):

$$(X_R^{i-1})_2 \oplus (X_L^{i-1})_0 \oplus (X_R^{i+2})_0 \oplus (X_L^{i+2})_2 = (K^i)_2 \oplus (K^{i+2})_2. \tag{4}$$

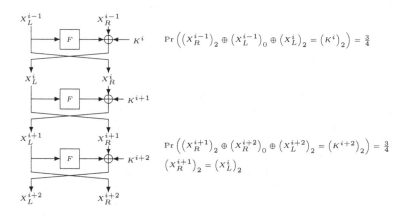

Fig. 1. A 3-round linear characteristic for SIMON.

Equation 4 can be used to produce a 7-round linear expression as

$$(X_R^{i-1})_2 \oplus (X_L^{i-1})_0 \oplus (X_R^{i+2})_0 \oplus (X_L^{i+2})_2 \oplus (X_R^{i+3})_2 \oplus (X_L^{i+3})_0 \oplus (X_R^{i+6})_0 \oplus (X_L^{i+6})_2$$
$$= (K^i)_2 \oplus (K^{i+2})_2 \oplus (K^{i+4})_2 \oplus (K^{i+6})_2$$

The above expression can be simplified to the following.

$$(X_R^{i-1})_2 \oplus (X_L^{i-1})_0 \oplus (F(X_L^{i+2}))_0 \oplus (X_R^{i+6})_0 \oplus (X_L^{i+6})_2$$
$$= (K^i)_2 \oplus (K^{i+2})_2 \oplus (K^{i+3})_0 \oplus (K^{i+4})_2 \oplus (K^{i+6})_2 \tag{5}$$

In Eq. 5, the only intermediate value is the term $(F(X_L^{i+2}))_0$. We can approximate $(F(X_L^{i+2}))_0$ with some bits of plaintext as

$$\Pr\left((F(X_L^{i+2}))_0 = (X_L^{i+2})_{14}\right) = 3/4$$
$$\Pr\left((X_L^{i+2})_{14} = (X_R^{i+1})_{14} \oplus (K^{i+2})_{14} \oplus (X_L^{i+1})_{12}\right) = 3/4$$
$$\Pr\left((X_R^{i+1})_{14} = (X_R^{i-1})_{14} \oplus (K^i)_{14} \oplus (X_L^{i-1})_{12}\right) = 3/4$$
$$\Pr\left((X_L^{i+1})_{12} = (X_L^{i-1})_{12} \oplus (K^{i+1})_{12} \oplus (X_L^i)_{10}\right) = 3/4$$
$$\Pr\left((X_L^i)_{10} = (X_R^{i-1})_{10} \oplus (K^i)_{10} \oplus (X_L^{i-1})_8\right) = 3/4$$

Then, with probability $(3/4)^5$ and bias 2^{-6}, we get the following expression for $F(X_L^{i+2}))_0$:

$$
\begin{aligned}
(F(X_L^{i+2}))_0 = {} & (X_R^{i-1})_{10} \oplus (X_R^{i-1})_{14} \oplus (X_L^{i-1})_8 \oplus (K^i)_{10} \\
& \oplus (K^i)_{14} \oplus (K^{i+1})_{12} \oplus (K^{i+2})_{14}
\end{aligned}
\tag{6}
$$

Using Eq. 6 in Eq. 5, we can extract a 7-round linear expression with bias 2^{-10}. It is possible to use Eq. 5 and produce a 11-round linear expression as

$$
\begin{aligned}
& (X_R^{i-1})_2 \oplus (X_L^{i-1})_0 \oplus (F(X_L^{i+2}))_0 \oplus (F(X_L^{i+6}))_0 \oplus (X_R^{i+10})_0 \oplus (X_L^{i+10})_2 \\
& = (K^i)_2 \oplus (K^{i+2})_2 \oplus (K^{i+3})_0 \oplus (K^{i+4})_2 \oplus (K^{i+6})_2 \\
& \oplus (K^{i+7})_0 \oplus (K^{i+8})_2 \oplus (K^{i+10})_2.
\end{aligned}
\tag{7}
$$

Thus, Eq. 7 will be an 11-round linear expression with bias 2^{-17}. We note that similar to $(F(X_L^{i+2}))_0$, we can approximate $(F(X_L^{i+6}))_0$ with some bits of X^{i+10} with probability $(3/4)^5$ and bias 2^{-6}. The bias is calculated using biases given in Table 1 and the piling-up lemma.

Table 1. The biases for an 11-round linear characteristic

Bias of 7-round linear expression	2^{-10}
Bias of $(F(X_L^{i+6}))_0$ approximate	2^{-6}
Bias of approximate 7–11	2^{-3}

Unfortunately this linear expression can not yield a successful linear attack because the required number of plaintexts exceeds the full codebook, i.e. 2^{32}. Later, we introduce an 11-round linear expression with bias 2^{-16}, but in this section we use the above method and calculate a 10-round linear expression. The bias of the 10-round linear characteristic is 2^{-14} as given in Table 2 and the expression is

$$
\begin{aligned}
& (X_R^{i-1})_2 \oplus (X_L^{i-1})_0 \oplus (F(X_L^{i+2}))_0 \oplus (F(X_L^{i+6}))_0 \oplus (X_R^{i+9})_2 \\
& = (K^i)_2 \oplus (K^{i+2})_2 \oplus (K^{i+3})_0 \oplus (K^{i+4})_2 \oplus (K^{i+6})_2 \oplus (K^{i+7})_0 \oplus (K^{i+8})_2.
\end{aligned}
$$

The approximation of $(F(X_L^{i+6}))_0$ can be simplified as follows, with bias 2^{-4}:

$$
(F(X_L^{i+6}))_0 = (X_R^{i+9})_{10} \oplus (X_L^{i+9})_{12} \oplus (X_R^{i+9})_{14} \oplus (K^{i+8})_{14} \oplus (K^{i+9})_{12}.
$$

Then the 10-round linear expression gets simplified as

$$
\begin{aligned}
& (X_R^{i-1})_2 \oplus (X_R^{i-1})_{10} \oplus (X_R^{i-1})_{14} \\
& \oplus (X_L^{i-1})_0 \oplus (X_L^{i-1})_8 \oplus (X_R^{i+9})_2 \\
& \oplus (X_R^{i+9})_{10} \oplus (X_R^{i+9})_{14} \oplus (X_L^{i+9})_{12}
\end{aligned}
=
\begin{aligned}
& (K^i)_2 \quad\ \oplus (K^i)_{10} \quad\ \oplus (K^i)_{14} \quad\ \oplus (K^{i+1})_{12} \\
& \oplus (K^{i+2})_2 \oplus (K^{i+2})_{14} \oplus (K^{i+3})_0 \\
& \oplus (K^{i+4})_2 \oplus (K^{i+6})_2 \oplus (K^{i+7})_0 \\
& \oplus (K^{i+8})_2 \oplus (K^{i+8})_{14} \oplus (K^{i+9})_{12}
\end{aligned}
$$

Table 2. The biases for a 10-round linear characteristic

Bias of 7-round linear approximation	2^{-10}
Bias of $(F(X_L^{i+6}))_0$ approximate	2^{-4}
Bias of approximate 7–10	2^{-2}

3.1 A 13-Round Linear Characteristic

In this section we extend our attack by one more round to get an 11-round linear expressions for SIMON 32/64 with bias 2^{-16}. Once we have such an 11-round linear characteristic we can add another one round to the beginning and one round to the end of each characteristic to extend the attack up to 13 rounds. The added rounds are related to the plaintext and ciphertext and free of any approximation, because we know the input of F functions for these rounds. In this way we have a 13-round linear characteristic for SIMON32/64.

To produce an 11-round linear characteristic, we consider the 10-round linear expression in the previous section and add a single round at its beginning to achieve an 11-round characteristic. In this case we have the following changes:

$$(X_R^{i-1})_2 = (X_L^{i-2})_2$$
$$\Pr\left((X_L^{i-1})_0 = (X_R^{i-2})_0 \oplus (K^{i-1})_0 \oplus (X_L^{i-2})_{14}\right) = 3/4$$
$$(X_R^{i-1})_{14} = (X_L^{i-2})_{14}$$
$$(X_R^{i-1})_{10} = (X_L^{i-2})_{10}$$
$$\Pr\left((X_L^{i-1})_8 = (X_R^{i-2})_8 \oplus (K^{i-1})_8 \oplus (X_L^{i-2})_6\right) = 3/4$$

Since the bias of the added round is 2^{-3}, the bias of the 11-round linear expression is 2^{-16}. Thus, when using Matsui's Algorithm 1 to recover the key, for the data complexity of 2^{32} the success probability of recovering 1 bit of the key would be 0.921 [18].

4 Impossible Differential Cryptanalysis

Impossible differential cryptanalysis was first mentioned in 1998 by Knudsen in the analysis of DEAL [15], and further extended to an attack on IDEA by Biham *et al.* at FSE 1999 [6]. The approach combines two certain properties (two differentials with probability 1), one in the forward direction and one in the backward direction, and uses a resulting conflict when both directions are joined. This miss-in-the-middle approach is used to obtain an impossibility result. This can be utilized in a chosen-plaintext attack by requesting encryptions of plaintext pairs with a fixed difference, guessing key material and checking for the impossibility property to discard wrong guesses. In our case, the forward and backward differentials are truncated.

Some impossible differentials rely on the round function F being a permutation, a prominent example being the general 5-round property on Feistel schemes presented in [15]. However, the F function of SIMON is not a bijection, and indeed the impossible differentials we present in the following do not rely on it being so.

One can determine the possible output differences of the F function of SIMON, using a fixed input difference, in the sense that we can determine the truncated output difference. We also noted that all possible output differences are equiprobable. We are interested in investigating for how many rounds a particular input difference can go before we are uncertain about all output difference bits, i.e. before we have asterisks on all positions. Intuitively, using an input difference of Hamming weight one will be the best approach, as each active bit in the input difference gives rise to 1, 2 or 3 active bits in the output difference, ignoring the possibility of cancellations, which is less predictable. For $n \in \{16, 24, 32\}$, we exhaustively tried all possible input differences and saw that this was indeed the case. For $n = 16$ and $n = 32$, there was another pattern of Hamming weight two, namely $(0 \cdots 00101)$ and any rotation of it, that covered equally many rounds in one direction. However, as there was no occurrence of both 0'es and 1's in the last truncated difference, the resulting impossible differential would cover lesser rounds than when using a Hamming weight one input difference. Table 3 shows how the truncated differences progress over the rounds of SIMON for $n = 16$. All progressions use the same input difference $(0 \cdots 01 \parallel 0 \cdots 0)$. Other Hamming weight one input differences would yield a progression of truncated differences that are rotated correspondingly.

Table 3. Truncated differential pattern propagation for SIMON using word size $n = 16$, with an input difference $(0 \cdots 01 \parallel 0 \cdots 0)$

| | 32-bit block | |
Rounds	Left	Right
0	0000000000000001	0000000000000000
1	0000000*000001*0	0000000000000001
2	00000**00001**0*	0000000*000001*0
3	000***0*01*****0	00000**00001**0*
4	0******1*****0*	000***0*01*****0
5	****************	0******1*****0*

Taking the $n = 16$ case as an example, we see that after 5 rounds of SIMON, we have with probability 1 the truncated output difference

$$(* * * * * * * * * * * * * * * * \parallel 0 * * * * * * 1 * * * * * * 0*).$$

By left rotating this right truncated difference by 7 or 9 positions, one of the 0's will be shifted to the position of the 1. Due to the symmetry of decryption and encryption of the Feistel scheme, we find that this provides us with two impossibility properties:

$$\Pr\left((0001 \parallel 0000) \rightarrow (0001 \lll 7 \parallel 0000)\right) = 0 \qquad \text{and}$$
$$\Pr\left((0001 \parallel 0000) \rightarrow (0001 \lll 9 \parallel 0000)\right) = 0,$$

where the impossible differential is over 10 rounds of SIMON. With this, we find two impossibility properties for each input difference of Hamming weight one, i.e. $2n$ in total. This property for the rotation by $q = 7$ is depicted in Fig. 3 of Appendix A. In the further description of the attack, we denote by Q the set of indices for such rotations of the output difference, relative to the input difference, and hence $|Q|$ is the number of impossible differentials using one input difference. For example, for Simon32/64, $Q = \{7, 9\}$.

Note that the attack described so far uses an input difference of the form $(\alpha \parallel 0)$. Thus, the impossible differentials described in this section can trivially be extended by two rounds on top of probability 1 yielding an extra 2 rounds attacked.

Referring to Appendix A, we see that for other values of n, we do not have both a 0 and 1 in the last truncated difference. Thus, we cannot use this for obtaining an impossibility property, because we need to make a 0 overlap with a 1. We can, however, trace back to the last round where the truncated output difference on the right half contains a 1, and match this up with the last truncated output difference containing a 0. This sacrifice means the impossible differential covers less rounds.

4.1 Key Recovery

As the case of key recovery using the standard differentials, we encrypt for two rounds more than the property covers. Consider a pair of output ciphertexts $(c_L \parallel c_R)$ and $(c'_L \parallel c'_R)$. The first filter in the recovery we can apply, is to test if

$$\Gamma := F(c_R) \oplus F(c'_R) \oplus c_L \oplus c'_L \tag{8}$$

equals the right half of one of the $|Q|$ impossible differentials, i.e. if it equals some $\alpha \lll q, q \in Q$.

If it does, we try all values v of the last round key and partially decrypt for one round to obtain the 1-round decrypted pair $(u_L \parallel u_R)$ and $(u'_L \parallel u'_R)$. We may now test if

$$F(u_R) \oplus F(u'_R) \oplus u_L \oplus u'_L \tag{9}$$

equals 0. If it does, then v can be discarded forever as a possible last round key. The attack procedure is summarized as pseudo-code in [4], and we refer to Fig. 2 for an illustration of the attack.

4.2 Analysis

In [4], we give the complexity analysis of the truncated differentials attack described. Our findings are summarized in Table 4. We note that in all cases, our data complexity, i.e. the required number of plaintext/ciphertext pairs, exceeds the size of the size of the message space. As such, our impossible differential cryptanalysis results presented *cannot be considered attacks* on the listed SIMON variants. However, we include the analysis here such that it may pose an open problem for others to consider.

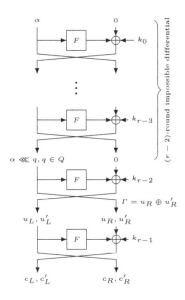

Fig. 2. Key recovery attack with impossible differentials on SIMON

Table 4. Results on key recovery on SIMON using $|Q| \cdot n$ impossible differentials. The number of pairs used, $n2^\ell$ is determined such that the expected size of $\mathcal{K}$, i.e. the remaining key candidates, is 1 % of the total subkey space 2^n. The complexities indicated with a † are computed an approximation (see [4] for the details).

Cipher	Rounds		$|Q|$	Pairs	Data	Memory	Time
	Total	Covered		$n2^\ell$	$2^\ell + n2^\ell$	2^ℓ	
Simon32/64	32	14	2	$2^{33.2}$	$2^{33.3}$	$2^{29.2}$	$2^{44.2}$
Simon48/72	36	15	1	$2^{50.2}$	$2^{50.3}$	$2^{45.6}$	$2^{69.1†}$
Simon48/96	36	15	1	$2^{50.2}$	$2^{50.3}$	$2^{45.6}$	$2^{69.1†}$
Simon64/96	42	16	2	$2^{65.2}$	$2^{65.2}$	$2^{60.2}$	$2^{92.0†}$
Simon64/128	44	16	2	$2^{65.2}$	$2^{65.2}$	$2^{60.2}$	$2^{92.0†}$
Simon96/92	52	19	2	$2^{97.2}$	$2^{97.2}$	$2^{91.6}$	$2^{139.7†}$
Simon96/144	54	19	2	$2^{97.2}$	$2^{97.2}$	$2^{91.6}$	$2^{139.7†}$
Simon128/128	68	22	2	$2^{129.2}$	$2^{129.2}$	$2^{123.2}$	$2^{187.5†}$
Simon128/192	69	22	2	$2^{129.2}$	$2^{129.2}$	$2^{123.2}$	$2^{187.5†}$
Simon128/256	72	22	2	$2^{129.2}$	$2^{129.2}$	$2^{123.2}$	$2^{187.5†}$

5 Further Observations

In this section we briefly describe other observations on SIMON that have not led to immediate attacks, but are interesting topics for further analysis. Specifically, we consider SIMON from a rotational cryptanalysis perspective, and consider analysis of repeating patterns in the key schedule.

As for rotational cryptanalysis, it is evident that the SIMON F function is invariant under rotation, i.e.

$$\forall x \in \mathbb{F}_2^n, \forall j = 0, \ldots, n-1 : F(x \lll j) = F(x) \lll j.$$

This property can be combined to achieve a rotational related-key behaviour that might be exploited as a weakness. When fixing two master keys to a related rotational difference, the consequent expanded round keys exhibit, to some extent, the same amount of rotation introduced. It is also notable through different experiments that there is a longest common subsequence evident for later round keys in the key scheduling.

As for repetitive patterns in the key schedule, it is still interesting to investigate the extent of the key repetition on a certain number of rounds, and what is the size of weak key classes that exhibits this property would be.

6   Connections Between Linear and Differential Characteristics for SIMON and Applications

Differential cryptanalysis [7] is a widely used chosen plaintext/ciphertext cryptanalytic attack technique. In a differential attack we look for an input pair with difference ΔX that propagates to an output pair with difference ΔY with a high probability p. This differential characteristic is denoted by $\Delta X \xrightarrow{p} \Delta Y$. In the round function of SIMON, the only non-linear operation is the bitwise AND. Hence, we can extract the following highly probable differential expressions for the F function:

$$
\begin{aligned}
\text{Differential characteristic 1}: \ & (\Delta X)_i \xrightarrow{1} (\Delta F(X))_{i+2} \\
\text{Differential characteristic 2}: \ & (\Delta X)_i \xrightarrow{\frac{1}{2}} (\Delta F(X))_{i+2,i+1} \\
\text{Differential characteristic 3}: \ & (\Delta X)_i \xrightarrow{\frac{1}{2}} (\Delta F(X))_{i+2,i+8} \\
\text{Differential characteristic 4}: \ & (\Delta X)_i \xrightarrow{\frac{1}{4}} (\Delta F(X))_{i+2,i+1,i+8}
\end{aligned}
\tag{10}
$$

where $(\Delta F(X))_{i+1,i+8}$ denotes differences in $(i+1)$-th and $(i+8)$-th bits for $\Delta F(X)$ to be 1 and remaining bit positions of $\Delta F(X)$ are 0, and similarly for the other expressions. Comparing Eqs. (10) with the related Eq. (2) for linear approximations, and the fact that for linear characteristic we approximate bits from output of F by bits from its input and for a differential characteristic we propagate differences in bits of input to the bits of output of F, we see a unique connection between Eqs. (2) and (10). In other words, each approximation in (2) can be mapped to a differential characteristic in (10). There are many other works which discuss connection between differential and linear characteristics [9,11]. Given this observation, for an r-round differential characteristic we can construct an equivalent r-round linear characteristic by employing the related approximation of each specific differential characteristic of F which has been used through an r-round differential characteristic.

Now we investigate the strength of different variants of SIMON against linear attacks, given the above observation and the known results on differential cryptanalysis of variants of SIMON from [1]. In Appendix C, Table 8 gives the propagation of our linear characteristics for SIMON32/64 (for the detail of each used approximation, see Eq. (2)). For SIMON32/64 reduced to 11 rounds, a linear characteristic based on the approach of [1] will have bias of 2^{-17}. However, we considered the propagation of the number of approximations for this variant of SIMON on more rounds, and obtained the following pattern (see Table 8):

$$\ldots, 1, 2, 1, 3, 2, 3, 1, 2, 1, 1, 0, 1, 1, 2, 1, 3, 2, 3, 1, 2, 1, 1, 0, 1, 1, 2, 1, 3, 2, 3 \ldots$$

Based on this pattern, it is possible to generate a pattern that has bias of 2^{-16} for 11 rounds, as

$$2, 3, 1, 2, 1, 1, 0, 1, 1, 2, 1.$$

This is in fact the pattern that we used in the previous section to provide a 13-round linear characteristic for SIMON32/64. Based on a similar strategy, it is possible to present linear characteristics for other variants of SIMON. We summarize the parameters of our linear attacks for the different variants of SIMON in Table 5. On the other hand, to use an approximation with the bias of ϵ to mount a linear attack the expected complexity is $O(\epsilon^{-2})$ [17]. Hence, we consider a case where $\epsilon \geq 2^{-n+2}$, where $2n$ is the block size, and with complexity

Table 5. Summary of our linear analysis for the different SIMON variants. KR denotes a linear characteristic that can be used through a key recovery attack; Dis denotes a linear characteristic that can be used through a distinguishing attack; App denotes the number of approximations and $\mathcal{A}_L$ and $\mathcal{A}_R$ denote active bit indices in the left, respectively right side.

SIMON	Linear expression				Rounds	App	Bias	Attack
	Start $\mathcal{A}_L$	Start $\mathcal{A}_R$	End $\mathcal{A}_L$	End $\mathcal{A}_R$				
32/64	10, 6, 2, 6, 14	8, 0	2, 10, 6, 2	4	11	15	2^{-16}	KR
32/64	4, 8, 4, 0	10, 6, 2	2, 14, 10	12	22	31	2^{-32}	Dis
48/96	2, 18, 14, 10	12	20, 0, 20, 16	2, 22, 18	14	22	2^{-23}	KR
48/96	2, 18, 14, 10	12	10, 22, 6, 6	8	23	46	2^{-47}	Dis
64/128	2, 26, 22, 18	20	2, 26, 22, 18	20	17	28	2^{-29}	KR
64/128	2, 26, 18, 28, 14, 28, 62, 24, 10	30, 0, 26, 12	2, 26, 18, 28, 14, 28, 62, 24, 10	30, 0, 26, 12	25	60	2^{-61}	Dis
96/144	2, 46, 42, 46, 38	0, 40	2, 46, 42	44	27	46	2^{-47}	KR
96/144	2, 42, 38, 34, 46, 38, 30	0, 40, 32	36, 0, 40, 36, 32	2, 42, 38, 34	36	70	2^{-71}	Dis
128/256	52, 0, 56, 52, 48	2, 58, 54, 50	2, 58, 54, 50	52	34	63	2^{-64}	KR
128/256	36, 0, 48, 40, 36, 32	2, 50, 42, 38, 34, 62, 46, 38, 30	2, 50, 42, 38, 34	0, 48, 40, 32	52	127	2^{-128}	Dis

Table 6. Summary of our linear analysis for the different SIMON variants s.t. we can mount a linear attack with success probability $p = 0.997$. App denotes the number of approximations and $\mathcal{A}_L$ and $\mathcal{A}_R$ denote active bit indices in the left, respectively right side.

SIMON	Linear expression				Rounds	App	Bias
	Start $\mathcal{A}_L$	Start $\mathcal{A}_R$	End $\mathcal{A}_L$	End $\mathcal{A}_R$			
32/64	10, 6, 2	4	0, 8, 0, 8, 4	2, 10, 6	10	13	2^{-14}
48/96	2, 18, 14, 10	12	2, 22, 18	20	13	19	2^{-20}
64/128	2, 26, 22, 18	20	2, 26, 22, 18	20	17	28	2^{-29}
96/144	2, 46, 42, 46, 38	0, 40	0, 0, 4	2, 46	26	45	2^{-46}
128/256	2, 58, 54, 50	52	2, 58, 54, 50	52	33	59	2^{-60}

$8\epsilon^{-2}$ the success probability of key recovery attack is 0.997 [1,17]. Our results for different variants of SIMON when $\epsilon \geq 2^{-n+2}$ are presented in Table 6.

In the following, let $(X)[i_1, \ldots, i_m]$ be short notation for the XOR of bits at indices i_j of X where $j = 1, \ldots, m$, i.e. $(X)[i_1, \ldots, i_m] = (X)_{i_1} \oplus \cdots \oplus (X)_{i_m}$. Using Table 8 as an example for SIMON32/64, it is possible to extract a linear expression for each SIMON variant that involves only input, output and key bits as follows.

11-round linear expression for SIMON32/64

$$
\begin{aligned}
(P_R)[0,8] \ \oplus \ (P_L)[2, 10, 14] \\
\oplus \ (C_R)[6, 10] \oplus (C_L)_4
\end{aligned}
=
\begin{aligned}
& (K^1)[0,8] \ \oplus \ (K^2)[2, 6, 10] \oplus (K^3)_4 \\
& \oplus \ (K^4)[6, 10] \ \oplus (K^5)_8 \ \ \ \ \ \ \oplus (K^6)_{10} \\
& \oplus \ (K^8)_{10} \ \ \ \ \ \oplus (K^9)_8 \ \ \ \ \ \ \oplus (K^{10})[6, 10] \oplus (K^{11})_4
\end{aligned}
\ . \quad (11)
$$

14-round linear expression for SIMON48/96

$$
\begin{aligned}
(P_R)_{12} \ \ \ \ \ \oplus (P_L)[2, 10, 14, 18] \\
\oplus (C_R)[0, 16] \oplus (C_L)[2, 18, 22]
\end{aligned}
=
\begin{aligned}
& (K^1)_{12} \ \ \ \ \ \ \ \ \oplus (K^2)[2, 14, 18] \oplus (K^3)[0, 16] \\
& \oplus (K^4)[2, 18, 22] \ \oplus (K^5)_{20} \ \ \ \ \ \oplus (K^6)[2, 22] \\
& \oplus (K^7)_0 \ \ \ \ \ \ \ \ \oplus (K^8)_2 \ \ \ \ \ \ \oplus (K^{10})_2 \\
& \oplus (K^{11})_0 \ \ \ \ \ \ \ \oplus (K^{12})[2, 22] \ \oplus (K^{13})_{20} \\
& \oplus (K^{14})[2, 18, 22]
\end{aligned}
\ . \quad (12)
$$

17-round linear expression for SIMON64/128

$$
\begin{aligned}
(P_R)_{20} \\
\oplus (P_L)[2, 18, 22, 26] \\
\oplus (C_R)[2, 18, 22, 26] \\
\oplus (C_L)_{20}
\end{aligned}
=
\begin{aligned}
& (K^1)_{20} \ \ \ \ \ \ \ \ \oplus (K^2)[2, 22, 26] \oplus (K^3)[0, 24] \\
& \oplus (K^4)[2, 26, 30] \ \oplus (K^5)_{28} \ \ \ \ \ \oplus (K^6)[2, 30] \\
& \oplus (K^7)_0 \ \ \ \ \ \ \ \ \oplus (K^8)_2 \ \ \ \ \ \ \oplus (K^{10})_2 \\
& \oplus (K^{11})_0 \ \ \ \ \ \ \ \oplus (K^{12})[2, 30] \ \oplus (K^{13})_{28} \\
& \oplus (K^{14})[2, 26, 30] \oplus (K^{15})[0, 24] \ \oplus (K^{16})[2, 22, 26] \\
& \oplus (K^{17})_{20}
\end{aligned}
\ . \quad (13)
$$

27-round linear expression for SIMON96/144

$$
\begin{aligned}
(P_R)[0,40] \\
\oplus (P_L)[2,38,42] \\
\oplus (C_R)[2,46,42] \\
\oplus (C_L)_{44}
\end{aligned}
=
\begin{aligned}
& (K^1)[0,40] && \oplus (K^2)[2,42,46] && \oplus (K^3)_{44} \\
& \oplus (K^4)[2,46] && \oplus (K^5)_0 && \oplus (K^6)_2 \\
& \oplus (K^8)_2 && \oplus (K^9)_0 && \oplus (K^{10})[2,46] \\
& \oplus (K^{11})_{44} && \oplus (K^{12})[2,42,46] && \oplus (K^{13})[0,40,41] \\
& \oplus (K^{14})[2,38,42] && \oplus (K^{15})[36,41,42] && \oplus (K^{16})[2,38,39,42] \\
& \oplus (K^{17})[0,40] && \oplus (K^{18})[2,42,46] && \oplus (K^{19})_{44} \\
& \oplus (K^{20})[2,46] && \oplus (K^{21})_0 && \oplus (K^{22})_2 \\
& \oplus (K^{24})_2 && \oplus (K^{25})_0 && \oplus (K^{26})[2,46] \\
& \oplus (K^{27})_{44}
\end{aligned}
\tag{14}
$$

34-round linear expression for SIMON128/256

$$
\begin{aligned}
(P_R)[2,50,54,58] \\
\oplus (P_L)[0,48,56] \\
\oplus (C_R)[2,50,54,58] \\
\oplus (C_L)_{52}
\end{aligned}
=
\begin{aligned}
& (K^1)[2,50,54,58] && \oplus (K^2)_{52} && \oplus (K^3)[2,54,58] \\
& \oplus (K^4)[0,56] && \oplus (K^5)[2,58,62] && \oplus (K^6)_{60} \\
& \oplus (K^7)[2,62] && \oplus (K^8)_0 && \oplus (K^9)_2 \\
& \oplus (K^{11})_2 && \oplus (K^{12})_0 && \oplus (K^{13})[2,62] \\
& \oplus (K^{14})_{60} && \oplus (K^{15})[2,58,62] && \oplus (K^{16})[0,56,57] \\
& \oplus (K^{17})[2,58,54] && \oplus (K^{18})[52,57,58] && \oplus (K^{19})[2,54,55,58] \\
& \oplus (K^{20})[0,56] && \oplus (K^{21})[2,62,58] && \oplus (K^{22})_{60} \\
& \oplus (K^{23})[2,62] && \oplus (K^{24})_0 && \oplus (K^{25})_2 \\
& \oplus (K^{27})_2 && \oplus (K^{28})_0 && \oplus (K^{29})[2,62] \\
& \oplus (K^{30})_{60} && \oplus (K^{31})[2,58,62] && \oplus (K^{32})[0,56] \\
& \oplus (K^{33})[2,58,54] && \oplus (K^{34})_{52}
\end{aligned}
\tag{15}
$$

7 Conclusion and Open Problems

In this paper we analyzed the security of SIMON family against linear-, impossible differential- and rotational cryptanalysis techniques. Based on this analysis we presented several attacks and observations. We have shown that there is a direct connection between linear characteristics and differential characteristics of SIMON. In particular, given a differential characteristic for an r-round variant of SIMON, it is possible to generate an r-round linear characteristic although the probability of these characteristics would not necessarily be the same. The significance of this approach is that any progress on providing a better differential characteristic may be directly used to provide a better linear characteristic. We exploited this property to provide the best known linear cryptanalysis results for reduced round variants of SIMON. Although the presented results are advanced compared to the previously known results on the linear cryptanalysis of SIMON, they only cover less than half of the cipher rounds. This work introduced several open problems that are worth exploring, e.g. in the possibility of improving complexities of impossible differential attacks presented or to

provide a better understanding of the linear hull behavior of SIMON over different number of rounds. Finally it would be interesting to use different properties
to utilize the differential and linear characteristics link to introduce better attack
results.

A   Addenda to Impossible Differentials Cryptanalysis

In this appendix, we provide an example on impossible differential for Simon32/64
in Fig. 3. A detailed description on the attack and its complexity analysis can be
found in an extended version of this part, see [4].

B   Experimental Results of Linear Cryptanalysis for SIMON32/64

We evaluated the theoretical results presented in Eq. 11 for 11-round SIMON32/64
experimentally. Table 7 presents the results. It shows that experimental results
justify the theory and the bias of the presented path is not less than 2^{-16}.

Table 7. Experimental results for the linear characteristic of 11-round SIMON32/64 of
Eq. 11. P_n is the number of known plaintexts; C_n is the number of plaintext/ciphertext
pairs that satisfy Eq. 11; $p = 1/2 + \epsilon$ is the probability that Eq. 11 holds.

P_n	$\log_2 P_n$	C_n	$p = 1/2 + \epsilon$	$\log_2 \epsilon$
179702664	27.42	89867759	0.5000914	-14.004
1073741824	30.00	536877274	0.500005925	-12.635
2526206249	31.23	1263137717	0.50001369	-15.078
4294967296	32.00	2147550464	0.500015557	-16.028

C   Sequences of Approximation Used Through Driving the Linear Characteristic of Each Variant of SIMON

In Table 8 we give the propagation of our linear characteristics for SIMON32/64.

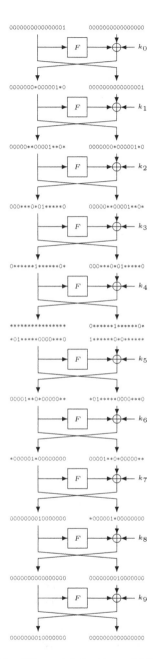

Fig. 3. A 10-round impossible differential for Simon32/64. Tracing truncated output differences in respectively forward and backward directions give a contradiction on the right half truncated mask after 5 rounds, where a 0 overlaps a 1.

Table 8. Sequences of approximation for SIMON32/64. $\mathcal{A}_L$ and $\mathcal{A}_R$ denote the active bits in the left and right side respectively and App. denotes the approximation used for the corresponding bit(s) of $\mathcal{A}_R$.

$\mathcal{A}_L$	$\mathcal{A}_R$	Used App.	# App.
10, 6, 2, 6, 14	8, 0	1; 1	2
4, 8, 4, 0	10, 6, 2	1; 1; 1	3
10, 6, 2	4	1	1
8, 8, 4	10, 6	1; 1	2
10, 6	8	1	1
8	10	1	1
10	–	–	0
8, 8	10	1	1
10, 6, 6	8	1	1
4, 8, 4	10, 6	1; 1	2
2, 10, 6, 2	4	1	1
0, 8, 0, 8, 4	2, 10, 6	1; 1; 1	3
2, 14, 10, 14, 6	0, 8	1; 1	2
12, 0, 12, 8	2, 14, 10	1; 1; 1	3
2, 14, 10	12	1	1
0, 0, 12	2, 14	1; 1	2
2, 14	0	1	1
0	2	1	1
2	–	–	0
0	2	1	1
2, 14	0	1	1
0, 0, 12	2, 14	1; 1	2
2, 14, 10	12	1	1
12, 0, 12, 8	2, 14, 10	1; 1; 1	3

References

1. Abed, F., List, E., Lucks, S., Wenzel, J.: Differential Cryptanalysis of Reduced-Round Simon. Cryptology ePrint Archive, Report 2013/526 (2013). http://eprint.iacr.org/

2. Abed, F., List, E., Lucks, S., Wenzel, J.: Differential cryptanalysis of round-reduced Simon and Speck. In: Preproceedings of Fast Software Encryption (FSE 2014) (2014, to appear)

3. Alizadeh, J., Bagheri, N., Gauravaram, P., Kumar, A., Sanadhya, S.K.: Linear Cryptanalysis of Round Reduced SIMON. Cryptology ePrint Archive, Report 2013/663 (2013) http://eprint.iacr.org/

4. Alkhzaimi, H.A., Lauridsen, M.M.: Cryptanalysis of the SIMON Family of Block Ciphers. Cryptology ePrint Archive, Report 2013/543 (2013). http://eprint.iacr.org/

5. Beaulieu, R., Shors, D., Smith, J., Treatman-Clark, S., Weeks, B., Wingers, L.: The SIMON and SPECK Families of Lightweight Block Ciphers. Cryptology ePrint Archive, Report 2013/404 (2013). http://eprint.iacr.org/

6. Biham, E., Biryukov, A., Shamir, A.: Miss in the middle attacks on IDEA and Khufu. In: Knudsen, L.R. (ed.) FSE 1999. LNCS, vol. 1636, p. 124. Springer, Heidelberg (1999)

7. Biham, E., Shamir, A.: Differential cryptanalysis of the full 16-round DES. In: Brickell, E.F. (ed.) CRYPTO 1992. LNCS, vol. 740, pp. 487–496. Springer, Heidelberg (1993)

8. Biryukov, A., Roy, A., Velichkov, V.: Differential analysis of block ciphers SIMON and SPECK. In: Preproceedings of Fast Software Encryption (FSE 2014) (2014, to appear)

9. Blondeau, C., Nyberg, K.: New links between differential and linear cryptanalysis. In: Johansson, T., Nguyen, P.Q. (eds.) EUROCRYPT 2013. LNCS, vol. 7881, pp. 388–404. Springer, Heidelberg (2013)

10. Bogdanov, A.A., Knudsen, L.R., Leander, G., Paar, C., Poschmann, A., Robshaw, M., Seurin, Y., Vikkelsoe, C.: PRESENT: an ultra-lightweight block cipher. In: Paillier, P., Verbauwhede, I. (eds.) CHES 2007. LNCS, vol. 4727, pp. 450–466. Springer, Heidelberg (2007)

11. Chabaud, F., Vaudenay, S.: Links between differential and linear cryptanalysis. In: De Santis, A. (ed.) EUROCRYPT 1994. LNCS, vol. 950, pp. 356–365. Springer, Heidelberg (1995)

12. Cho, J.Y., Hermelin, M., Nyberg, K.: A new technique for multidimensional linear cryptanalysis with applications on reduced round serpent. In: Lee, P.J., Cheon, J.H. (eds.) ICISC 2008. LNCS, vol. 5461, pp. 383–398. Springer, Heidelberg (2009)

13. ISO/IEC 29192-2. Information technology - Security techniques - Lightweight cryptography - Part 2: Block ciphers. Technical report, International Organization for Standardization

14. Nakahara Jr., J., Preneel, B., Vandewalle, J.: Linear cryptanalysis of reduced-round versions of the SAFER block cipher family. In: Schneier, B. (ed.) FSE 2000. LNCS, vol. 1978, p. 244. Springer, Heidelberg (2001)

15. Knudsen, L.R.: DEAL - A 128-bit Block Cipher (1998)

16. Li, T., Lim, T.-L.: RFID Anticounterfeiting: An Architectural Perspective (2008)

17. Matsui, M.: Linear cryptanalysis method for DES cipher. In: Helleseth, T. (ed.) EUROCRYPT 1993. LNCS, vol. 765, pp. 386–397. Springer, Heidelberg (1994)

18. Nyberg, K.: Linear Cryptanalysis. Icebreak 2013 (2013). http://ice.mat.dtu.dk/slides/kaisa_1.pdf

19. Saarinen, M.-J.O., Engels, D.: A Do-It-All-Cipher for RFID: Design Requirements (Extended Abstract). Cryptology ePrint Archive, Report 2012/317 (2012). http://eprint.iacr.org/

20. Shirai, T., Shibutani, K., Akishita, T., Moriai, S., Iwata, T.: The 128-bit blockcipher CLEFIA (extended abstract). In: Biryukov, A. (ed.) FSE 2007. LNCS, vol. 4593, pp. 181–195. Springer, Heidelberg (2007)

21. Tardy-Corfdir, A., Gilbert, H.: A known plaintext attack of FEAL-4 and FEAL-6. In: Feigenbaum, J. (ed.) CRYPTO 1991. LNCS, vol. 576, pp. 172–182. Springer, Heidelberg (1992)

Privacy-Preserving Authorized RFID Authentication Protocols

Nan Li[1]($\boxtimes$), Yi Mu[1], Willy Susilo[1], Fuchun Guo[1], and Vijay Varadharajan[2]

[1] Centre for Computer and Information Security Research,
School of Computer Science and Software Engineering,
University of Wollongong, Wollongong, Australia
{nl864,ymu,wsusilo,fuchun}@uow.edu.au
[2] Faculty of Science, Information and Networked Systems Security Research,
Department of Computing, Macquarie University, Sydney, Australia
vijay.varadharajan@mq.edu.au

Abstract. Radio Frequency Identification (RFID) has been widely ad-opted for object identification. An RFID system comprises three essential components, namely RFID tags, readers and a backend server. Conventionally, the system is considered to be controlled by a single party who maintains all the secret information. However, in some practical scenarios, RFID tags, readers and servers could be operated by different parties. Although the private information should not be shared, the system should allow a valid tag to be authenticated by a legal reader. The challenge in designing the system is preserving the tag and reader's privacy. In this paper, we propose a novel concept of *authorized RFID authentication*. The proposed protocols allow the tag to be merely identifiable by an authorized reader and the server cannot reveal the tag during the reader-server interaction. We provide a formal definition of privacy and security models of authorized authentication protocols under the strong and weak notions and propose three provably secure protocols.

1 Introduction

A Radio Frequency Identification (RFID) system comprises three components: RFID tags, RFID readers and a backend server. An RFID tag is associated with a unique identifier which is allocated by the backend server. The typical RFID system is established by a single party who initiates the secret keys. To identify a tag, a reader communicates with the tag and sends the tag's response to the backend server. The server checks the tag's identity by using the shared keys and informs the reader whether the tag is valid.

Many RFID authentication protocols [13,14,23,24] have been proposed to preserve the tag privacy in conventional systems. These protocols assume that a reader and a server are held by a single entity. However, in some practical scenarios, we found that tag, reader and server are relatively independent, and

This work is supported by the Australian Research Council Discovery Project DP110101951.

ⓒ Springer International Publishing Switzerland 2014
N. Saxena and A.-R. Sadeghi (Eds.): RFIDSec 2014, LNCS 8651, pp. 108–122, 2014.
DOI: 10.1007/978-3-319-13066-8_7

hence, the existing solutions of RFID authentication protocols are deemed to be impractical. Consider the following scenario.

In an priviledged membership club, there are sole facilities provided for their members exclusively, such as restaurant, massage and sauna. Each of these facilities is operated by different business owners, who are paid by the owner of the club, who is also taking membership fees from its members. Hence, these facilities will allow exclusive club members only to access them and enjoy the service provided. In order to provide this benefit to the members, the club issues a membership card that is used to identify each member's identity. Nevertheless, to ensure the privacy of each member, the member would like to ensure that his/her identity will remain private whenever he/she is enjoying those services. Otherwise, these facilities will not be attractive to the members, if they have to sacrifice their privacy to trade for the facilities offered. In addition, the facilities are also expected to prevent the sensitive customer information from being exposed to the club, even though the members are indeed paying the membership fee to the club. The current solution may sound feasible to be implemented with an RFID system. Nevertheless, the requirement to maintain both privacy and accountability at the same time is seemingly contradictory.

The challenge in designing authentication protocols for the above scenario is the tag and reader's privacy. A strong tag privacy prevents a tag being linked in two different sessions even if the tag is completely corrupted. Most previous protocols consider the tag untraceability under the assumption that the server is honest and the reader can authenticate all the tags. However, it is suitable to our scenario where the server and the reader are relatively independent. The adversary who plays as an authorized reader can attempt to disclose a tag which is not intended to be identifiable. The reader's privacy is considered as whether the backend server can reveal the tag's identity during the protocol run. Specifically, the tag is merely identifiable by the authorized reader rather than the server; otherwise the server can obtain the merchant's (reader) client information and trace the tag. Unfortunately, to the best of our knowledge, existing protocols ignore this requirement and there is no protocol that cater the reader's privacy. Therefore, we need new models to evaluate a protocol's privacy and a novel protocol is desired.

Tag impersonation is one of crucial security problems of authentication protocols. Normally, it is hard to resist this attack if the tag is compromised. However, in our system, the untrusted server can cheat the reader without corrupting the tag by using the tag's shared secret. Hence, the protocol needs to prevent abuse of the shared information by the server.

Our Contributions. We introduce a novel notion of authorized RFID authentication (ARA, for short) protocols. In an ARA protocol, a reader is required to be authorized prior to identifying a tag and the server is blind regarding the tag which is being identified. The exiting protocols allow the server to disclose the tag's identity, which is not desirable for systems which require strong privacy protection. In this paper, provide three constructions. First, we propose a concrete construction based on the symmetric key cryptography. The protocol provides a weak privacy while the tag only needs to perform hash computations. To improve the privacy, we provide two protocols which achieve the strong privacy. The second protocol provides constant authentication time on the reader, while the communication cost is dependent on the number of authorized tags. The third protocol supports the constant communication cost, while it requires exhaustive key search.

We discuss the privacy and security requirements of ARA protocols. Firstly, a reader is only allowed to authenticate a specified group of tags which are currently authorized. It indicates the tag's forward privacy and backward privacy. These two notions are different from the traditional definitions. We give the definition in Sect. 4.2. Then, the security of a tag is considered such that the server cannot forge a tag unless it corrupts the tag. According to the proposed threat model, the privacy and security models are classified in strong and weak. We prove that our proposed ARA protocols are secure.

Related Work. Vaudenay [26] proposed a strong privacy model which is considered as the most complete one. The privacy of an RFID tag authentication protocol is classified in several levels which are strong, destructive, forward and weak. Each level is with respect to a different adversary with a set of oracle calls. A strong adversary is allowed to corrupt a tag and continues future interactions with the compromised tag.

Another strong privacy model was introduced by Juels and Weis [15]. The model is based on the IND-CCA experiment and the adversary of the experiment aims to distinguish two different tags. Later, Hermans, Pashalidis, Vercautern and Preneel [12] proposed a new practical RFID privacy model. They defined the "left" and "right" world that an adversary needs to decide which world is simulated in the experiment. Many other RFID privacy models (e.g., [5–7,20]) are also presented in the literature.

Nithyanand, Tsudik and Uzun [21,22] considered the reader revocation problem in the public key infrastructure based RFID system. This problem is prominent as the (passive) tag could not check the time information during the protocol execution. The proposed solution requires a tag to equip a date display and a user checks during the certificate verification.

The elliptic curve cryptography (ECC) based RFID authentication protocols are acceptable by low-cost RFID tags [11,19]. Many ECC based RFID authentication protocols [2,16–18,25] were proposed. The main purpose of the ECC based protocol is to provide the strong privacy. However, most of existing schemes have been unfortunately broken later in [4,8–10,16].

2   System Model

In this section, we describe the entities of the ARA system and the formal definition of ARA protocols. The system defines the following entities: Tags, Readers and Servers.

– **Tag** T_i: Has a small storage and is not temper-resistant. It stores the keys in a non-volatile memory and requires capabilities to perform hash computations and ECC computations depends on the protocols. It can be considered as a membership card held by the member who initiates the tag's secret key.

- **Reader** R_i: A powerful device which is authorized by a server to authenticate a group of tags with the given period key. R_i is controlled by a merchant who has an individual backend server.
- **Server** S_i: S_i provides the membership registration for customers and aids the reader to authenticate a tag. The server can authorize the reader to authenticate a group of tags and revoke the reader when it is no longer qualified.

The ARA protocol is executed by tag, reader and server. In the system, a server creates a tag and publishes a set of public information, such as the public key of the server. The member initiates the tag with the server's information and the keys which are chosen by himself. The public key of the tag is given to the server when the card is activated, while the private key is unknown to the server. To authorize a reader, the server generates a period key for the reader. During the tag authentication, the reader needs to cooperate with the server. However, the server cannot discover the identity of the tag which is involved in the session. To revoke a reader, the server can let the reader's period key be expired.

Our protocol consists of four algorithms: server key generation (ServerKey-Gen), tag key generation (TagKeyGen), reader authorization (ReaderAuth) and tag authentication (Auth). The definition of algorithms are depicted as follows.

- ServerKeyGen$(k) \rightarrow (PK, SK)$: Taking as input a security parameter k, it generates the server's public/private key pair (PK, SK).
- TagKeyGen$(T, k) \rightarrow (pk, sk)$: Taking as input a security parameter k for the tag T, it outputs T's public key pk and private key sk.
- ReaderAuth$(\{pk_i\}, \mathbb{T}_R, sk, R) \rightarrow (rsk, rpk)$: Taking as input a set of public keys $\{pk_i\}$ of tags $\mathbb{T}_R$, the server's private key SK and a reader R, it outputs a secret rsk and the reader's period key rpk. rpk is given to the reader and rsk is given to the server. For each run of this algorithm, the reader's current keys are revoked.
- Auth$(sk, PK, rsk, rpk) \rightarrow \{T, \bot\}$: The tag takes as input a private key sk and a server's public key PK, a reader takes as input a period key rpk and the server takes as input a secret rsk, it outputs T if the tag is authenticated, $\bot$ otherwise.

3   Proposed Protocols

The concrete constructions of proposed ARA protocols are presented in this section. The protocol in Sect. 3.1 is based on symmetric key cryptography and it achieves basic requirements of ARA protocols. Section 3.2 shows the drawbacks of protocol 1 and describe an ECC-based solution which the server handles most computations of the protocol execution. Optionally, Sect. 3.3 introduces a protocol which only requires constant communication cost during the authentication and provides the false output detection. As an overview, Table 1 summarizes the security and privacy properties of three protocols along with communication cost, computational efficiency and tag capabilities.

We define three cryptographic hash functions H_1, H_2, H_3, where $H_1 : \{0,1\}^* \rightarrow \{0,1\}^l$, $H_2 : \{0,1\}^* \rightarrow \mathbb{Z}_p^*$, $H_3 : \{0,1\}^* \rightarrow \mathbb{G}$ and employ the pairing group $(g, h, p, \hat{e}, \mathbb{G}, \mathbb{G}_T)$. $\mathbb{G}$ and $\mathbb{G}_T$ are two multiplicative cyclic groups of the same prime order p. g, h are two generators of group $\mathbb{G}$. The map $\hat{e} : \mathbb{G} \times \mathbb{G} \rightarrow \mathbb{G}_T$ is a symmetric bilinear mapping.

Table 1. Comparison of proposed protocols and tag capabilities. $\sqrt{}$: the protocol achieves this property; $\times$: the protocol cannot provide this property; $\blacklozenge$: the protocol achieves this property without tag corruption operations; H: requires hash computations; PK: requires ECC computations. Note that tag unforgeability is against a malicious server who cannot corrupt tags.

	Forward Privacy	Backward Privacy	Reader Privacy	Tag Unforgeability	Constant Com. Cost	Constant Reader Auth.	Tag Cap.
P1	$\blacklozenge$	$\blacklozenge$	$\sqrt{}$	$\times$	$\times$	$\sqrt{}$	H
P2	$\sqrt{}$	$\sqrt{}$	$\sqrt{}$	$\sqrt{}$	$\times$	$\sqrt{}$	H, PK
P3	$\sqrt{}$	$\sqrt{}$	$\sqrt{}$	$\sqrt{}$	$\sqrt{}$	$\times$	H, PK

3.1   Protocol 1

Our proposed protocol 1 is based on the symmetric key cryptography. It only requires a tag to compute hash values. The protocol achieves basic privacy requirements of ARA protocols with a relaxed condition. We analyze the privacy in Appendix A. The protocol is presented in Fig. 1.

- ServerKeyGen: The server generates a key space $\mathcal{K}$.
- TagKeyGen: The member randomly chooses $x \in \mathcal{K}$ and sets $(pk, sk) = (\cdot, x)$. The secret key sk is stored in the tag and given to the server.
- ReaderAuth: To authorize the reader R to identify a specified set of tags $\mathbb{T}_R$, the server randomly chooses $\gamma \in \{0,1\}^l$, and sets $(rpk, rsk) = (\gamma, \gamma)$.
- Auth:To authenticate a tag, the tag, reader and server interact as follows
  1. The reader randomly chooses $s \in \{0,1\}^l$ and send (s, γ) to the tag.
  2. Upon receiving (s, γ), the tag selects $a \in \{0,1\}^l$ and sends the reader the response (a, C), where $C = H_1(x, a, s, \gamma)$.
  3. Upon receiving the tag's response C, the reader sends (a, s) to the server.
  4. Upon receiving (a, s), the server retrieves $(\mathbb{T}_R, \gamma)$. For each $T_i \in \mathbb{T}_R$, the server computes $C' = H_1(x_i, a, s, \gamma)$ then sends the reader a set $\{(T_i, C_i') : T_i \in \mathbb{T}_R\}$.
  5. Finally, the reader outputs T_i if $C \in \{(T_i, C_i') : T_i \in \mathbb{T}_R\}$.

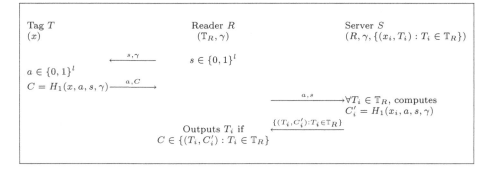

Fig. 1. Authorized RFID authentication protocol 1.

3.2 Protocol 2

In ARA system model, tag, reader and server are relatively independent. The key of a tag is expected to be unknown by the server since the server could abuse the key to forge the tag. It is difficult to prevent forging a tag by the server from using symmetric key based protocols. A trivial solution may be that the tag sends a signed nonce to the reader. However, in this case, the tag's response is publicly verifiable that an adversary can identify the tag by exhaustive public key search. Thus, tag's identity needs to be concealed and only an authorized reader is entitled to reveal. We then present Protocol 2 with ECC to tackle this issue. The protocol is presented in Fig. 2.

- ServerKeyGen: The server randomly picks $\alpha \in \mathbb{Z}_p^*$, and sets the public/private key pair $(PK, SK) = (g^\alpha, \alpha)$.
- TagKeyGen: The member randomly chooses $x \in \mathbb{Z}_p^*$, and computes the tag's public and private keys $(pk, sk) = (g^x, x)$. (g, sk, pk, PK) are stored in the tag and pk is given to the server.
- ReaderAuth: To authorize the reader R to identify a specified set of tags $\mathbb{T}_R$, the server randomly chooses $\gamma \in \mathbb{Z}_p^*$, and sets the reader's period $rpk = \{\gamma, (T_i, g^{x_i}) : T_i \in \mathbb{T}_R\}$ and secret key $rsk = (\gamma, \alpha)$. The server stores $(R, rsk, \mathbb{T}_R)$ and sends rpk to the reader R.
- Auth: To authenticate a tag, the tag, reader and server communicate as follows.
  1. The reader randomly selects $B \in \mathbb{G}$ and sends (B, γ) to the tag.
  2. Upon receiving (B, γ) from the reader, the tag randomly chooses $r \in \mathbb{Z}_p^*$, and computes (w, s, C_1, C_2, C_3). It sends (C_1, C_2, C_3) as the response to the reader. Note that C_1 is to assist reader identify a tag and hide the value s, otherwise the tag's response is publicly verifiable.
  3. Upon receiving (C_1, C_2, C_3), the reader forwards (B, C_3) to the server.
  4. Upon receiving the message (B, C_3) from the reader R, for each $T_i \in \mathbb{T}_R$, the server computes (w', V_i, U_i). Then the server replies $\{(T_i, V_i, U_i) : T_i \in \mathbb{T}_R\}$.
  5. Finally, the reader outputs T_i if $C_1 = U_i$ and $\hat{e}(C_2, g^{x_i+V_i}) = \hat{e}(g, g)$, otherwise rejects.

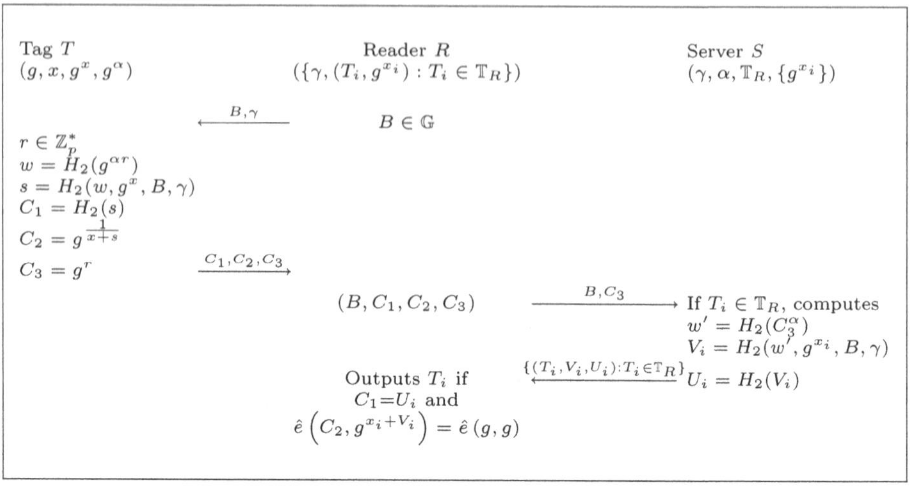

Fig. 2. Authorized RFID authentication protocol 2.

3.3 Protocol 3

ARA protocol 2 engages the reader to perform constant computations during the tag authentication. Instead, the server needs to send the reader a set of possible values for tag identification. In some scenarios where the communication bandwith is limited, it is desired to reduce the size of the set. Hence, we introduce third protocol which only transfers one group element from the server to the reader. Additionally, we consider a new attack that the server may cheat a reader by replying a random value which is called *false output*. Then, the reader could not successfully authenticate a tag even the tag is valid. This attack cannot be detected in neither protocol 1 nor protocol 2. Fortunately, our protocol 3 below shows that it is able to determine whether the received value is a false output. The protocol is depicted as in Fig. 3.

- ServerKeyGen: The server picks α, where $\alpha \in \mathbb{Z}_p^*$, and sets the public key $PK = h^\alpha$ and the private key $SK = \alpha$.
- TagKeyGen: The member randomly chooses $x \in \mathbb{Z}_p^*$ and computes the tag's public and private keys $(pk, sk) = (h^x, g^x)$. (g, sk, PK) are stored in the tag and pk is given to the server.
- ReaderAuth: To authorize the reader R to identify a specified set of tags $\mathbb{T}_R$, the server randomly chooses a secret $\gamma \in \mathbb{Z}_p^*$, and computes g^γ. For each tag $T_i \in \mathbb{T}_R$, the server computes $(h^{x_i})^{\alpha\gamma}$ and sets the reader's period key $rpk = \{g^\gamma, (T_i, h^{\alpha x_i \gamma}) : T_i \in \mathbb{T}_R\}$ and the secret $rsk = (\gamma, \alpha)$. The server stores $(R, rsk, \mathbb{T}_R)$ and sends rpk to the reader R.
- Auth: To authenticate a tag, the following steps are implemented.
  1. The reader randomly selects $B \in \mathbb{G}$ and sends (B, g^γ) to the tag.
  2. Upon receiving (B, g^γ) from the reader, the tag chooses two random numbers $r, s \in \mathbb{Z}_p^*$, and computes a tuple $(C_1, C_2, C_3, C_4, C_5)$. It sends the tuple to the reader as a response.

3. Upon receiving the response, the reader checks $\hat{e}(C_2, C_4) \stackrel{?}{=} \hat{e}(g, A)$. If it holds, the reader forwards (B, C_3, C_4, C_5) to the server.
4. Upon receiving the message (B, C_3, C_4, C_5) from the reader R, the server retrieves (γ, g^γ) and check $\hat{e}(C_3, A') \stackrel{?}{=} \hat{e}(h^\alpha, C_5)$. If it holds, the server calculates and sends $V = C_3^\gamma$ to the reader.
5. Finally, the reader authenticate the tag according to the server's response. Firstly, the checks the equation $\hat{e}(V, g) \stackrel{?}{=} \hat{e}(C_3, g^\gamma)$. If the equation does not hold, the reader outputs false. After that, the reader computes $\hat{e}(V, C_1)$ and checks whether there exists a pair $(T_i, h^{\alpha x_i \gamma}) \in rpk$, such that $\hat{e}(V, C_1) = \hat{e}(h^{\alpha x_i \gamma}, C_2)$. The reader outputs T_i if the above equation holds, otherwise rejects.

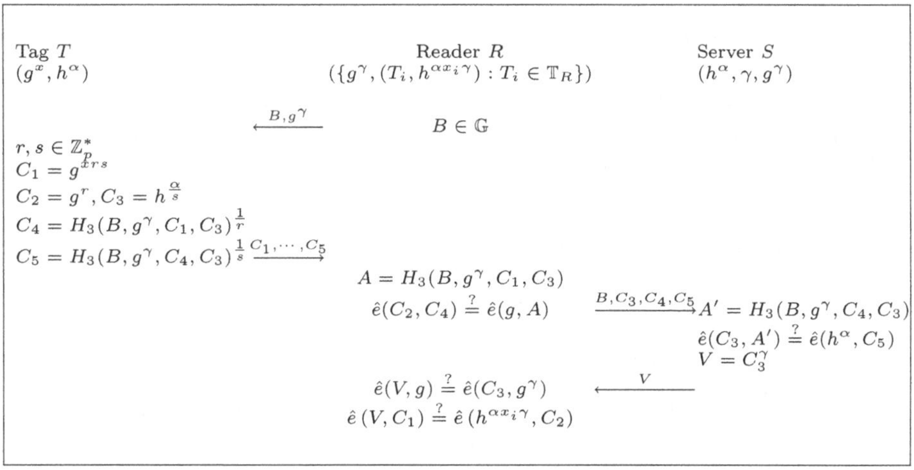

Tag T	Reader R	Server S
(g^x, h^α)	$(\{g^\gamma, (T_i, h^{\alpha x_i \gamma}) : T_i \in \mathbb{T}_R\})$	$(h^\alpha, \gamma, g^\gamma)$

$\xleftarrow{\quad B, g^\gamma \quad}$ $\qquad B \in \mathbb{G}$

$r, s \in \mathbb{Z}_p^*$
$C_1 = g^{\frac{1}{x} rs}$
$C_2 = g^r, C_3 = h^{\frac{\alpha}{s}}$
$C_4 = H_3(B, g^\gamma, C_1, C_3)^{\frac{1}{r}}$
$C_5 = H_3(B, g^\gamma, C_4, C_3)^{\frac{1}{s}} \xrightarrow{C_1, \cdots, C_5}$

$A = H_3(B, g^\gamma, C_1, C_3)$
$\hat{e}(C_2, C_4) \stackrel{?}{=} \hat{e}(g, A)$ $\xrightarrow{B, C_3, C_4, C_5} A' = H_3(B, g^\gamma, C_4, C_3)$
$\hat{e}(C_3, A') \stackrel{?}{=} \hat{e}(h^\alpha, C_5)$
$V = C_3^\gamma$

$\hat{e}(V, g) \stackrel{?}{=} \hat{e}(C_3, g^\gamma)$ $\xleftarrow{\quad V \quad}$
$\hat{e}(V, C_1) \stackrel{?}{=} \hat{e}(h^{\alpha x_i \gamma}, C_2)$

Fig. 3. Authorized RFID authentication Protocol 3.

3.4 Efficiency

We compare the efficiency in Table 2. In Protocol 2, C_1 is used for the reader to quickly identify the tag, and C_2 is for identity verification. The main computational cost of reader is dominated by computing $g^{H_2(V_i, B)}$ and $\hat{e}(C_2, g^{x_i} \cdot g^{H_2(V_i, B)})$ for the verification, where $\hat{e}(g, g)$ can be pre-computed. This protocol requires the server to compute all potential hash values for the reader. The communication cost therefore is all V_i for each tag in $\mathbb{T}_R$. The server can send all hash values in sequences to eliminate sending T_i. In protocol 3, the communication cost and the computational cost of server is constant-size and independent of the size of $\mathbb{T}_R$. The price to pay of this protocol is a liner computation cost on the reader. The reader needs to identify the potential tag one by one until the correct one is found. The computation time therefore is linear in n for $|\mathbb{T}_R| = n$.

Note that Protocol 2 is suitable for computationally weak readers without bandwidth limitation, while Protocol 3 fits for scenarios of limited bandwidth.

Table 2. Efficiency of two Protocols. Here, we assume the reader can identify n tags (i.e., $|\mathbb{T}_R| = n$).

Protocols	Reader Computation Cost	Communication Cost	Server Computation Cost
Protocol 2	$\mathbb{G}+\hat{e}$	$2n|\mathbb{Z}_p|$	$\mathbb{G} + 2nH_2$
Protocol 3	$(n + 1)\hat{e}$	$|\mathbb{G}|$	$\mathbb{G} + \hat{e}$

4   Privacy and Security Models

In this section, we consider the privacy and security models of authorized authentication protocols. We assume that the communication channel between the reader and the server is secure.

4.1   Adversaries and Oracles

We define a set of oracles and four attacks which respectively aim at different goals. In the particular attack, the ability of an adversary is regarded as the actions executed by oracle calls.

Definition 1 (Oracles). *The adversary plays with the challenger by given public information of the system and the following oracles.*

- TagCorrupt(T) $\rightarrow sk$: *On input a tag T, it outputs the tag's private key sk.*
- ReaderAuth($\mathbb{T}_R$) $\rightarrow rpk$: *On input a set of tags $\mathbb{T}_R$, it outputs the reader's period key rpk.*
- SendTag(T, m, π) $\rightarrow m'$: *On input a tag T, a message m and a session π, it sends the message m to the tag and receives the tag's response m'.*
- SendServer(m) $\rightarrow m'$: *On input a message m, it sends the message m to the server and receives the response m'.*
- Challenge(m^*, T^*) $\rightarrow C^*$: *On input a message m^* and a target tag T^* which is not issued to ReaderAuth oracle, it flips a coin b and outputs a response C^* regarding to the tag T^* (if $b = 1$) or a random tag $T^{*\prime}$ (if $b = 0$). This oracle can be called at most once of a game.*

Definition 2 (Strong and weak adversaries). *We define four types of attacks as follows.*

- Forward *attack: The adversary plays as a malicious reader who attempts to trace the tags' previous communications after it has been authorized by the server.*

– Backward *attack: The adversary plays as a malicious reader who attempts to trace the tags' future communications after it has been revoked by the server.*
– Outside *attack: The adversary plays as a dishonest server who attempts to discover the tag which is authenticating by the reader.*
– Impersonation *attack: The adversary plays as an impersonator who is not the tag holder attempts to impersonate the tag which is not compromised without being detected.*

A strong adversary can access all above oracles and launch all above attacks while a weak adversary cannot access the TagCorrupt(·) *oracle.*

4.2   Privacy and Security Models

Forward Privacy. The forward privacy game allows the adversary $\mathcal{A}$ to launch the forward attack. In the ARA system, a reader R may be authorized to authenticate a tag T in a certain period P of time. However, R shall not be able to interpret T's sessions prior to P since R is unauthorized to authenticate T outside the time P. In the forward privacy game, $\mathcal{A}$ is given the reader's current period key and attempts to decide whether the tag which can be authenticated currently was involved in the *previous* interactions.

The forward privacy game is defines in two phases, which are Forward Phase and Backward Phase. $\mathcal{A}$ plays with the challenger as follows.

– Setup: The challenger runs the algorithms ServerKeyGen and TagKeyGen to generate the server and tags' public/private keys (PK, SK) and $\{(pk_i, sk_i)\}$, respectively. The challenger gives public keys to $\mathcal{A}$.
– Forward Phase: The challenger sets the reader's period key and $\mathcal{A}$ can query Challenge(·) for the challenge. $\mathcal{A}$ interacts with the challenger through the oracles which can be accessed by the classified type of $\mathcal{A}$.
– Backward Phase: The challenger refreshes the reader's period key and $\mathcal{A}$ interacts with the challenger through the oracles which can be accessed by the classified type of $\mathcal{A}$.
– Guess: $\mathcal{A}$ outputs a bit b' and wins the game if $b' = b$.

Definition 3. *An authorized authentication scheme provides forward privacy if there is no $\mathcal{A}$ who wins the above game with the probability $\Pr[b' = b] \geq \frac{1}{2} + \epsilon$, where ϵ is negligible.*

Backward Privacy. The backward privacy game allows the adversary $\mathcal{A}$ to launch the backward attack. It is different from the forward attack that a reader R attempts to trace the tag after R has been revoked. In the backward privacy game, $\mathcal{A}$ is given the reader's current period key to authenticate the tags, while $\mathcal{A}$ needs to decide whether a tag involves in the *future* interactions after the reader was revoked.

The backward privacy game is defined in two phases, which are Forward Phase and Backward Phase. $\mathcal{A}$ plays with the challenger as follows.

- Setup: The challenger runs the algorithms ServerKeyGen and TagKeyGen to generate the server and tags' public/private keys (PK, SK) and $\{(pk_i, sk_i)\}$, respectively. The challenger gives public keys to $\mathcal{A}$.
- Forward Phase: The challenger sets the reader's period key and $\mathcal{A}$ interacts with the challenger through the oracles which can be accessed by the classified type of $\mathcal{A}$.
- Backward Phase: The challenger refreshes the reader's period key and $\mathcal{A}$ can query Challenge$(\cdot)$ for the challenge. $\mathcal{A}$ interacts with the challenger through the oracles which can be accessed by the classified type of $\mathcal{A}$.
- Guess: $\mathcal{A}_{\mathcal{F}}$ outputs a bit b' and wins the game if $b' = b$.

Definition 4. *An authorized authentication scheme provides backward unlinkability if there is no $\mathcal{A}$ who wins the above game with the probability $\Pr[b' = b] \geq \frac{1}{2} + \epsilon$, where ϵ is negligible.*

Reader Privacy. The reader privacy game allows the adversary $\mathcal{A}$ to launch the outside attack. Conventionally, the reader and the server are mutually trusted in RFID systems. However, the reader's privacy is needed to be considered in ARA protocols. For instance, the server may intend to learn the identity of the tag which is authenticating by the reader. Since the reader and the server are operated by different parties, the reader/tag interaction should be invisible to the server. In the reader privacy game, $\mathcal{A}$ is given the secret of the server and attempts to distinguish the tags during the server/reader interactions. $\mathcal{A}$ interacts with the challenger as follows.

- Setup: The challenger runs the algorithms ServerKeyGen, TagKeyGen and ReaderAuth to respectively generate the server's public and private keys (PK, SK), tag's public and private keys (pk, sk) and reader's keys (rpk, rsk). The challenger gives the server and tags' public/private keys and the reader's period key rpk to $\mathcal{A}$.
- Query: The adversary is allowed to make queries to the oracle SendServer$(\cdot)$.
- Challenge: The adversary outputs two tags T_0 and T_1 to the challenger. The challenger randomly chooses a bit $b \in \{0, 1\}$. Let M_t be the output of SendTag$(\cdot)$ with respect to the tag T_b and M_s be the corresponding query to SendServer$(\cdot)$. The challenger sends M_s to the adversary.
- Guess: $\mathcal{A}$ outputs a bit b' and wins the game if $b' = b$.

Definition 5. *An authorized authentication scheme provides reader privacy if there is no $\mathcal{A}$ who wins the above game with the probability $\Pr[b' = b] \geq \frac{1}{2} + \epsilon$, where ϵ is negligible. We say that it unconditionally preserves the reader privacy if $\epsilon = 0$.*

Tag Unforgeability. The tag unforgeability is with respect to the security of the protocol and the attacker is referred to a malicious sever. This game allows an adversary $\mathcal{A}$ to launch the impersonation attack. Clearly, it is hard to prevent the impersonation attack if the tag is corrupted. Symmetry-key based protocols are not secure against this attack as a server obtains secret keys of tags during the system setup. Hence, TagCorrupt($\cdot$) oracle cannot be queried during the game. $\mathcal{A}$ attempts to forge a tag's response to pass the authentication. It allows $\mathcal{A}$ to access the secret of the server and the reader. $\mathcal{A}$ interacts with the challenger as follows.

- Setup: The challenger runs the algorithms ServerKeyGen, TagKeyGen and ReaderAuth to respectively generate the server's public and private keys (PK, SK), tag's public and private keys (pk, sk) and reader's keys (rpk, rsk). The challenger gives the server's private key, tags' public key and reader's keys to $\mathcal{A}$.
- Query: The adversary can query the oracle SendTag($\cdot$) to the challenger.
- Forgery: $\mathcal{A}$ outputs a valid session π which is not queried to the SendTag($\cdot$) oracle.

Definition 6. *An authorized authentication scheme provides tag unforgeability if there is no $\mathcal{A}$ who can outputs a valid forgery of the tag with the non-negligible advantage ϵ.*

5   Privacy and Security Analysis

To analyze the privacy and security of protocols, we define two new complexity assumptions which are given in Appendix A. Due to the page limitation, we refer the readers to the full version of this paper for the proof of theorems[1].

Theorem 1. *Our ARA protocol 1 provides forward privacy and backward privacy against the weak adversary if H_1 is pre-image resistant and provides unconditional reader privacy.*

Theorem 2. *Our ARA protocol 2 provides forward privacy and backward privacy against the strong adversary if the ODH assumption holds, tag unforgeability if BB signature [3] is secure and unconditional reader privacy.*

Theorem 3. *Our ARA protocol 3 provides forward privacy and backward privacy against the strong adversary if the V-l-wDBDHI assumption holds, reader privacy if the EDBDH assumption holds and tag unforgeability if $k+1$-Exponent assumption holds.*

6   Conclusion

In this paper, we introduced a novel concept of authorized RFID authentication protocols. The reader's privacy is considered as a new issue that it prevents the server disclosing the identity of the tag which is authenticated by the reader. Three protocols were proposed based on the different efficiency requirements. We provided the formal definition of privacy and security models of authorized authentication protocols and proved that our protocols are secure against the various adversaries.

---

[1] The full version of the paper can be requested from the authors.

A   Complexity Assumptions

Definition 7 (Oracle Diffie-Hellman Assumption [1]). *Given g^a, g^b, a function $H : \{0,1\}^* \to \{0,1\}^l$ and an oracle $\mathcal{O} = H(X^b)$, where $X \neq g^a$, the advantage of an adversary $\mathcal{A}$ in violating the ODH assumption is*

$$Adv_{\mathcal{A},H}^{odh} = \left| \Pr\left[a, b : \mathcal{A}^{\mathcal{O}}(g^a, g^b, H(g^{ab})) = 1\right] - \Pr\left[a, b : \mathcal{A}^{\mathcal{O}}(g^a, g^b, t) = 1\right] \right|,$$

where $t \in \{0,1\}^l$ We say that the ODH assumption holds, if $Adv_{\mathcal{A},H}^{odh}$ is negligible.

Definition 8 (EDBDH Assumption). *Let $(g, p, \mathbb{G}, \mathbb{G}_T)$ be a pairing group. Given (g, g^a, g^b, g^c, g^t), the Extended Decisional Bilinear Diffie-Hellman problem is to determine whether $g^t = g^{abc}$. We say that the EDBDH assumption holds, if no PPT algorithm $\mathcal{A}$ can solve the problem with non-negligible advantage.*

Definition 9 (V-l-wDBDHI Assumption). *Let $(g, h, p, \mathbb{G}, \mathbb{G}_T)$ be a pairing group. Given $(g, h, g^a, g^{a^2}, \cdots, g^{a^l}, h^a, h^{a^2}, \cdots, h^{a^l}, g^t)$, the Variant l-weak Decisional Bilinear Diffie-Hellman Inversion problem is to determine whether $g^t = g^{a^{2l+1}}$. We say that the V-l-wDBDHI assumption holds, if no PPT algorithm $\mathcal{A}$ can solve the problem with non-negligible advantage.*

Definition 10 ($k+1$-Exponent Assumption). *Given $(g, g^a, g^{a^2}, \cdots, g^{a^k})$, the $k+1$-Exponent problem is to compute $g^{a^{k+1}}$. We say that the $k+1$-Exponent assumption holds, if no PPT algorithm $\mathcal{A}$ can solve the problem with non-negligible advantage.*

We show that the security of EDBDH assumption is related to the security of Decisional Bilinear Diffie-Hellman (DBDH) assumption.

Lemma 1. *The EDBDH assumption holds if the DBDH assumption holds.*

Proof. Suppose that there is a PPT algorithm $\mathcal{A}$ who can break the EDBDH assumption. Given an instance (g, g^a, g^b, g^c, g^t), $\mathcal{A}$ can output whether $g^t = g^{abc}$ in polynomial time with non-negligible advantage. It implies that $\mathcal{A}$ decides whether $\hat{e}(g, g^t) = \hat{e}(g, g^{abc})$ which is a solution of DBDH problem. Therefore, if DBDH problem is intractable then the EDBDH assumption holds.   □

In terms of V-l-wDBDHI, a solution of V-l-wDBDHI problem also implies that the algorithm $\mathcal{A}$ can decide whether

$$\hat{e}(g, g^t) = \hat{e}(g, g^{a^{2l+1}}).$$

Since that V-l-wDBDHI problem is modified from l-wDBDHI problem, its security can be bounded by using the similar strategy in the generic group model.

References

1. Abdalla, M., Bellare, M., Rogaway, P.: The oracle Diffie-Hellman assumptions and an analysis of DHIES. In: Naccache, D. (ed.) CT-RSA 2001. LNCS, vol. 2020, p. 143. Springer, Heidelberg (2001)
2. Batina, L., Seys, S., Singelée, D., Verbauwhede, I.: Hierarchical ECC-based RFID authentication protocol. In: Juels, A., Paar, C. (eds.) RFIDSec 2011. LNCS, vol. 7055, pp. 183–201. Springer, Heidelberg (2012)
3. Boneh, D., Boyen, X.: Short signatures without random oracles. In: Cachin, C., Camenisch, J.L. (eds.) EUROCRYPT 2004. LNCS, vol. 3027, pp. 56–73. Springer, Heidelberg (2004)
4. Bringer, J., Chabanne, H., Icart, T.: Cryptanalysis of EC-RAC, a RFID identification protocol. In: Franklin, M.K., Hui, L.C.K., Wong, D.S. (eds.) CANS 2008. LNCS, vol. 5339, pp. 149–161. Springer, Heidelberg (2008)
5. Burmester, M., Le, T.V., de Medeiros, B., Tsudik, G.: Universally composable RFID identification and authentication protocols. ACM Trans. Inf. Syst. Secur. **12**(4), 1–33 (2009)
6. Canard, S., Coisel, I., Etrog, J., Girault, M.: Privacy-preserving RFID systems: model and constructions. IACR Cryptology ePrint Archive **2010**, 405 (2010)
7. Deng, R.H., Li, Y., Yung, M., Zhao, Y.: A new framework for RFID privacy. In: Gritzalis, D., Preneel, B., Theoharidou, M. (eds.) ESORICS 2010. LNCS, vol. 6345, pp. 1–18. Springer, Heidelberg (2010)
8. van Deursen, T., Radomirović, S.: Untraceable RFID protocols are not trivially composable: attacks on the rvision of ec-rac. IACR Cryptol. ePrint Archive **2009**, 332 (2009)
9. van Deursen, T., Radomirović, S.: EC-RAC: enriching a capacious RFID attack collection. In: Ors Yalcin, S.B. (ed.) RFIDSec 2010. LNCS, vol. 6370, pp. 75–90. Springer, Heidelberg (2010)
10. Fan, J., Hermans, J., Vercauteren, F.: On the claimed privacy of EC-RAC III. In: Ors Yalcin, S.B. (ed.) RFIDSec 2010. LNCS, vol. 6370, pp. 66–74. Springer, Heidelberg (2010)
11. Hein, D., Wolkerstorfer, J., Felber, N.: ECC is ready for RFID – a proof in silicon. In: Avanzi, R.M., Keliher, L., Sica, F. (eds.) SAC 2008. LNCS, vol. 5381, pp. 401–413. Springer, Heidelberg (2009)
12. Hermans, J., Pashalidis, A., Vercauteren, F., Preneel, B.: A new RFID privacy model. In: Atluri, V., Diaz, C. (eds.) ESORICS 2011. LNCS, vol. 6879, pp. 568–587. Springer, Heidelberg (2011)
13. Hopper, N.J., Blum, M.: Secure human identification protocols. In: Boyd, C. (ed.) ASIACRYPT 2001. LNCS, vol. 2248, p. 52. Springer, Heidelberg (2001)
14. Juels, A., Weis, S.A.: Authenticating pervasive devices with human protocols. In: Shoup, V. (ed.) CRYPTO 2005. LNCS, vol. 3621, pp. 293–308. Springer, Heidelberg (2005)
15. Juels, A., Weis, S.A.: Defining strong privacy for RFID. In: PerCom Workshops, pp. 342–347. IEEE Computer Society (2007)
16. Lee, Y.K., Batina, L., Verbauwhede, I.: Ec-rac (ecdlp based randomized access control): Provably secure RFID authentication protocol. In: 2008 IEEE International Conference on RFID, pp. 97–104 (2008)
17. Lee, Y.K., Batina, L., Verbauwhede, I.: Untraceable RFID authentication protocols: Revision of EC-RAC. In: 2009 IEEE International Conference on RFID, pp. 178–185 (2009)

18. Lee, Y.K., Batina, L., Singelée, D., Verbauwhede, I.: Wide–weak privacy-preserving RFID authentication protocols. In: Chatzimisios, P., Verikoukis, C., Santamaría, I., Laddomada, M., Hoffmann, O. (eds.) MOBILIGHT 2010. LNICST, vol. 45, pp. 254–267. Springer, Heidelberg (2010)
19. Lee, Y.K., Sakiyama, K., Batina, L., Verbauwhede, I.: Elliptic-curve-based security processor for RFID. IEEE Trans. Computers **57**(11), 1514–1527 (2008)
20. Ng, C.Y., Susilo, W., Mu, Y., Safavi-Naini, R.: RFID privacy models revisited. In: Jajodia, S., Lopez, J. (eds.) ESORICS 2008. LNCS, vol. 5283, pp. 251–266. Springer, Heidelberg (2008)
21. Nithyanand, R., Tsudik, G., Uzun, E.: Readers behaving badly. In: Gritzalis, D., Preneel, B., Theoharidou, M. (eds.) ESORICS 2010. LNCS, vol. 6345, pp. 19–36. Springer, Heidelberg (2010)
22. Nithyanand, R., Tsudik, G., Uzun, E.: User-aided reader revocation in PKI-based RFID systems. J. Comput. Secur. **19**(6), 1147–1172 (2011)
23. Song, B., Mitchell, C.J.: RFID authentication protocol for low-cost tags. In: Gligor, V.D., Hubaux, J.P., Poovendran, R. (eds.) WISEC, pp. 140–147. ACM (2008)
24. Tsudik, G.: Ya-trap: Yet another trivial RFID authentication protocol. In: PerCom Workshops, pp. 640–643. IEEE Computer Society (2006)
25. Tuyls, P., Batina, L.: RFID-tags for anti-counterfeiting. In: Pointcheval, D. (ed.) CT-RSA 2006. LNCS, vol. 3860, pp. 115–131. Springer, Heidelberg (2006)
26. Vaudenay, S.: On privacy models for RFID. In: Kurosawa, K. (ed.) ASIACRYPT 2007. LNCS, vol. 4833, pp. 68–87. Springer, Heidelberg (2007)

Energy Budget Analysis for Signature Protocols on a Self-powered Wireless Sensor Node

Krishna Pabbuleti, Deepak Mane, and Patrick Schaumont[($\boxtimes$)]

Secure Embedded Systems, Bradley Department of ECE, Center for Embedded Systems for Critical Applications, Virginia Tech, Blacksburg, VA 24061, USA
{kriscp4,mdeepak,schaum}@vt.edu

Abstract. The Internet of Things will include many resource-constrained wireless sensing devices, hungry for energy, bandwidth and compute cycles. The sheer amount of devices involved will require new solutions to handle issues such as identification and power provisioning. In this contribution, we analyze the energy needs of several public-key based authentication protocols, taking into account the energy cost of communication as well as of computation. We have built an autonomous, energy-harvesting sensor node which includes a micro-controller, RF-unit, and energy harvester. We investigate the Elliptic Curve Digital Signature Algorithm (ECDSA), the Lamport-Diffie one-time hash-based signature scheme (LD-OTS) and the Winternitz one-time hash-based signature scheme (W-OTS). We demonstrate that there's a trade-off between energy used for communication, energy used for computation, and security level. However, when we consider the energy needs for the overall system, we show that all schemes are within one order of magnitude from each another.

Keywords: Wireless sensor node · Public key cryptography · Digital signatures · Elliptic curves · Hashing

1 Introduction

Wireless Sensor Nodes (WSN) systems have been extensively investigated over the past decade and a half. These small, resource constrained devices monitor their surroundings and they provide a real-time, distributed view on a physical process. The Internet-of-Things, which may turn every WSN into an Internet host, is an important opportunity for this class of devices. This contribution looks at a specific type of WSN, one which is in capability just above a passive RFID. We consider a wireless sensor node which harvests energy from its surroundings [27]. Energy harvesting considerably simplifies the installation and maintenance of such devices. Without battery replacement or wiring requirements, they can be installed in physically challenging or inaccessible environments - and their lifetime appears to become infinite. The downside of energy harvesting is that it severely limits the energy budget available for WSN

© Springer International Publishing Switzerland 2014
N. Saxena and A.-R. Sadeghi (Eds.): RFIDSec 2014, LNCS 8651, pp. 123–136, 2014.
DOI: 10.1007/978-3-319-13066-8_8

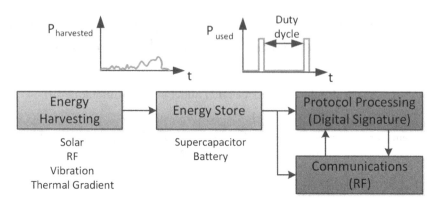

Fig. 1. Energy harvested Embedded System

operation [17]. For example, vibration-based [13] or piezo-electric based harvesters [18] deliver a few microwatt up to a milliwatt; solar-based harvesters deliver a few tens to hundreds of milliwatt [23].

Figure 1 demonstrates the topology of an energy-harvested WSN. An energy store collects energy from a harvester. The energy store then powers up a microcontroller and a radio. This system needs to balance the influx of energy from the harvester with the energy consumed in computing and communicating. The WSN will therefore operate in a duty cycle that periodically activates the communication/computation subsystem, and that otherwise powers it off or keeps it in a low-power standby mode.

We studied the implementation of public-key cryptographic primitives on an energy harvested node. In a public-key identification protocol, a verifier sends a random challenge to the WSN and requests a signature for it. Afterwards, the verifier checks the signature using the WSN public key. When large numbers of WSN are involved, PKC is a better choice than symmetric-key cryptography because of easier key distribution and key handling. The energy cost of PKC authentication using elliptic-curve cryptography (ECC) has been previously studied and the conclusions are as follows [15]: the strategy that minimizes the energy cost per signature is one that runs the microcontroller as fast as possible, while keeping it in a low-power state otherwise. This minimizes the loss through static energy dissipation. Hence, in the energy-harvested sensor node of Fig. 1, it is best to hold off on activities until the energy store has sufficient energy to support at least one complete iteration of the signature protocol. This contribution goes beyond this earlier effort by expanding the analysis to include the communication overhead.

Contributions:

1. We demonstrate a WSN platform that integrates a microcontroller, a radio, an energy-harvester, and an energy-measurement subsystem. We can accurately measure performance as well as energy consumption of individual components

in this system. The WSN connects to a host workstation that takes the role of server. For example, when implementing an identification protocol, the host workstation acts as the verifier. Our design is based on COTS components leading to a physical proof-of-concept.

2. We measure the energy-performance characteristics of three identification protocols, each using a different public-key algorithm. The three PKC signing systems include the Elliptic Curve Digital Signature Algorithm (ECDSA), the Lamport Diffie One Time Signature Algorithm (LD-OTS), and the Winternitz One Time Signature Algorithm (W-OTS). The first is based on Elliptic Curve Cryptography, while the latter two are based on hash functions. For each type of signature, we measure both the computation energy as well as the communication energy.

3. We perform an in-depth analysis of the energy needs for each PKC, isolating the energy required for computations from the energy required for communications. These three PKC have very different characteristics. ECSDA is computationally expensive, but it has relatively short signatures (e.g. 512 bit for 128-bit security level). Hence, for a protocol based on ECDSA, the dominating energy factor is attributed to computations. LD-OTS is computationally much simpler, but it carries very long signatures (e.g. 16 Kbytes for 128-bit security level). In a protocol based on LD-OTS, the dominating energy factor is attributed to communications. Finally, W-OTS enables a trade-off between communication cost and computation cost: by increasing the amount of hashes, a shorter signature can be obtained (e.g. 532 bytes for 128-bit security level). Therefore, we conclude that it's important to perform a comprehensive analysis when assessing the energy needs from a WSN that implements a PKC based protocol. Both the computational load, as well as the communication load, are important factors.

Related Work: The implementation of PKC in constrained environments is a challenging problem, and there is an extensive body of work on efficient implementation of ECC-based and hash-based signatures. Most of this work emphasizes *performance* optimization of the cryptographic algorithms. Indeed, assuming that the microcontroller power dissipation is constant, then the energy dissipation of an algorithm is directly proportional to its execution time. Some examples include work by Liu [14], Mane [15], Cervenka [10], Wenger [29,30] and Pendl [22] for public-key cryptography, by Batina for symmetric-key cryptography [7] and by Rohde for hash-based signatures [25]. An additional factor in energy budget analysis is the energy needed for communications, which leads to additional optimization opportunities [26]. A methodology for this analysis was previously proposed by de Meulenaer *et al.* for ECDSA [16], and by Wander *et al.* for ECDSA and RSA [28]. Our efforts expand on this previous work in three aspects: (a) we present actual measurement data rather than estimates, (b) we investigate the impact of security level, and (c) we include results for hash-based signatures.

Finally, the energy-harvesting itself poses a special challenge for the optimization of cryptographic algorithms. The uncertainty in the source of energy has prompted researchers to propose checkpointing strategies [24] or scheduling techniques that optimize the duty schedule of activity [9]. Furthermore, pre-computing techniques have been proposed that can move some parts of the calculations to an off-line phase [6]. This contribution does not yet include these more advanced strategies, but we recognize the significance of these techniques to enable the full potential of energy harvesting.

The remainder of the paper is organized as follows. In the next section, we describe the target protocols used for authentication. In Sect. 3, we explain our system architecture and the experimental setup. Section 4 describes different operating modes of a sensor node. Next, we explain our energy model used to configure the node. The resulting comparison between different signature schemes is presented in Sect. 5. Section 6 concludes the paper.

2   Target Protocols: Signatures Based on ECC and Hashing

In this section, we describe the identification protocols running on the energy-harvesting WSN. We are comparing three different methods of implementing PKC signatures, while the top-level protocol remains identical in each case. The next few subsections describe the top-level protocol, and they briefly review each of the PKC algorithms.

2.1   Two-Pass Unilateral Authentication

The ISO/IEC 9798-3 standard describes a mechanism for a two-pass authentication protocol using signatures. It is based on the following steps:

$$Server \to WSN : N_S \tag{1}$$

$$WSN \to Server : N_S, N_W, ID_S, Sig_W(N_W, N_S, ID_S) \tag{2}$$

In this protocol, N_S and N_W are nonces generated by the server and WSN, respectively, ID_S is a public server ID, and $Sig_W()$ is a signature scheme executed by the WSN. The nonces guarantee freshness, while the server ID prevents man-in-the-middle attacks. An alternate one-pass protocol is possible provided that the Server and WSN maintain a synchronized counter or timer. In that case, the ISO/IEC 9798-3 standard describes the following case:

$$WSN \to Server : T_W, ID_S, Sig_W(T_W, ID_S) \tag{3}$$

In this protocol, T_W is a timestamp, assumed to be available on the WSN as well as the server. We can implement either protocol in our setup. The signature $Sig_W()$ can be implemented in any of the three different algorithms as described in the following subsections.

2.2   Signatures Using ECC: ECDSA

ECDSA is a well known signature mechanism based on elliptic curve cryptography [12]. We have implemented ECDSA using two different prime-field curves, `secp160r1` and `nistp256`, which have a security level of 80 bit and 128 bit respectively. In ECDSA, signing costs one point multiplication, while verification costs two. Our code is written using the RELIC library [21], and with the following parameters. The scalar multiplication is implemented using a left-to-right window-3 NAF multiplication, and with Jacobian Projective Coordinates. The field operations are basic Comba multiplication and squaring, with Montgomery reduction. SHA-1 is used for hashing and as a pseudo-random generator.

2.3   Signatures Using Hash Algorithms: LD-OTS and LD-OTS-C

The second signature algorithm uses hash functions. It was first proposed by Lamport and Diffie as a one-time-signature scheme (LD-OTS): this implies that a single key pair can be used for exactly one signature. The LD-OTS scheme works as follows [8]. For a security level b, the signer generates a secret key of $4b$ random strings, each $2b$ bits long. The $4b$ random strings of the secret key can be thought of as two arrays of $2b$ random strings: $x(0,0), .., x(0, 2b-1)$ and $x(1,0), .., x(1, 2b-1)$.

At 128-bit security, the signer will create a 16 KByte secret key. The public key is obtained by computing the digest of each of the $4b$ strings: $y(0,0) = H(x(0,0)), .., y(0, 2b-1) = H(x(0, 2b-1))$ and $y(1,0) = H(x(1,0)), .., y(1, 2b-1) = H(x(1, 2b-1))$. Each digest is $2b$ bits long. At 128-bit security level, we use SHA256. To sign a message m, the signer computes a digest over the salted message $H(m,r)$, and breaks this digest into $2b$ bits: $D(0) .. D(2b-1)$. The signature is now formed by selecting a subset of the random strings from the secret key: $x(D(0),0) .. x(D(2b-1), 2b-1)$. A signature thus is 8 Kbyte plus the length of the salt r. To verify the signature, the verifier computes the hash of each string in the signature: $H(x(D(0),0)) .. H(x(D(2b-1), 2b-1))$. The verifier also computes the digest of the salted message $H(m,r)$, splits the digest into bits $v(0) .. v(2b-1)$, and finally checks if $y(v(0),0) = H(x(D(0),0)), .., y(v(2b-1), 2b-1) = H(x(D(2b-1), 2b-1))$. Generating the key costs $4b$ hash operations, verifying a signature costs $2b$ hash operations.

The LD-OTS scheme is simple, easy to compute, but it has a large signature and key pair. Furthermore, the key can only be used a single time. This last drawback can be eliminated by *chaining*: at each signing, a new key pair is generated, the new public key is signed, and appended to the signature. This triples the length of the message (from 8 Kbyte to 24 Kbyte), and it requires the verifier to check all signatures in sequence. In our experimental setup, we have implemented chaining in order to obtain a fair comparison with ECDSA. We refer to this scheme as LD-OTS-C (with the C indicating chaining). Merkle has proposed improvements to chaining using a hash-three, but we have not implemented these.

In our implementation of LD-OTS-C, we paid attention to the memory usage. Indeed, a secret key of 128-bit equivalent security requires 16 KByte, which is well over the capabilities of most microcontrollers, and which is at the limit of the MSP430F5438 device we have used. To address this problem, we generate the LD-OTS secret key on the fly from a 128-bit secret seed and AES in counter mode. This drastically reduces memory usage at the overhead of recomputing the secret key (and the public key) during signing. We have implemented two security levels for LD-OTS: one at 80-bit security level using SHA1 as a hash function, and a second one at 128-bit security level using SHA256 as a hash function.

2.4 Signatures Using Hash Algorithms: W-OTS and W-OTS-C

Another improvement to the LD-OTS scheme was made by Winternitz [11]. In the following description, we summarize the idea but have omitted some details for brevity: refer to the literature for a formal definition.

The fundamental insight from Winternitz was to construct signatures from hash chains rather than from isolated hash digests. A hash chain is a sequence of digests computed as $x_1 = H(x_0)$, $x_2 = H(x_1)$, and so forth. In the Winternitz One Time Signature (W-OTS) scheme, the secret key is located at the start of the hash chain, and the public key is located at the end. A hash chain of length l can sign a bit field of length $log_2(l)$ bits. To see how, consider this field of $log_2(l)$ bits as an index v into the chain and return element $l - v$ from the digest chain as the signature for this field. Verification is now done by continuing the hash chain for v more steps; the final element found should correspond to the public key. To sign messages longer than a field of $log_2(l)$ bits, one can define multiple hash chains. For a message of fixed length (say, 256 bits), there is a trade-off between the depth of the hash chains and the number of chains (or field length). For example, a 256 bit message can be signed using 256 chains of length 2, or 128 chains of length 4, or 64 chains of length 8, or 32 chains of length 16. The length of the hash chains, in turn, determines the computational overhead of signing and verification.

Since the public key only includes the endpoints of the chains, there is a considerable reduction in signature length possible by using fewer, but longer, chains. In our experiments, we have experimented with chain lengths of length 2, 4, 8, and 16 and a security level of 256 bit. These require a public key size of 4 Kbytes, 2 Kbyte, 1 Kbyte and 512 byte respectively. We settled on a chain length of 4, which resulted in signature sizes that are halfway between ECDSA-128 and LD-OTS-128.

Rohde *et al.* describe an implementation of W-OTS and a Merkle hash tree, on constrained devices: they confirm that the implementation on AVR is feasible, but they do not show energy consumption [25]. To get around the one-time nature of W-OTS, we apply chaining in a similar fasion as for LD-OTS, and we use W-OTS-C in our experiments. Table 1 shows the five schemes that we have evaluated in our experiments: two security levels for each of ECDSA and LD-OTS-C, and one security level of W-OTS-C.

Table 1. Security Parameters, Algorithms, Key Sizes, and Operation Counts

Scheme	Alg	Public (byte)	Secret (byte)	Sig (w chain) (byte)	Sign (Ops)	Verify (Ops)
ECDSA-80	secp160r1	20	20	40	1 Pt Mul	2 Pt Mul
ECDSA-128	nistp256	32	32	64	1 Pt Mul	2 Pt Mul
LD-OTS-C-80	SHA1	3200	3200	9600	320 SHA1	160 SHA1
LD-OTS-C-128	SHA256	8192	8192	24576	512 SHA2	256 SHA2
W-OTS-C-128*	SHA256	2128	2128	4256	256 SHA2	256 SHA2

* For hash chains of length 4. Average operation counts.

3   System Architecture

Figure 2 shows the block diagram of our experimental setup. It consists of three parts: (a) an energy-harvesting wireless node, (b) a server and (c) an energy-measurement subsystem. The server authenticates the wireless node by performing a standard unilateral authentication protocol over a low-cost wireless link. The wireless node includes an solar-powered energy harvester, a microcontroller, and an RF frontend. The energy measurement unit monitors the energy dissipation of the wireless node. It can distinguish communication energy from computation energy. By controlling the timing of the energy measurement from

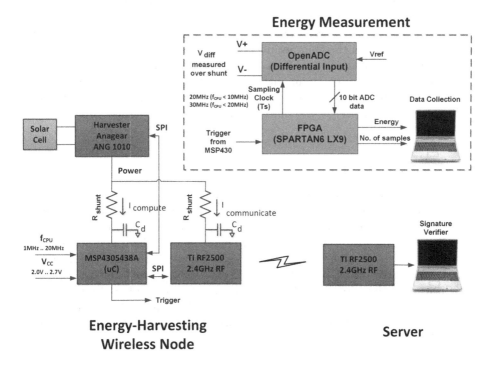

Fig. 2. Wireless sensor node block diagram

within the microcontroller, we achieve precise synchronization. In the following subsections, we describe each of the components in Fig. 2 in further detail.

3.1 Microcontroller

The MSP430F5438A [3] computes signatures on a node. The MSP430F5438A is an ultra-low power microcontroller, optimized for resource-constrained platforms [4]. It features a 16-bit CPU, 256 KB flash, 16 KB SRAM, up to 25 MHz CPU clock and a 32 bit hardware multiplier. The full MSP430 family contains many members, and the selected controller is a relatively high-end member of the family. The MSP430F5438A combines active mode and five low power modes, in which subsections of the microcontroller are disabled. Furthermore, the microcontroller supports a wide range of operating frequencies and operating voltages. It has an on-board configurable power management unit to adjust the core voltage under such conditions. The logical integration of other peripherals of the wireless node with the microcontroller is done through a 4-wire SPI interface.

3.2 RF Transceiver

CC2500 (Texas Instruments) is a low-power RF transceiver [2]. It operates in the 2.4 GHz ISM band and supports various programmable modulation schemes and power levels. It has an SPI interface for configuration and data transfer. It can perform polling-based and interrupt-based data transfers. It supports two low power modes: the Power-Down mode, and the Wake-on-Radio mode. In Power down mode, all the chip peripherals including radio frontend and digital circuitry are off, consuming only 2 uA current. During this mode, the transceiver is effectively blind for RF communications. In the Wake-On-Radio mode, the RF receiver periodically wakes up to check for RF packets. It automatically goes back to sleep if no packet is available. The period and stay-awake time are both configurable.

3.3 Energy Harvester

The wireless node is passively powered through an energy harvester chip that charges a low-leakage supercapacitor. We used the ANG 1010 chip from Anagear, which includes a boost converter as well as autonomous logic for independent operation [1]. The idea is that the chip can independently boot and perform initial harvesting to bring the system into a state where a sufficient level of energy is available. Then, it will awake the microcontroller which will further complete initialization of the wireless node, configure the RF frontend, and initialize the ECC protocol. During operation, the microcontroller can check the level of harvested energy (the level of the supercapacitor voltage) through an SPI interface on the Anagear chip.

3.4 Server

The verifier-part of the protocol is implemented on a PC with an integrated RF transceiver. The PC software is written in C. Using a portable cryptographic library (RELIC, [21]), we can quickly build a protocol that runs on the MSP430 as well as on the PC.

3.5 Energy Measurement Unit

This unit precisely calculates the computation and communication energy for an authentication. It consists of OpenADC [19, 20] attached to a Spartan FPGA [5] that accumulates the sampled current values. The OpenADC samples the differential voltage measured over a shunt resistor in the power line of the wireless node microcontroller or the wireless node RF frontend. The $1\,k\Omega$ shunt resistor is high-precision, high-bandwidth. The accumulation process in the FPGA is under control of the MSP430 by means of a trigger signal. This way, we can easily evaluate the energy and timing of a specific set of events. The sample frequency of the OpenADC depends on the clock frequency of the MSP430 microcontroller. Below $10\,MHz$, we set it at $20\,MHz$. Above $10\,MHz$, we increase the OpenADC sample frequency to $30\,MHz$. We justify the relatively slow sample rate by observing that we are not interested in the high-frequency components of the power, but in the accumulated value. Furthermore, the decoupling capacitors of the chip ensure that the measured current will approach the average current per clock cycle.

4 Energy Model

In this section, we introduce a model that estimates the total energy needed for an authentication that guides the design of energy harvester.

In order to calculate required energy for one authentication, we need to precisely measure both computation as well as communication energy. The required supercapacitor voltage is calculated as follows. We consider a safety margin of twice the required energy. As solar panel harvests energy, supercapacitor voltage increases and MSP430 periodically monitors this level. We require:

Energy stored in capacitor $>$ Computation $+$ Communication Energy

$$\frac{C.V^2}{2} > 2.(E_c + E_{rf}) + E_{ov}$$

$$\frac{C.V^2}{2} > \frac{2.(E_c + E_{rf}) + 125}{1000}$$

$$V > \sqrt{\frac{2.(E_c + E_{rf}) + 125}{500.C}}$$

where C is supercapacitor value in Farad, V is supercapacitor voltage in Volts, E_c is computational energy in mJ, E_{rf} is communication energy in mJ, E_{ov} is energy harvester overhead which is 125mJ.

The relation between solar panel rating, the energy needed for one signature and the signing duty cycle can be expressed as follows.

$$V_{solar}.I_{solar} = P_{sleep} + E_{sig}.Dutycycle \tag{4}$$

where V_{solar} is the rated voltage of solar panel, I_{solar} is the rated current of solar panel, P_{sleep} is the sleep mode power of the system, E_{sig} is the energy needed for one signature and $Dutycycle$ denotes how often the signature is generated.

5   Results

In this section, we present experimental results of our energy measurements and compare the performance of three signature schemes. We measure the energy needed for computation of one signature on MSP430 and transmitting it over RF. We also measure the signature generation and transmission time to find the throughput of the system, i.e., number of authentications performed per second. We use the gcc 4.6.3 cross-compiler for MSP430 family of microcontrollers. Table 2 shows the footprint of different signature protocol implementations. Figure 3a compares the energy consumption of different signature schemes at 10 MHz. ECDSA is based on point multiplication over finite fields which is computationally expensive. Hence, computational energy for ECDSA is higher and it scales up cubically as we increase the required security level from 80–128. However, ECDSA has smaller signature lengths. LD-OTS and W-OTS based signatures use hash functions to generate key and signature and are relatively easier to compute, but have longer signatures which result in higher energy for communication. Compared to ECDSA, our results show that LD-OTS requires 8 times less computational energy at security level of 80 bit, and 30 times less computational energy for a security level of 128 bit. On the other hand, these hash based signatures require 100–300 times more energy for transmitting a signature compared to the short signatures of ECDSA. This clearly demonstrates the trade-off between communication and computation.

Table 2. Code size (Bytes) of the implementations on the MSP430F5438A

	ECDSA-80	ECDSA-128	LD-OTS-C-80	LD-OTS-C-128	W-OTS-C-128
Flash	35,058	38,174	21,210	23,234	17,088
RAM	2,046	2,365	3,634	8,654	406

Figure 3b shows total energy per signature as a function of the operating frequency of the micro-controller. In general, schemes at a higher security level are computationally more expensive, and they have a higher energy cost. The energy increases at lower microcontroller frequencies. This is explained by the higher proportion of static (parasitic) energy consumption in the microcontroller.

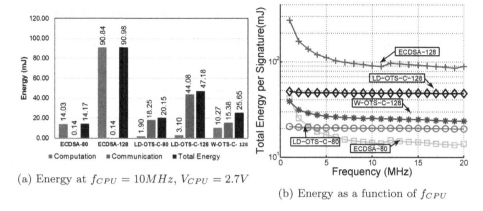

(a) Energy at $f_{CPU} = 10MHz$, $V_{CPU} = 2.7V$

(b) Energy as a function of f_{CPU}

Fig. 3. Energy consumption per authentication for ECDSA, LD-OTS-C and W-OTS-C

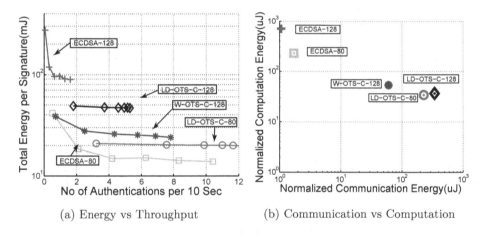

(a) Energy vs Throughput

(b) Communication vs Computation

Fig. 4. Energy trade-off for ECDSA, LD-OTS-C, and W-OTS-C

The faster it runs, the smaller the proportion of this static part. We notice that the ECC based schemes are more sensitive to the microcontroller frequency than the hash-based schemes. This is because in ECC based schemes, the energy dissipation is largely determined by the computations, while in hash-based schemes, the energy cost is dominated by the communication energy cost (which does not depend on the microcontroller operating frequency). Finally, one can also note a discontinuity in the ECC curve at 12 MHz. This is caused by reprogramming of the power management system of MSP430. Internal core voltage needs to be increased in order to operate MSP430 at higher frequencies [4].

Figure 4a shows total energy per signature and as a function of signature throughput. The different points in each curve correspond to different microcontroller frequencies. We believe this curve is, from an application point-of-view, more useful than Fig. 3b because it relates throughput, security-level and energy.

For example, this chart can tell, for a given throughput and energy budget, what security-level is available and what algorithm can be used. Conversely, for a given throughput and selected algorithm, this chart will tell how much energy is needed per signature.

Figure 4b shows the normalized energy for computation and computation at a throughput of one signature per five seconds. The energy is normalized for one bit of equivalent security level offered by the scheme. ECC based schemes and hash based schemes are relatively close to one another in terms of energy, when we consider computation as well as communication. In fact, for all algorithms, the total normalized energy (the sum of X and Y coordinates in Fig. 4b), falls within one order of magnitude.

6   Conclusion

This work has demonstrated the exciting design space of communication, computation, and energy-harvesting for the case of cryptographic signatures. We show an end-to-end methodology which enables complete measurement of every aspect of a signature protocol. We apply the methodology to several different signature schemes, including ECC-based and hash-based signature schemes. This demonstrates the trade-off between computation energy and communication energy in PKC signature schemes.

Our work also opens up a couple of interesting perspectives. A first aspect are signature schemes that *jointly* optimize computation and communication overhead at a given security level. For example, one could investigate how to reduce communication overhead in hash-based schemes, or how to apply precomputation techniques in ECC-based schemes. A full and fair comparison of energy-harvested cryptosystes should always consider both aspects: communication and computation.

A second perspective is the further optimization of our measurement and prototype platform. We are developing an integrated version of Fig. 2 which combines all components on a single PCB, and which scales down the microcontroller to a smaller family member. We expect that this will provide significant reduction of energy overhead.

Finally, we wish to acknowledge the support of the National Science Foundation, grant no 1314598.

References

1. Anagear Power Management. http://www.anagear.com/content/ANG1010
2. Texas Instruments Low Power 2.4 GHz RF Transceiver. http://www.ti.com/lit/ds/swrs040c/swrs040c.pdf
3. Texas Instruments MSP430F5438A Mixed Signal Microcontroller. http://www.ti.com/lit/ds/symlink/msp430f5438a.pdf
4. Texas Instruments MSP430x5xx and MSP430x6xx Family User's Guide 2013. http://www.ti.com/lit/ug/slau208m/slau208m.pdf

5. Xilinx Spartan-6 FPGA LX9 MicroBoard. http://www.em.avnet.com/en-us/design/drc/Pages/Xilinx-Spartan-6-FPGA-LX9-MicroBoard.aspx

6. Ateniese, G., Bianchi, G., Capossele, A., Petrioli, C.: Low-cost standard signatures in wireless sensor networks: a case for reviving pre-computation techniques? In: NDSS (2013)

7. Batina, L., Das, A., Ege, B., Kavun, E.B., Mentens, N., Paar, C., Verbauwhede, I., Yalçin, T.: Dietary recommendations for lightweight block ciphers: power, energy and area analysis of recently developed architectures. In: Hutter, M., Schmidt, J.-M. (eds.) RFIDsec 2013. LNCS, vol. 8262, pp. 101–110. Springer, Heidelberg (2013)

8. Buchmann, J., Dahmen, E., Szydlo, M.: Hash-based digital signature schemes. In: Bernstein, D.J., Buchmann, J., Dahmen, E. (eds.) Post-Quantum Cryptography, pp. 35–93. Springer, Heidelberg (2009). http://dx.doi.org/10.1007/978-3-540-88702-7_3

9. Buettner, M., Greenstein, B., Wetherall, D.: Dewdrop: An energy-aware runtime for computational RFID. In: NSDI (2011)

10. Cervenka, V., Komosny, D., Malina, L., Mraz, L.: Energy efficient public key cryptography in wireless sensor networks. In: Elleithy, K., Sobh, T. (eds.) Innovations and Advances in Computer, Information, Systems Sciences, and Engineering. Lecture Notes in Electrical Engineering, vol. 152, pp. 497–509. Springer, New York (2013). http://dx.doi.org/10.1007/978-1-4614-3535-8_42

11. Dods, C., Smart, N.P., Stam, M.: Hash based digital signature schemes. In: Smart, N.P. (ed.) Cryptography and Coding 2005. LNCS, vol. 3796, pp. 96–115. Springer, Heidelberg (2005). http://dx.doi.org/10.1007/11586821_8

12. Hankerson, D., Menezes, A.J., Vanstone, S.: Guide to Elliptic Curve Cryptography. Springer, New York (2003)

13. Lai, E., Redfern, A., Wright, P.: Vibration powered battery-assisted passive RFID tag. In: Enokido, T., Yan, L., Xiao, B., Kim, D.Y., Dai, Y.-S., Yang, L.T. (eds.) EUC-WS 2005. LNCS, vol. 3823, pp. 1058–1068. Springer, Heidelberg (2005)

14. Liu, A., Ning, P.: TinyECC: a configurable library for elliptic curve cryptography in wireless sensor networks. In: Proceedings of the 7th International Conference on Information Processing in Sensor Networks, IPSN '08, pp. 245–256. IEEE Computer Society, Washington, DC (2008). http://dx.doi.org/10.1109/IPSN.2008.47

15. Mane, D., Schaumont, P.: Energy-architecture tuning for ECC-based RFID tags. In: Hutter, M., Schmidt, J.-M. (eds.) RFIDsec 2013. LNCS, vol. 8262, pp. 145–158. Springer, Heidelberg (2013)

16. de Meulenaer, G., Gosset, F., Standaert, O.X., Pereira, O.: On the energy cost of communication and cryptography in wireless sensor networks. In: 2008 IEEE International Conference on Wireless and Mobile Computing Networking and Communications, WIMOB '08, pp. 580–585, October 2008

17. Mitcheson, P., Yeatman, E., Rao, G., Holmes, A., Green, T.: Energy harvesting from human and machine motion for wireless electronic devices. Proc. IEEE **96**(9), 1457–1486 (2008)

18. Kong, N., Cochran, T., Ha, D., Lin, H., Inman, D.: A self-powered power management circuit for energy harvested by a piezoelectric cantilever. In: Applied Power Electronics Conference and Exposition (APEC), 2010 Twenty-Fifth Annual IEEE, APEC2010 (2010). http://www.mics.ece.vt.edu/Research/Publications/ByFaculty/Papers/Ha/10APEC2010_Published.pdf

19. O'Flynn, C.: OPENADC (2012). http://newae.com/tiki-index.php?page=OpenADC

20. O'Flynn, C.: Power analysis for cheapskates (2012). https://media.blackhat.com/ad-12/O%27Flynn/bh-ad-12-for-cheapskates-o%27flynn-WP.pdf

21. Oliveira, L.B., Aranha, D.F., Gouvêa, C.P.L., Scott, M., Câmara, D.F., López, J., Dahab, R.: TinyPBC: pairings for authenticated identity-based non-interactive key distribution in sensor networks. Comput. Commun. **34**(3), 485–493 (2011)

22. Pendl, C., Pelnar, M., Hutter, M.: Elliptic curve cryptography on the WISP UHF RFID tag. In: Juels, A., Paar, C. (eds.) RFIDSec 2011. LNCS, vol. 7055, pp. 32–47. Springer, Heidelberg (2012)

23. Raghunathan, V., Kansal, A., Hsu, J., Friedman, J., Srivastava, M.: Design considerations for solar energy harvesting wireless embedded systems. In: Proceedings of the 4th International Symposium on Information Processing in Sensor Networks, IPSN '05, IEEE Press, Piscataway, NJ, USA (2005). http://dl.acm.org/citation.cfm?id=1147685.1147764

24. Ransford, B., Sorber, J., Fu, K.: Mementos: system support for long-running computation on RFID-scale devices. In: ASPLOS, pp. 159–170 (2011)

25. Rohde, S., Eisenbarth, T., Dahmen, E., Buchmann, J., Paar, C.: Fast hash-based signatures on constrained devices. In: Grimaud, G., Standaert, F.-X. (eds.) CARDIS 2008. LNCS, vol. 5189, pp. 104–117. Springer, Heidelberg (2008)

26. Struik, R.: AEAD ciphers for highly constrained networks. In: DIAC (2013). http://2013.diac.cr.yp.to/slides/struik.pdf

27. Vullers, R., Schaijk, R., Visser, H., Penders, J., Hoof, C.: Energy harvesting for autonomous wireless sensor networks. IEEE Solid State Circ. Mag. **2**(2), 29–38 (2010)

28. Wander, A., Gura, N., Eberle, H., Gupta, V., Shantz, S.: Energy analysis of public-key cryptography for wireless sensor networks. In: 2005 Third IEEE International Conference on Pervasive Computing and Communications, PerCom 2005, pp. 324–328, March 2005

29. Wenger, E., Feldhofer, M., Felber, N.: Low-resource hardware design of an elliptic curve processor for contactless devices. In: Chung, Y., Yung, M. (eds.) WISA 2010. LNCS, vol. 6513, pp. 92–106. Springer, Heidelberg (2011)

30. Wenger, E., Werner, M.: Evaluating 16-bit processors for elliptic curve cryptography. In: Prouff, E. (ed.) CARDIS 2011. LNCS, vol. 7079, pp. 166–181. Springer, Heidelberg (2011)

High Throughput in Slices: The Case of PRESENT, PRINCE and KATAN64 Ciphers

Kostas Papapagiannopoulos[✉]

Department of Digital Security, Radboud University Nijmegen,
Nijmegen, The Netherlands
kostaspap88@gmail.com

Abstract. This paper presents high-throughput assembly implementations of PRESENT, PRINCE and KATAN64 ciphers for the ATtiny family of AVR microcontrollers. We report new throughput records, achieving the speed of 2967 clock cycles per block encryption for PRESENT, 1803 cycles for PRINCE and 23671 cycles for KATAN64. In addition, we offer insight into the 'slicing' techniques used for high throughput and their application to lightweight cryptographic implementations. We also demonstrate the speed-memory tradeoff by constructing high-throughput implementations with large memory requirements.

Keywords: PRESENT · PRINCE · KATAN64 · AVR · ATtiny · High-speed assembly implementation

1 Introduction

During the recent years, our society experienced big changes in the IT landscape. Starting from the development of wireless connectivity and embedded systems, we have observed an extensive deployment of tiny computing devices in our environment. Everyday objects transform into sophisticated appliances, enhanced with communication and computation capabilities. Ubiquitous computing is gradually becoming a reality and researchers have already identified a wide range of security and privacy risks stemming from it.

In this new fully-interconnected, always-online environment, we rely heavily on a huge number of daily transactions that are carried over a large distributed infrastructure and can be security-critical or privacy-related. RFID tags on commercial products, cardiac pacemakers, fire-detecting sensor nodes, traffic jam detectors and vehicular ad-hoc communication systems have one thing in common: they need to establish a *secure* and *privacy-friendly* modus operandi, under a particularly restricted environment, *e.g.* limited processing capabilities, low energy consumption and/or demanding network protocols.

To provide sufficient security in such a setting, we need security primitives that have a small footprint (low gate number and construction complexity), reduced power consumption (since we often rely on a limited battery or on an external electromagnetic field to supply the required energy) and sufficient speed

© Springer International Publishing Switzerland 2014
N. Saxena and A.-R. Sadeghi (Eds.): RFIDSec 2014, LNCS 8651, pp. 137–155, 2014.
DOI: 10.1007/978-3-319-13066-8_9

(to be able to communicate in real time). The new pervasive computing requirements, in combination with the lack of a suitable candidate (AES is usually too expensive, despite various approaches that have been proposed to reduce the costs of hardware and software implementations [32]), has led researchers to establish new ciphers that are tailor-made for pervasive computing and are often referred to as lightweight ciphers. Among the best studied algorithms are the block ciphers CLEFIA [43], Hight [29], KATAN, KTAN-TAN [16], Klein [25], LED [27], PRESENT [11], the stream ciphers Grain [28], Mickey [7] and Trivium [17] and more recently lightweight hash functions such as SPONGENT [10], PHOTON [26] and QUARK [6].

Our contribution. This work focuses on the software speed aspect of lightweight cryptography, usually with CTR mode of encryption. For AVR devices with the ATtiny RISC architecture [20] (ATtiny85 and ATtiny45), we present new encryption throughput records for ciphers PRESENT and KATAN64 that improve the current state of the art ([21,39,41]) and we also present the first high-throughput implementation of PRINCE cipher. Our main tools for high-throughput are 'slicing' techniques, namely the traditional 'bitslicing' for PRESENT, a variant called 'nibble-slicing' for PRINCE and finally, hardware slices in KATAN64. We note that all these optimization techniques incur a large overhead in memory requirements. The ATtiny devices are low-power 8-bit AVR microcontrollers that employ SRAM, flash and EEPROM types of memory, as well as 32 registers, an ALU[1] and other peripherals. In Sects. 2, 3, 4 we explain these techniques and their effects in detail for PRESENT, PRINCE and KATAN64 respectively and provide comparisons between them. We measure directly the number of clock cycles, SRAM memory bytes and flash memory bytes that they require. We conclude in Sect. 5.

2   PRESENT Cipher: Bitslicing with 8-Bit Processors

This section of this work suggests a novel, bitsliced PRESENT cipher implementation that achieves high throughput performance, namely $2.9\times$ the throughput of the fastest non-bitsliced implementation (Papagiannopoulos, Verstegen [38,39]) and $2.1\times$ the throughput of the fastest bitsliced implementation to our knowledge (Rauzy, Guilley, Najm [41]). The second focal point of this section is to demonstrate the effects of 'slicing' techniques on cipher implementations. By opting for bitsliced PRESENT, we examine the speedups achieved in the permutation layer but also the repercussions occurring in the substitution layer under this non-standard, bitsliced representation.

Algorithm outline. PRESENT [11] is an ultra-lightweight, 64-bit symmetric block cipher, using 80-bit or 128-bit keys. It is based on a substitution/permutation network and as of 2012, was adopted as a standard for lightweight block ciphers (ISO/IEC 29192-2:2012 [3]). The full algorithm has been resistant to attempts at

---

[1] Arithmetic Logic Unit.

Table 1. Substitution layer. The S-box used in PRESENT is a 4-bit to 4-bit function S.

x	0	1	2	3	4	5	6	7	8	9	A	B	C	D	E	F
S[x]	C	5	6	B	9	0	A	D	3	E	F	8	4	7	1	2

Table 2. Permutation layer. The bit-oriented permutation network used in PRESENT. Bit in position i of state is moved to bit position $P(i)$.

i	0	1	2	3	4	5	6	7	8	9	10	11	12	13	14	15
P(i)	0	16	32	48	1	17	33	49	2	18	34	50	3	19	35	51
i	16	17	18	19	20	21	22	23	24	25	26	27	28	29	30	31
P(i)	4	20	36	52	5	21	37	53	6	22	38	54	7	23	39	55
i	32	33	34	35	36	37	38	39	40	41	42	43	44	45	46	47
P(i)	8	24	40	56	9	25	41	57	10	26	42	58	11	27	43	59
i	48	49	50	51	52	53	54	55	56	57	58	59	60	61	62	63
P(i)	12	28	44	60	13	29	45	61	14	30	46	62	15	31	47	63

cryptanalysis, although attacks have shown that up to 15 of its 31 rounds can be broken with $2^{35.6}$ plaintext-ciphertext pairs in 2^{20} operations [4,18,36].

PRESENT uses exclusive-or as its round key operation, a 4-bit substitution layer, a bit permutation network with a 4-bit period, over 31 rounds and a final round key operation. Key scheduling is a combination of bit rotation, S-box application and exclusive-or with the round counter. Constructions found in PRESENT are also encountered in hash functions SPONGENT [10], H-PRESENT [12] and in ciphers Maya [24] and SMALL PRESENT [33]. Thus the optimizations presented here are also directly applicable to these algorithms or to any cipher that uses either a bit-oriented permutation network or the PRESENT S-box (*e.g.* the LED cipher [27]).

The cipher's key register is supplied with the 80-bit cipher key and in every encryption round the first 64 bits of the 80-bit key register form the round key. To encrypt a single 64-bit block, during each encryption round, PRESENT applies an exclusive-or with the current round key followed by a substitution and a permutation layer. The substitution layer applies nibble-wise (4-bit) S-boxes to the state (Table 1), while the permutation layer re-arranges the bits in the state following a 4-bit period (Table 2). Key scheduling is done by rotating the key register 61 bit positions to the left, applying the S-box to the top nibble of the key register and XORing bits 15 through 19 with the round counter. There is a total of 31 such rounds and finally we perform one last exclusive-or with the round key (Fig. 1).

2.1 Permutation Layer Under Bitslicing

Bitslicing was first introduced by Biham [8] in order to improve the performance of bit permutations of DES in software. We note that there exist structural

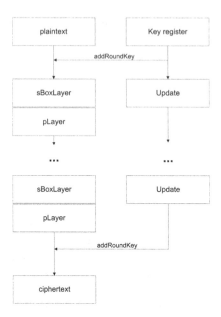

Fig. 1. Overview schematic of the PRESENT cipher. It consists of 31 rounds, including exclusive-or addRoundKey application, nibble-wise substitution (sBoxLayer), bit position permutation (pLayer) and key update.

similarities between DES and PRESENT; although DES is a Feistel instead of an SP network, both are hardware-oriented ciphers that rely heavily on bit permutations which are efficient with circuit wirings, yet slow in software. Bitslicing views our 8-bit microprocessor as a SIMD[2] computer with 8 single-bit processors running in parallel. Thus, we use a non-standard, bitsliced representation for our 64-bit PRESENT cipher block: 64 SRAM cells (each cell consisting of 8 bits) represent the 64 bit positions of the block. Due to the 8-bit size of our cells/positions, we are able to permute 8 cipher blocks in parallel. *i.e.* we achieve a bitslice factor of 8.

Normally, the permutation layer under this representation would be reduced to simple memory cell renaming according to the permutation pattern (Table 2) and should cost zero clock cycles. However, cell renaming for 31 cipher rounds requires full loop unrolling, resulting in infeasible code size. Thus, we use the following approach:

1. Load four 8-way-bitsliced cells from the SRAM to four registers.
2. Perform the nibble-based substitution layer (Sect. 2.2).
3. Store the substituted result back to SRAM cells in a permuted fashion (Table 2).
4. Repeat this for all nibbles in the cipher block.

---

[2] Single instruction, multiple data (SIMD), is a class of parallel computers in Flynn's taxonomy [23]. It describes computers with multiple processing elements that perform the same operation on multiple data points simultaneously.

Essentially, the computational cost of the permutation layer drops to 64 memory loads and 64 memory stores. In order to load cells in a sequential manner and to store in a permuted fashion, we use direct SRAM addressing (instructions `lds, sts`). The bitsliced permutation approach is substantially faster (in terms of throughput) when compared to LUT approaches like merged SP lookup tables [39] or permutation lookup tables [9]. Likewise, instruction-set-based approaches such as bit-level manipulation/masking techniques that employ the `bld, bst` instructions [37] or logical shifts [21] are also outperformed. The ineffectiveness of several ISAs[3] w.r.t. permutation operations has also been addressed by Lee *et al.* [34,42], who suggested extensions to existing instruction sets in order to compute arbitrary *n-bit* permutations.

2.2   Substitution Layer Under Bitslicing

Despite the large throughput boost on the permutation layer, bitslicing increases the complexity of the substitution operation and has even led to bitslicing-oriented compilers [40]. When assuming 4-bit S-boxes, a cipher block size of 64 bits and an 8-bit architecture, performing a substitution directly via lookup tables becomes impossible; the LUT size and addressing mode is infeasible for the AVR ATtiny. A more viable alternative would be to first *extract* the bits required out of the bitsliced representation, *i.e.* temporarily revert to the original form (un-bitslicing), perform a lookup and then store back in the bitsliced representation. Still, this procedure also implies a large performance overhead.

The best solution that has been identified so far for computing efficiently the substitution layer of a cipher in bitsliced representation is by interpreting the S-box as a boolean function. Bitslicing uses 8-bit cells (Sect. 2.1), each pertaining to a position withing the cipher block. When implementing any boolean function under bitslicing, we still maintain the SIMD parallelization, *i.e.* any logical operation between two 8-way-bitsliced cells performs 8 single-bit logical operations in parallel.

Efficient software implementation of boolean functions. In order to efficiently implement a boolean function in software we point out its close resemblance to hardware construction of optimal circuits; in fact, we will demonstrate that boolean function implementation in software can be solved using the same techniques, albeit with slightly different constraints. Constructing optimal combinational circuits and 'technology mapping' in general is an intractable problem under almost any meaningful metric (gate count, depth, energy consumption, *etc.*). In practice, even a boolean function with as few as 8 inputs and a single output would require searching over a space of 2^{256} such outputs and this naturally leads us to heuristic methods.

Boyar-Peralta heuristic and Courtois extension. In 2008, Boyar and Peralta introduced an efficient new heuristic methodology to minimize the complexity of digital circuits [2,14,15]. Their focal point was to construct efficient cipher

---

[3] Instruction Set Architectures.

implementations based on the notion of *Multiplicative Complexity* (number of AND gates) and they produced a 2-stage methodology to optimize the circuit over the basis $\{\oplus, \wedge, 1\}$ by first minimizing the non-linear (AND) components and consequently the linear (XOR) components.

Courtois, Hulme and Mourouzis [19] extended this conjecture and applied the heuristic to several S-boxes modeled by $GF(2)^4 \rightarrow GF(2)^4$ boolean functions (including the PRESENT cipher S-box). In addition to the existing multiplicative complexity metric, Courtois *et al.* introduced the notion of *Bitslice Gate complexity* as the minimum number of 2-input gates of types XOR, OR, AND and single-input gates of type NOT needed to construct the circuit. For a silicon implementation this notion is helpful but definitely non-optimal: certain gates are more costly to implement, given the fact that silicon mapping often tries to minimize the number of the cheap NAND gates. Still, *we observe a case where software-efficient boolean functions differentiate from hardware-efficient boolean functions.* AVR ATtiny instructions for XOR, OR, AND, NOT operations cost a single clock cycle whereas there exists no native NAND operation. Consequently, mapping the PRESENT S-boxes to XOR, OR, AND, NOT gates and translating to software instructions outperforms any hardware-oriented mapping to NAND gates and subsequent translation to software operations. In the 'technology mapping' context, we can view these two approaches as mappings to different cell libraries, where the different component cost indicates the difference between hardware and software implementation.

The results of the Courtois form the basis of an efficient software-based bit-sliced implementation of the PRESENT cipher, both for the AVR architecture (this work) and C-based implementations [35]. Courtois applied the 2-stage Boyar-Peralta heuristic in combination with SAT solvers, resulting in the following representation for the PRESENT Sbox that has very low bitsliced gate complexity.

```
T1=X2^X1; T2=X1&T1; T3=X0^T2; Y3=X3^T3; T2=T1&T3; T1^=Y3; T2^=X1;
T4=X3|T2; Y2=T1^T4; X3=~X3; T2^=X3; Y0=Y2^T2; T2|=T1; Y1=T3^T2;
```

where X_i=input, Y_i=output and T_i=intermediate values.

This is the final form that we use for computing the PRESENT substitution layer in the AVR ATtiny architecture and it requires 14 gates. Note that the set of operations uses the 'operator destination, sourceA, sourceB' instruction format instead of the native ATtiny 'operator destination, source' format. The inherent problem is that it is not possible to reuse a computed value, unless we store it temporarily elsewhere. With careful register usage, we maintain this penalty to a minimum and our final implementation requires 19 clock cycles to compute the output of a single PRESENT S-box. As a result, the 16 S-box operations used in the bitsliced representation require $19 \cdot 16 = 304$ clock cycles for 8 cipher blocks in parallel.

Table 3. Size (pertaining to flash and SRAM bytes) and throughput (clock cycles per block) of AES (row 1) and PRESENT (rows 2 to 5) cipher implementations.

Implementation	Flash (bytes)	SRAM (bytes)	Throughput (cc/block)	Bitsliced
AES, [1]	3098	-	2474	no
Eisenbarth *et al.* [21]	1000	18	10723	no
Papag. [38,39] ATtiny45	1794	0	8721	no
Rauzy *et al.*, ATtiny45 [41]	1194	144	6473	yes
This work, ATtiny85	3816	256	2967	yes

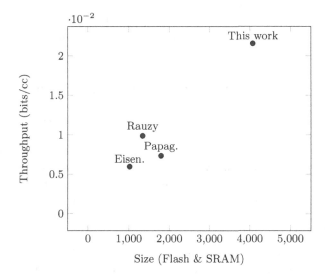

Fig. 2. Throughput *vs.* Size diagram for various implementations of the PRESENT cipher.

2.3 PRESENT Performance

The suggested implementation manages to outperform all existing implementations with respect to throughput. Comparing this work with the non-bitsliced work by Eisenbarth *et al.* [21], we can draw several conclusions regarding bitsliced representations. Eisenbarth's substitution layer is extremely efficient, consisting of a single flash memory lookup (4 clock cycles) per 8 bits (0.5 cc[4] per bit). Our boolean-function-oriented implementation requires 19 clock cycles for an S-box computation, *i.e.* 0.59 cc per bit, so slightly slower. However, this hindrance is unimportant when considering the very slow permutation layer of Eisenbarth *et al.* (154 cc per round) compared to ours (32 cc per round). We also outperform Papagiannopoulos and Verstegen [39] due to the fact that they replace the whole

---

[4] Clock cycles.

SP network with lookup tables and this results in a large number of flash memory accesses (1 memory access per 2 bits of state). However, we must stress the fact that the bitsliced version of PRESENT increased the memory requirements by a factor of 4, when compared to straightforward implementations [21]. Comparing our bitsliced version with Rauzy *et al.* [41], we observe that we achieve a *2.1×* boost in throughput. Since the authors do not elaborate on the implementation of the boolean function in use, memory accesses or other secondary operations (addRoundKey, keyUpdate *etc.*) we cannot identify the source of this speed-up, although we note that the authors were more efficient in terms of code size. When examining latency, we note that all bitsliced implementations perform inherently multiple blocks in parallel (equal to the bitslice factor). In our case, we perform 8 block encryptions in parallel within 23736 clock cycles, resulting in poor latency performance. It is also worth pointing out that AES [1] can out-perform PRESENT in terms of both latency and throughput, since it encrypts a 128-bit block (twice the PRESENT block) in fewer cycles (Fig. 2 and Table 3).

3   PRINCE: Nibble-Slicing in 8-Bit Microprocessors

In this section, we present the first (to our knowledge) 'sliced' implementation of the PRINCE cipher [13] for the ATtiny architecture. Our focal points are the substitution and the nibble (4 bits) permutation operations of the cipher. We suggest a novel idea, namely a variation of the bitslicing technique called nibble-slicing, in order to efficiently compute these operations. We also offer insight w.r.t. the effects of slicing on the permutation and substitution layer and provide a comparison between bitslicing (used in PRESENT) and nibble-slicing (used in PRINCE).

Algorithm outline. PRINCE is a 64-bit block cipher with a 128-bit keys, based on the F–X construction [13,31]. The key k is split into two parts of 64 bits each, *i.e.* $k = k_1 || k_2$ and extended to 192 bits via the following mapping:

$$k_0 || k_1 \rightarrow k_0 || k_0' || k_1 = (k_0 || k_0 >>> 1) \oplus (k_0 >> 63 || k_1) \qquad (1)$$

Now, k_0 and k_0' are used as whitening keys, while k_1 is the main 64-bit used by the 12 rounds of the cipher without any key updates. Figure 3 shows the 12 rounds of encryption. The encryption consists of a nibble-based substitution layer S, a Shift Rows operation (SR) and a matrix multiplication M'. Operations M' and SR (in this order) construct the operation M (Tables 4, 5).

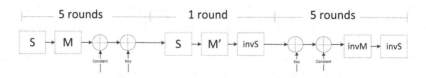

Fig. 3. The 12 rounds of the PRINCE cipher. k_1 denotes the core cipher key, RC_is are constants, S the substitution layer and M the diffusion layer.

Table 4. The S-Box of the PRINCE cipher, used for the S operation.

x	0	1	2	3	4	5	6	7	8	9	A	B	C	D	E	F
S[x]	B	F	3	2	A	C	9	1	6	7	8	0	E	5	D	4

Table 5. Nibble permutation of the PRINCE cipher in the SR operation (from old nibble position to new nibble position).

Old	0	1	2	3	4	5	6	7	8	9	10	11	12	13	14	15
New	0	5	10	15	4	9	14	3	8	13	2	7	12	1	6	11

3.1 Diffusion Layer Under Nibble-Slicing

Shift Rows. When comparing the substitution-permutation network of PRESENT with that of PRINCE we can observe similarities and differences. The substitution operation is fairly identical in nature and similarities do exist between the Shift Rows operation (nibble permutation) and the PRESENT bit permutation network; the SR operation is a permutation with fewer degrees of freedom when compared to single-bit permutations. Based on this observation, we have identified a technique stemming from bitslicing (we call it *nibble-slicing*) that is custom-made for nibble-oriented permutation layers and manages to avoid memory accesses, despite the fact that we operate on a 64-bit cipher state (Fig. 4).

$$M' = \begin{pmatrix} M_a & 0 & 0 & 0 \\ 0 & M_b & 0 & 0 \\ 0 & 0 & M_b & 0 \\ 0 & 0 & 0 & M_a \end{pmatrix}$$

$$M_a = \begin{pmatrix} M_0 & M_1 & M_2 & M_3 \\ M_1 & M_2 & M_3 & M_0 \\ M_2 & M_3 & M_0 & M_1 \\ M_3 & M_0 & M_1 & M_2 \end{pmatrix} \quad M_b = \begin{pmatrix} M_1 & M_2 & M_3 & M_0 \\ M_2 & M_3 & M_0 & M_1 \\ M_3 & M_0 & M_1 & M_2 \\ M_0 & M_1 & M_2 & M_3 \end{pmatrix}$$

$$M_0 = \begin{pmatrix} 0&0&0&0 \\ 0&1&0&0 \\ 0&0&1&0 \\ 0&0&0&1 \end{pmatrix} \ M_1 = \begin{pmatrix} 1&0&0&0 \\ 0&0&0&0 \\ 0&0&1&0 \\ 0&0&0&1 \end{pmatrix} \ M_2 = \begin{pmatrix} 1&0&0&0 \\ 0&1&0&0 \\ 0&0&0&0 \\ 0&0&0&1 \end{pmatrix} \ M_3 = \begin{pmatrix} 1&0&0&0 \\ 0&1&0&0 \\ 0&0&1&0 \\ 0&0&0&0 \end{pmatrix}$$

Fig. 4. The M' operation, analyzed from top to bottom.

Nibble-slicing uses the following representation: every 8-bit register is split into two parts (high and low, 4 bits each) and we use a total of 16 registers (thus avoiding SRAM usage, something impossible for bitsliced representations on ATtiny). The whole representation consists of 128 bits, *i.e.* two separate cipher states (we refer to them as block 1 and block 2 – see Fig. 5). Block 1 is stored in all high parts of the 16 registers and block 2 in all low parts of the corresponding registers. Nibble-slicing presents similarities with vectorized computations on larger processors and to digit-slicing or byte-slicing techniques used to improve speed of AES [30]. In our context, nibble-slicing essentially removes the need to compute the SR operation and could be of similar usage for other lightweight ciphers with a nibble-oriented permutation network (*e.g.* KLEIN or LED).

Fig. 5. Nibble-sliced representation of two PRINCE cipher blocks.

Matrix multiplication. Matrix multiplication (M') is the most computationally expensive operation of the PRINCE cipher. To increase speed, we try to exploit the diagonal structure of the matrix: we view the matrix as a set of 4 by 4 matrices, then we multiply with the state nibbles with the main diagonal of every 4 by 4 matrix. This approach works well under the nibble-sliced representation; both high and low parts of the register are multiplied with the same diagonal.

3.2 Substitution Layer Under Nibble-Slicing

A negative effect of nibble-slicing is the following: under this non-standard representation, we have lost our maximum parallel processing capability; instead of storing 8 different cipher states within a single register (bitslice factor of 8) we store only two (bitslice factor of 2). However, this novel representation is faster when implementing PRINCE in the AVR context compared to the original bit-slicing method for the following reasons:

1. As mentioned, nibble-slicing in 16 registers results in an implementation that fully avoids usage of SRAM and the penalty associated with it. Storing two separate cipher states in such a way fits into registers and thus avoids spills to SRAM.
2. Second, although it is still possible, we no longer have to compute the S-box via a boolean function and we can use LUTs which are more efficient in the ATtiny context.

Although we demonstrated in Sect. 2.2 that boolean functions are fairly efficient for S-box computation, we remind that they are still slower than direct flash memory lookups. Bitsliced PRESENT could not use lookup tables for the substitution layer, but that is not the case for nibble-sliced PRINCE. Each register contains two separate 4-bit values. Based on the guidelines by Eisenbarth *et al.* [21] and Papagiannopoulos and Verstegen [39], we use a 'squared', byte-oriented lookup table for S-box computation. During the lookup, each one of

Table 6. Performance of the high-throughput of the AES (row 1) and PRINCE (rows 2 to 4) ciphers.

Implementation	Flash (bytes)	SRAM (bytes)	Throughput (cc/block)
AES [1]	3098	-	2474
Shahverdi *et al.*, T-box	1990	232	4292
Shahverdi *et al.*, parallel	1574	24	3253
This work, ATtiny85	2382	220	1803

the 4-bit halves is substituted separately. The whole process is carried out efficiently via 8-bit flash memory lookups from 256-byte tables in flash memory. In fact, we merge the S operation with the SR operation; every time we perform a lookup, we take into account that values need to be stored back in registers in a permuted fashion.

3.3   PRINCE Performance

Nibble-slicing lacks in terms of throughput compared to the 'traditional' bitslicing approach. However, the fact that LUTs are a viable option for the substitution layer compensates to some extent. Our PRINCE cipher implementation encrypts two 64-bit blocks in 3606 cc, *i.e.* a throughput of 1803 cc per block. Comparing to a straightforward implementation that uses T-tables (Shahverdi *et al.* [5]), we observe a throughput increase of 2.3, while memory consumption increased by a factor of 1.16. Comparing to a parallel PRINCE implementation (Shahverdi *et al.* [5]), we achieve throughput increase by a factor of 1.8 and memory requirements increase by a factor of 1.61. AES [1] still outperforms PRINCE (0.051 bits/cc *vs.* 0.035 bits/cc) (Table 6).

4   KATAN64: Hardware Parallelism Translated to Software Slices

The third section of this work examines a different type of cipher that is not related to SP networks and resembles a stream cipher. However, as we will point out, certain parallel constructs in hardware can also lead us to a non-standard representation in software that taps into parallelism – not unlike bitslicing. We identify these cases as 'hardware slices'.

Algorithm outline. The outline is provided in Fig. 6. The KATAN cipher [16] was designed as a secure 80-bit block cipher with a minimal number of hardware gates, while it demonstrates very slow software performance. Following the design of KeeLoq [22], the designers chose a structure similar to a stream cipher, resembling the two-register variant of Trivium [17], known as Bivium.

The cipher's plaintext is loaded into two linear feedback shift registers (LFSRs) L1 and L2. Each round several bits are taken from the registers and the cipher key. Those bits enter two non-linear boolean functions (f_a and f_b), while the output of the boolean functions is loaded to the least-significant bits of the registers after they are shifted (or 'clocked'). Computing the two boolean functions f_a, f_b requires AND and XOR operations between the state bits, the cipher keys and a constant value IR (irregular update) that increases diffusion. The KATAN cipher executes a fairly large number of rounds (254) and comes in three variants: KATAN32, KATAN48 and KATAN64 (the suffix denotes the size of the cipher state – the key size is always 80 bits). Our implementation focuses solely on the 64-bit version, which presents additional interest w.r.t. slicing.

As mentioned, KATAN64 uses two non-linear function f_a and f_b in each round which are computed as follows.

$$f_a(L_1) = L_1[24] \oplus L_1[15] \oplus (L_1[20] \cdot L_1[11]) \oplus (L_1[9] \cdot IR) \oplus k_a \qquad (2)$$

$$f_b(L_2) = L_2[38] \oplus L_2[25] \oplus (L_2[33] \cdot L_2[21]) \oplus (L_2[14] \cdot L_2[9]) \oplus k_b \qquad (3)$$

where $L_1[i]$ and $L_2[i]$ denote bit positions on the two LFSR registers, IR denotes the irregular update (constant) and k_a, k_b denote the two subkey bits of every KATAN64 round. After the computation of the non-linear functions, the registers L1 and L2 are shifted. The MSB falls off into the corresponding non-linear function and the LSB is loaded with the output of the second non-linear function, *i.e.*, after the round, the LSB of L1 is the output of f_b and the LSB of L2 is the output of f_a.

A specific feature of the KATAN64 construction with respect to the non-linear functions is the following. In KATAN64, each round applies f_a and f_b *three times* with the same key bits k_a, k_b. An efficient hardware implementation can implement these three steps in parallel, a fact that will also lead us to software parallelism.

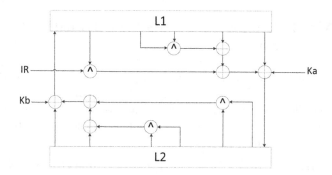

Fig. 6. The core operation of the KATAN cipher. The two LFSR L1, L2 store the cipher state. Several bits are extracted from L1, L2, from the cipher key (k_a, k_b) and from IR in order to compute the non-linear functions f_a, f_b (via XOR/AND operations) and to update the cipher state.

The key schedule of the KATAN64 cipher loads the 80-bit key into an LFSR (the least significant bit of the key is loaded to position 0 of the LFSR). Every round, positions 0 and 1 of the LFSR are used as the round's subkey k_{2i} and k_{2i+1}, and the LFSR is clocked twice according to the following feedback polynomial:

$$x^{80} + x^{61} + x^{50} + x^{13} + 1 \tag{4}$$

The subkey of round i can be described as $k_a \| k_b = k_{2i} \| k_{2i+1}$ where $k_i = K_i$ for $i \in \{0, 1, \ldots, 79\}$ (K being the 80-bit input key) or alternatively $k_i = k_{i-80} \oplus k_{i-61} \oplus k_{i-50} \oplus k_{i-13}$.

4.1 KATAN64 Non-linear Functions Under Slicing

The KATAN cipher has an interesting hardware-related property that has not been yet translated to software implementations. During each cipher round, the 64-bit version of KATAN applies the non-linear functions f_a, f_b three times and these computations can be carried out in parallel (if the extra hardware gates are available). Eisenbarth *et al.* suggest that implementing this property may result in complicated shifting/masking that will increase the code size with little or no performance gain, yet we attempt to rebut this statement.

Computing the functions f_a, f_b sequentially via the `bld`,`bst` bit-level instructions is very time-consuming. A single run of f_b would require 7 extract (`bld`), 7 deposit (`blst`), 2 AND, 3 XOR operations and as a result $3 \cdot 19 \cdot 254 = 14478$ clock cycles for a full encryption (the factor 3 due to the 3-way parallelizable step being done sequentially). Analogously, f_a also costs roughly the same amount. Bitslicing would solve this issue but it would entail a huge SRAM transfer overhead due to the large number of rounds. Thus, we turn to register-oriented approaches.

Achieving 3-way parallelizability involves using masking and instructions that operate on register level and not bit-level operations. In addition, it involves a slightly different representation of the cipher state: instead of storing the 64 bit state in 8 registers (each containing 8 bits), we employ 9 registers that store the representation in a slid fashion (see Fig. 7). First, observe that there exist several triadic bit groups that contribute to the computation of the next cipher state. For instance, KATAN64 uses (among others) bit 9 of the the L2 LFSR to compute a single bit of the next state and since this operation has to be carried out 3 times within a KATAN64 round, the same procedure is applied to bits 8 and 7 correspondingly. There exist 6 such triads in the L2 LFSR (9/8/7, 14/13/12, 21/20/19, 25/24/23, 33/32/31, 38/37/36) and 5 such triads in the L1 LFSR (9/8/7, 11/10/9, 15/14/13, 20/19/18, 24/23/22). This non-standard representation displayed in Fig. 7 attempts to arrange all bit triads used for the new state computation in a way that never splits a triad between two separate registers. Having established that, we can use register-level operations that carry out the new state computations, while maintaining 3-way parallelizability. We have essentially created 3 slices in our representation.

Under the new representation, computing *3 parallel output bits* costs 19 clock cycles for function f_b and 19 clock cycles for function f_a. Compared to the sequential approach of the previous paragraph, we observe a *3*× performance boost when parallelizing the operations in software; f_a and f_b used to cost $57 = 3 \cdot 19$ cycles each for a 3 bit output. Note also that the new representation does not fully utilize all registers, since registers r0, r5 and r8 have bits indicated as *null* (*i.e.* non-relevant in our representation). A side-effect is that bit rotation (also denoted as LFSR clocking) becomes slightly slower; it costs us 39 clock cycles in order to carry out 3 bit rotations to all 9 registers that are transparent to the *null* register positions, *i.e.* sliding all registers to the right and transferring overflow bits from L2 to L1 and L1 to L2 correspondingly while taking into account the null bits. A standard representation (using 8 registers without *null* bit elements) would rotate in 24 clock cycles ($24 = 3 \cdot 8$, *i.e.* 3 single bit rotations carried on 8 registers) Fig. 8.

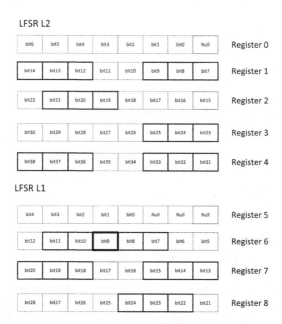

Fig. 7. Cipher state of KATAN64, stored in a slid manner, using 9 registers. The bit triads required for computing the new cipher state are highlighted in bold.

4.2 KATAN64 Performance

The only known implementation of KATAN64 in AVR architecture is presented by Eisenbarth *et al.* [21] and it focuses on low size, not high throughput. Our implementation manages a full KATAN64 encryption in 23671 clock cycles, while Eisenbarth *et al.* manages a full encryption in 72063 clock cycles, *i.e.* we improve the throughput by a factor of 3. Although the two implementations are not directly comparable (due to different implementation objectives) it is still useful to compare and observe the tradeoffs. Specifically, we disagree with the statement that the 3-way KATAN64 parallelizability cannot be sufficiently exploited

```
function fb          function fa

mov t1,s1            mov t3,s6
swap t1              lsr t3
lsr t1               eor t3,s8
and t1,s1

mov t2,s2            eor t3,s8
swap t2              lsr t3
and t2,s4            eor t3,s7

eor t1,t2            mov t4,s7
eor t1,s3            lsr t4
                     and t4,s6
swap t1              swap t4
lsl t1               eor t4,t3
eor t1, s4
```

Fig. 8. Register-oriented code to compute f_a, f_b, while performing operations in parallel (excluding key XOR operations and irregular update XORing). Variables s_i denote cipher state (Fig. 7 register i corresponds to s_i), and variable t_j denotes temporary values.

in software; with the penalty of a single extra register, we manage to increase the throughput of the non-linear layer threefold. Although we exploit a form of parallelizability, we do not compute many blocks in parallel; thus, throughput improvement translates automatically to latency improvement. Finally, our implementation precomputes the cipher round key and requires extra SRAM space for lowering the latency (Table 7).

Table 7. Throughput of KATAN64 cipher implementations for AVR architecture, *i.e.*, clock cycles required for a single encryption round.

KATAN64 implementation	Throughput (cc)	Size (bytes)
Eisenbarth *et al.* [21]	72063	338 flash, 18 SRAM
This work, ATtiny45	23671	380 flash, 96 SRAM

5   Conclusion

Summarizing, this work has managed to improve the throughput aspect of three lightweight ciphers (PRESENT, PRINCE, KATAN64). We displayed the 'slicing' techniques, then determined which is applicable for each cipher and finally, we investigated their effects on substitution, permutation and other operations.

Our results demonstrate a 2.1× improvement for PRESENT throughput, 3×
improvement for KATAN64 (throughput and latency) and the first high-speed
implementation of PRINCE for ATtiny devices. Code is available online here:
https://github.com/kostaspap88?tab=repositories. Future directions include
high-throughput implementations for ciphers or hash functions that present
structural similarities with the three ciphers discussed in this paper. Finally, an
interesting direction would be an attempt to analytically model the behavior of
e.g. SP networks and rigidly link computational efficiency in software with other
important properties such as cryptanalysis resistance, power consumption and
hardware performance. Establishing trade-offs between these design parameters
in a analytic manner could link to more efficient designs in the future.

Acknowledgments. We would like to thank P. Schwabe and the rest of the reviewers
of this paper for their contribution. This work was supported in part by the Technology
Foundation STW (project 12624 – SIDES), The Netherlands Organization for Scientific
Research NWO (project ProFIL – 628.001.007) and the ICT COST action IC1204
TRUDEVICE.

References

1. Avr, AES: The AES block cipher on AVR controllers. http://point-at-infinity.org/
   avraes/
2. Circuit minimization results obtained at Yale University. http://cs-www.cs.yale.
   edu/homes/peralta/CircuitStuff/CMT.html. (Accessed 15 November 2013)
3. ISO/IEC 29192–2:2011, Information technology - Security techniques - Lightweight
   cryptography - Part 2: Block ciphers (2011)
4. Abed, F., Forler, C., List, E., Lucks, S., Wenzel, J.: Biclique cryptanalysis of the
   PRESENT, LED and KLEIN. IACR Cryptol. ePrint Arch., 591 (2012). http://
   eprint.iacr.org/2012/591.pdf. (Accessed 18 November 2013)
5. Aria, S., Eisenbarth, T.: AVRprince - An Efficient Implementation of PRINCE for
   8-bit Microprocessors. http://users.wpi.edu/teisenbarth/pdf/avrPRINCEv01.pdf.
6. Aumasson, J-P., Henzen, L., Meier, W., Naya-Plasencia, M.: Quark: A lightweight
   hash. J. Cryptol. 26(2), 313–339 (2013). https://131002.net/quark/quark_full.pdf.
   (Accessed 18 November 2013)
7. Babbage, S., Dodd, M.: The stream cipher MICKEY 2.0, ECRYPT stream
   cipher (2006). http://www.ecrypt.eu.org/stream/p3ciphers/mickey/mickey_p3.
   pdf. (Accessed 18 November 2013)
8. Biham, E.: A fast new DES implementation in software. In: Biham, E. (ed.) FSE
   1997. LNCS, vol. 1267, pp. 260–272. Springer, Heidelberg (1997). http://citeseerx.
   ist.psu.edu/viewdoc/download?
9. Bishop, M.: An application of a fast data encryption standard implementation. Comput. Syst. 1(3): 221–254 (1988). http://www.cs.dartmouth.edu/reports/
   TR88-138.pdf. (Accessed 18 November 2013)
10. Bogdanov, A., Knežević, M., Leander, G., Toz, D., Varıcı, K., Verbauwhede,
    I.: SPONGENT: a lightweight hash function. In: Preneel, B., Takagi, T. (eds.)
    CHES 2011. LNCS, vol. 6917, pp. 312–325. Springer, Heidelberg (2011).
    http://homes.esat.kuleuven.be/abogdano/papers/spongent_ches11.pdf

11. Bogdanov, A.A., Knudsen, L.R., Leander, G., Paar, C., Poschmann, A., Robshaw, M., Seurin, Y., Vikkelsoe, C.: PRESENT: An Ultra-Lightweight Block Cipher. In: Paillier, P., Verbauwhede, I. (eds.) CHES 2007. LNCS, vol. 4727, pp. 450–466. Springer, Heidelberg (2007). http://homes.esat.kuleuven.be/abogdano/papers/present_ches07.pdf

12. Bogdanov, A., Leander, G., Paar, C., Poschmann, A., Robshaw, M.J.B., Seurin, Y.: Hash functions and RFID tags: mind the gap. In: Oswald, E., Rohatgi, P. (eds.) CHES 2008. LNCS, vol. 5154, pp. 283–299. Springer, Heidelberg (2008). http://www.iacr.org/archive/ches2008/51540279/51540279.pdf

13. Borghoff, J., Canteaut, A., Güneysu, T., Kavun, E.B., Knezevic, M., Knudsen, L.R., Leander, G., Nikov, V., Paar, C., Rechberger, C., Rombouts, P., Thomsen, S.S., Yalçın, T.: PRINCE – a low-latency block cipher for pervasive computing applications. In: Wang, X., Sako, K. (eds.) ASIACRYPT 2012. LNCS, vol. 7658, pp. 208–225. Springer, Heidelberg (2012). http://eprint.iacr.org/2012/529.pdf

14. Boyar, J., Peralta, R.: A new combinational logic minimization technique with applications to cryptology. In: Festa, P. (ed.) SEA 2010. LNCS, vol. 6049, pp. 178–189. Springer, Heidelberg (2010). http://eprint.iacr.org/2009/191.pdf

15. Boyar, J., Peralta, R.: A small depth-16 circuit for the AES S-box. In: Gritzalis, D., Furnell, S., Theoharidou, M. (eds.) SEC 2012. IFIP AICT, vol. 376, pp. 287–298. Springer, Heidelberg (2012). http://eprint.iacr.org/2011/332.pdf

16. De Cannière, C., Dunkelman, O., Knežević, M.: KATAN and KTANTAN — a family of small and efficient hardware-oriented block ciphers. In: Clavier, C., Gaj, K. (eds.) CHES 2009. LNCS, vol. 5747, pp. 272–288. Springer, Heidelberg (2009). http://www.cs.technion.ac.il/orrd/KATAN/CHES2009.pdf

17. De Cannière, C., Preneel, B.: TRIVIUM. In: Robshaw, M., Billet, O. (eds.) New Stream Cipher Designs. LNCS, vol. 4986, pp. 244–266. Springer, Heidelberg (2008). http://www.ecrypt.eu.org/stream/p3ciphers/trivium/trivium_p3.pdf

18. Collard, B., Standaert, F.-X.: A statistical saturation attack against the block cipher PRESENT. In: Fischlin, M. (ed.) CT-RSA 2009. LNCS, vol. 5473, pp. 195–210. Springer, Heidelberg (2009)

19. Courtois, N., Hulme, D., Mourouzis, T.: Solving circuit optimisation problems in cryptography and cryptanalysis. IACR Cryptol. ePrint Arch. 2011:475 (2011). http://www.ima.org.uk/_db/_documents/Courtois.pdf. (Accessed 18 November 2013)

20. Atmel datasheet. Atmel 8-bit AVR microcontroller datasheet. http://tinyurl.com/klld65e. (Accessed 18 November 2013)

21. Eisenbarth, T., Gong, Z., Güneysu, T., Heyse, S., Indesteege, S., Kerckhof, S., Koeune, F., Nad, T., Plos, T., Regazzoni, F., Standaert, F.-X., van Oldeneel tot Oldenzeel, L.: Compact implementation and performance evaluation of block ciphers in attiny devices. In: Mitrokotsa, A., Vaudenay, S. (eds.) AFRICACRYPT 2012. LNCS, vol. 7374, pp. 172–187. Springer, Heidelberg (2012). http://perso.uclouvain.be/fstandae/PUBLIS/108.pdf

22. Eisenbarth, T., Kasper, T., Paar, C., Indesteege, S.: Encyclopedia of Cryptography and Security, 2nd edn. Springer (2011)

23. Flynn, M.J.: Some computer organizations and their effectiveness. IEEE Trans. Comput. C-21(9): 948–960, September (1972)

24. Gomathisankaran, M., Lee, R.B.: Maya: a novel block encryption function (2009). http://palms.princeton.edu/system/files/maya.pdf. (Accessed 18 November 2013)

25. Gong, Z., Nikova, S., Law, Y.W.: KLEIN: a new family of lightweight block ciphers. In: Juels, A., Paar, C. (eds.) RFIDSec 2011. LNCS, vol. 7055, pp. 1–18. Springer, Heidelberg (2012). http://doc.utwente.nl/73129/1/The_KLEIN_Block_Cipher.pdf

26. Guo, J., Peyrin, T., Poschmann, A.: The PHOTON family of lightweight. In: Rogaway, p (ed.) Advances in Cryptology – CRYPTO 2011. LNCS, vol. 6841, pp. 222–239. Springer, Heidelberg (2011). http://www.ecrypt.eu.org/hash2011/proceedings/hash2011_04.pdf

27. Guo, J., Peyrin, T., Poschmann, A., Robshaw, M.: The LED block cipher. In: Preneel, B., Takagi, T. (eds.) CHES 2011. LNCS, vol. 6917, pp. 326–341. Springer, Heidelberg (2011). http://eprint.iacr.org/2012/600.pdf

28. Hell, M., Johansson, T., Meier, W.: Grain: a stream cipher for constrained environments. Int. J. Wireless Mobile Comput. 2, 86–93 (2007). http://www.ecrypt.eu.org/stream/ciphers/grain/grain.pdf. (Accessed 18 November 2013)

29. Hong, D., Sung, J., Hong, S.H., Lim, J.-I., Lee, S.-J., Koo, B.-S., Lee, C.-H., Chang, D., Lee, J., Jeong, K., Kim, H., Kim, J.-S., Chee, S.: HIGHT: a new block cipher suitable for low-resource device. In: Goubin, L., Matsui, M. (eds.) CHES 2006. LNCS, vol. 4249, pp. 46–59. Springer, Heidelberg (2006). http://www.iacr.org/cryptodb/archive/2006/CHES/04/04.pdf

30. Käsper, E., Schwabe, P.: Faster and timing-attack resistant AES-GCM. In: Clavier, C., Gaj, K. (eds.) CHES 2009. LNCS, vol. 5747, pp. 1–17. Springer, Heidelberg (2009). http://eprint.iacr.org/2009/129

31. Kilian, J., Rogaway, P.: How to protect DES against exhaustive eey search. In: Koblitz, N. (ed.) CRYPTO 1996. LNCS, vol. 1109, pp. 252–267. Springer, Heidelberg (1996). http://www.cs.ucdavis.edu/rogaway/papers/desx.pdf

32. Könighofer, R.: A fast and cache-timing resistant implementation of the AES. In: Malkin, T. (ed.) CT-RSA 2008. LNCS, vol. 4964, pp. 187–202. Springer, Heidelberg (2008). https://online.tugraz.at/tug_online/voe_main2.getvolltext?pCurrPk=47852

33. Leander, G.: Small scale variants of the block cipher present. IACR Cryptol. ePrint Arch. 2010:143 (2010). http://eprint.iacr.org/2010/143.pdf. (Accessed 18 November 2013)

34. Lee, R.B., Shi, Z., Yang, X.: Cryptography efficient permutation instructions for fast software. IEEE Micro. 21, 56–69 (2001). http://palms.ee.princeton.edu/PALMSopen/lee01efficient.pdf. (Accessed 18 November 2013)

35. Hulme, D., Song, G., Albrecht, M., Courtois, N.T.: Bit-slice implementation of PRESENT in pure standard C. https://bitbucket.org/malb/research-snippets/src. (Accessed 18 November 2013)

36. Nakahara Jr., J., Sepehrdad, P., Zhang, B., Wang, M.: Linear (hull) and algebraic cryptanalysis of the block cipher PRESENT. In: Garay, J.A., Miyaji, A., Otsuka, A. (eds.) CANS 2009. LNCS, vol. 5888, pp. 58–75. Springer, Heidelberg (2009). http://www.ioc.ee/tarmo/tday-meintack/zhang-slides.pdf

37. Papagiannopoulos, k.: Present with bld, bst instructions. https://github.com/kostaspap88/sc_res_present. (Accessed 18 November 2013)

38. Papagiannopoulos, K.: Speed-optimized implementation of PRESENT in AVR assembly (2013). https://github.com/kostaspap88/PRESENT_speed_implementation/ (Accessed 18 November 2013)

39. Papagiannopoulos, K., Verstegen, A.: Speed and size-optimized implementations of the PRESENT cipher for tiny AVR devices. In: Hutter, M., Schmidt, J.-M. (eds.) RFIDsec 2013. LNCS, vol. 8262, pp. 159–173. Springer, Heidelberg (2013)

40. Pornin, T.: Automatic software optimization of block ciphers using bit-slicing techniques.http://citeseerx.ist.psu.edu/viewdoc/download?doi=10.1.1.48.3085&rep=rep1&type=pdf.

41. Rauzy, P., Guilley, S., Najm, Z.: Formally proved security of assembly code against leakage. IACR Cryptol. ePrint Arch. 554 (2013). http://eprint.iacr.org/2013/554.pdf. (Accessed 18 November 2013)
42. Shi, Z., Lee, R.B.: Bit permutation instructions for accelerating software cryptography. In: Proceedings of the IEEE International Conference on Application-Specific Systems, Architectures and Processors, pp. 138–148, 2000. http://www.princeton.edu/rblee/PUpapers/shi_asap00.pdf
43. Shirai, T., Shibutani, K., Akishita, T., Moriai, S., Iwata, T.: The 128-bit block-cipher CLEFIA (extended abstract). In: Biryukov, A. (ed.) FSE 2007. LNCS, vol. 4593, pp. 181–195. Springer, Heidelberg (2007). http://www.iacr.org/archive/fse2007/45930182/45930182.pdf

Curved Tags – A Low-Resource ECDSA Implementation Tailored for RFID

Peter Pessl[(⊠)] and Michael Hutter

Institute for Applied Information Processing and Communications (IAIK),
Graz University of Technology, Inffeldgasse 16a, 8010 Graz, Austria
{Peter.Pessl,Michael.Hutter}@iaik.tugraz.at

Abstract. In recent years, a lot of effort was made to deploy asymmetric cryptography based on ECC to affordable RFID tags. However, many proposed hardware designs suffer from long execution times and high resource requirements. In this paper, we address this issue by presenting a low-resource implementation of a 160-bit ECDSA signature generation algorithm. As a novelty, we make use of the new KECCAK hashing algorithm. Moreover, we applied state of the art techniques such as co-Z ECC formulæ, a pipelined multiplication unit, RAM macros, and we evaluated fixed-base comb methods to improve the efficiency of ECDSA on passive tags. Furthermore, our design runs with constant runtime and provides basic resistance against common implementation attacks. It requires a total area of 12 448 GEs (including memory) and can generate a message digest within 140 kCycles, which is both smaller and considerably faster than comparable work. It has a power consumption of 42.7 μW at 1 MHz on a low-leakage 130 nm CMOS process technology. Our implementation can compete with binary-field based ECC solutions not only in terms of area and power but also in speed.

Keywords: Low-resource ASIC design · ECC · Keccak · SHA-3

1 Introduction

Implementing strong cryptography on Radio Frequency Identification (RFID) tags is a challenging but necessary task. Passively powered tags draw the required energy from the electromagnetic field of a reader; thus, much effort has to be put into low-power hardware designs to achieve high reading ranges. Moreover, tags must be cheap in order to keep production costs low, so the entire circuit has to be as small as possible.

Asymmetric cryptography is considered to be more resource consuming than symmetric cryptography. However, it has the big advantage that it makes key-distribution problems easier which is an important requirement especially in cases where RFID tags are going to be deployed in a large scale. Amongst many cryptographic services, the Elliptic Curve Digital Signature Algorithm (ECDSA) has been constituted over many years to provide most of the required needs

© Springer International Publishing Switzerland 2014
N. Saxena and A.-R. Sadeghi (Eds.): RFIDSec 2014, LNCS 8651, pp. 156–172, 2014.
DOI: 10.1007/978-3-319-13066-8_10

for practical applications. It is a building block that can be used within several authentication protocols, e.g., embedded in identification schemes to allow entity authentication or in signature schemes to offer message authentication. The latter service is thereby an important feature to implement proof-of-origin applications—a feature that can help to prevent the exponential rise in counterfeiting activity.

There already exist many low-resource hardware implementations of ECDSA. However, many of these designs suffer from either being very large in size or they have horrible execution times. This makes the designs often not well suitable for various RFID applications where the costs are limited or fast tag response times are mandatory.

Our Contribution. In order to tackle these problems, we present a highly optimized hardware implementation of ECDSA over the 160-bit prime-field curve secp160r1. Instead of integrating SHA-1 or SHA-2 into ECDSA, we integrate the KECCAK algorithm that is the winner of the NIST SHA-3 competition. We present a novel hardware architecture of KECCAK by applying a *factor-4 interleaving* method that improves the performance compared to related work. Concerning ECC point-scalar multiplication, we apply new techniques on various implementation levels, e.g., we use a 32-bit datapath width but integrate a 16-bit pipelined multiplication unit, we make use of an efficient RAM macro that is available for our targeted 130 nm CMOS process technology, we consider new explicit co-Z formulæ requiring 7 field registers, and evaluate a fixed-base comb scalar multiplication technique on passive RFID tags. Especially the latter offers a tremendous speed-up (factor 4) at the low cost of 800 GEs. These results offer valuable insights to obtain good trade-offs between speed and production costs.

Our work requires an area of 12 448 GEs (or 63 700 μm² in 130 nm), has a mean power consumption of 42.7 μW per MHz, and generates a digital signature in less than 140 kCycles. These results make our design smaller and considerably faster than previously presented designs of comparable implementations. With the applied techniques our design is on a par with related work on low-resource binary-field elliptic curve implementations. This is not surprising because we used a fixed-base comb technique but it is interesting for the RFID community and industry to achieve performances similar to binary-field based curve implementations while keeping the resource requirements low.

Outlook. The paper is organized as follows. In Sect. 2, we first give a brief introduction to ECC and ECDSA. After that, we list the imposed requirements and most important design decisions. Our low-resource architecture is then presented in Sect. 3. Section 4 discusses the KECCAK architecture and its integration into the design. Countermeasures aimed at securing the device against SCA are given in Sect. 5. Results are presented in Sect. 6.

Algorithm 1. ECDSA signature generation.

Require: Domain Parameters $T = \{p, a, b, G, n, h\}$, private key d, message m.
Ensure: Signature (r, s).
1: Compute hash $e = \text{Hash}(m)$, truncate to bit length of n.
2: Select random $k \in [1, n-1]$.
3: Compute $(x, y) = kG$, $r = x \mod n$, if $r = 0$ goto 1.
4: Compute $s = k^{-1}(e + rd) \mod n$, if $s = 0$ goto 1.
5: **return** (r, s).

---

2 Design Space Exploration

In this section, we first give a short introduction to ECC and ECDSA. Afterwards, we discuss the requirements and the needed properties of our design. Finally, we list all design choices for our targeted RFID-tag architecture.

ECC and the ECDSA. Elliptic curves are the base for many cryptographic primitives. An elliptic curve E defined over a finite-field $\mathbb{F}_p$ can be given in short Weierstrass form $y^2 = x^3 + ax + b$, with publicly known parameters $a, b \in \mathbb{F}_p$. Pairs of (x, y), with $x, y \in \mathbb{F}_p$, satisfying this equation are points $P \in E$. For a fixed point P with prime order n and a large integer $k \in [1, n-1]$, one can easily compute the point multiplication $Q = kP$. The inverse operation, i.e., finding k with given Q, P, is computationally hard and known as the Elliptic Curve Discrete Logarithm Problem (ECDLP). Point-scalar multiplications are carried out by means of the group operations point doubling and point addition. Efficient curve addition and doubling formulæ, typically using some sort of projective coordinates, try to reduce the required field operations, especially the more expensive field multiplications (M) and squarings (S).

ECDSA is the elliptic-curve counterpart of the Digital Signature Algorithm (DSA). Before signing, all parties must agree on domain parameters T, which specify a curve alongside a base point G with prime order n. For signature generation (Algorithm 1), the message m is hashed, then the base point G is multiplied with the nonce k. The resultant x coordinate and the variable s form the signature pair (r, s).

The Requirements. Goal of this work was to design an ASIC implementation of the ECDSA signature-generation algorithm. Our aim was to implement a low-cost coprocessor that features message authentication services and thus allows proof-of-origin authentication of RFID-tagged goods, for example, to tackle the problem of product counterfeiting. Signature verification is not supported and we did not include a random-number generator. To limit the tag requirements, we decided to base our implementation on the 160-bit standardized `secp160r1` [7,8] elliptic curve that features 80-bit security[1]. Starting from now the variables

---

[1] Note that many standardization bodies removed 160-bit prime curves from their recommendation standards but a 80-bit security level is still sufficient for many low-cost RFID applications.

p, n refer to the primes defined in the standard, $\mathbb{F}_p$ and $\mathbb{F}_n$ denote the respective finite fields.

As opposed to many other hardware implementations that use the (older) SHA-1 or SHA-2 algorithms, we decided to evaluate the recently announced NIST SHA-3 competition winner, i.e., the KECCAK hashing algorithm [4]. A subset of the algorithm will be incorporated into the Secure Hash Standard (SHS). KECCAK is highly tunable, the security level can be controlled by setting the security parameter c (which stands for *capacity*). For a chosen capacity c, KECCAK offers both a preimage and collision resistance of $c/2$ bits [3], so in order to match the security of the curve it was decided to set $c = 160$. The state size is also selectable, so we decided to use an 800-bit state instead of the 1 600-bit (full state) version to reduce the memory requirements. Thus, the exact used KECCAK instance is called KECCAK[r=640, c=160].

For designs meant to be deployed on (passive) RFID tags, low-power and low-area requirements are a prime goal (to obtain appropriate reading ranges and to be cheap in the production costs). So in the past, many designers that met these requirements payed the price of horrible execution times. To give an example, the work of Wenger et al. [31,32] needs more than 1 million clock cycles for signature generation, which corresponds to about 10 s if the tag is clocked with 100 kHz. So in addition to the previous goals, we aim to drastically reduce the execution time of ECDSA in this paper while keeping the resource requirements as low as related work.

2.1   Basic Design Choices

In order to fulfill the requirements, we made the following design choices.

Storage Type. Previous work, e.g., [15–17,20], often used some sort of synthesized dual-ported memory for storage of large data. The advantage of dual-port memory is that the core can access two words within one clock cycle. The major disadvantage, however, is that the size is almost twice as large as single-port memories. For example, the 2 048 bit dual-port register file RAM macro for UMC 130 nm CMOS from Faraday [10] requires 0.028 mm^2 while the single-port variant requires only 0.018 mm^2. We therefore decided to use a single-ported RAM macro as main storage element. Such specialized macros typically require much less resources than standard-cell based memory blocks.

Datapath and Memory Width. We decided to implement a 32-bit datapath and use a 32-bit memory interface to achieve our targeted computation speeds. To keep the power consumption low, we integrated a 16×16-bit multiplier core that is used to perform a 32×32-bit multiplication within 4 clock cycles. Note that a 32×32-bit multiplier would speed up the computation but would drastically increase area and power requirements because it dominates the ECDSA datapath complexity. Also, the single-port memory is not able to deliver data fast enough to keep such a large multiplier busy.

ECSM with Fixed-Base Comb Methods. The elliptic-curve scalar multiplication is by far the most time consuming part of ECDSA, so it is essential to speed up this process. Comb methods, first proposed by Lim and Lee [23], allow a drastic speed improvement for schemes with a fixed-base point P. For a chosen width w, one needs to precompute all $[\alpha_{w-1}, \ldots, \alpha_1, \alpha_0]P = \alpha_{w-1}2^{(w-1)\ell}P + \cdots + \alpha_1 2^{\ell}P + \alpha_0 P$ and store these points in a (read-only) memory. Comb methods then rearrange the n-bit scalar k in a matrix with dimension $w \times \ell$, with $\ell = \lceil n/w \rceil$. The columns of this matrix are then processed from left to right, in a simple double-and-add fashion. Typical implementations, e.g., [6], have one major problem: if all column bits are equal to zero then the point addition step must be skipped. Such behavior is detectable by Simple Power Analysis (SPA) attacks and should therefore be avoided.

Hedabou et al. [14] presented a comb scheme resistant to SPA. The scalar k is first recoded using the *Zeroless Signed Digit* (ZSD) scheme. This recoding technique represents an odd integer with digits in $\{-1, 1\}$ and is based on the observation that $1 = 2^w - \sum_{i=0}^{m-1} 2^i, \forall w > 0$. Hence, all blocks of $000\ldots01$ (w bits) can be replaced by w signed digits $1\bar{1}\bar{1}\ldots\bar{1}\bar{1}$, with $\bar{1} = -1$ [13]. This representation can be obtained by simply shifting k to the right and reinterpreting all 0 bits as $\bar{1}$. The hardware costs of obtaining the ZSD representation is therefore almost zero. In fact, all-zero columns can obviously not appear when using a *zeroless* representation. Also, usage of a signed-digit representation allows to reduce the memory requirements from $2^w - 1$ [6] to 2^{w-1} precomputed points by utilizing the fact that point negations are easy to compute.

For this work, $w = 4$ was chosen. The reason for this is that it offers a good speed-up (factor 4) while keeping the hardware requirements low, i.e., 8 points need to be precomputed and stored in a ROM, which requires in total 2 560 bits (modern hardware synthesizers can implement these ROMs with less than 1 000 GEs).

EC Addition Formulæ. Execution of a comb method requires so-called point doubling-additions, i.e., point operations of the form $R = 2P + Q$. For this work, the doubling-addition formulæ by Longa and Miri [24] are used, they require 11 field multiplications (M) and 7 squarings (S), and can be executed with 7 field registers. They are based on Meloni's co-Z addition formulæ [25]. Note that there exist faster point doubling-addition formulæ based on co-Z notation, e.g., as shown in [13,18]. However, they need to update the added point with a new Z coordinate after each doubling-addition. For the case of comb methods, the added point is selected out of a set of precomputed points stored in ROM, so the faster co-Z algorithms are not efficiently applicable there.

Field Inversions. Field inversions should be computed by means of a modular exponentiation, i.e., by applying Fermat's little theorem that states $a^p \equiv a \bmod p$, for all primes p. Then the inverse $a^{-1} \equiv a^{p-2} \bmod p$. Other algorithms, e.g., the binary or Montgomery inversion algorithm, are typically faster, but involve non-constant runtime loops or branch conditions and are therefore susceptible to side-channel attacks.

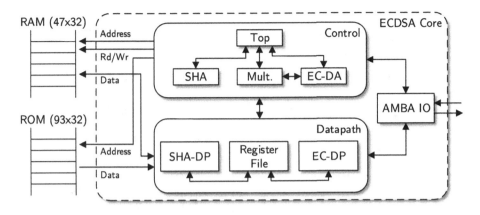

Fig. 1. Top-level view of the ECDSA core

3 A Low-Resource ECDSA Hardware Architecture

In this section, we present our low-resource ECDSA hardware architecture. We first give an overview and then discuss the datapath in more detail. Afterwards, we illustrate the implemented modular-reduction mechanisms and present optimized inversion algorithms.

3.1 Implementation Overview

Figure 1 shows the top-level structure of our design. The computation core contains a datapath, a controlling block, and an 8-bit AMBA APB interface. The Advanced Microcontroller Bus Architecture (AMBA) Advanced Peripheral Bus (APB), a very simple yet standardized interface, allows communication with the outside world, i.e., a bus master. The datapath (DP) can be split into separate modules, the SHA-DP is dedicated to the KECCAK hashing algorithm and the EC-DP handles all other computations required for ECDSA, both parts share a common register file. The controlling block is comprised of multiple sub-controllers and a top-level controller, which is in charge of overseeing the signing process and steering the subcontrollers. The multiplication controller handles modular multiplication in both fields $\mathbb{F}_p$ and $\mathbb{F}_n$ by implementing two reduction techniques. The EC-DA controller houses the control logic required for performing elliptic-curve doubling-additions. Finally, the KECCAK controller is dedicated to steering the hashing process. The controllers are implemented using a mixed approach, both finite-state machines and microcontroller-like programming are used.

The core is connected to a 47×32 bit (single-ported) RAM and a 93×32 bit ROM that stores all necessary constants (ECC comb points, prime modulus n, etc.).

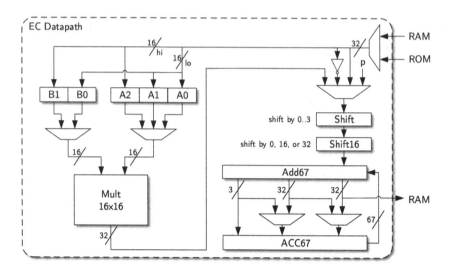

Fig. 2. The implemented ECDSA datapath

3.2 The Datapath

The datapath, shown in Fig. 2, is comprised of a multiplication (left) and an accumulation path (right). A 67-bit accumulator register (ACC) alongside a 67-bit adder form an accumulation unit. Multiplexers allow shifting the current adder output by 32 bits to the right.

The accumulation operand can be selected from the inverted or non-inverted RAM output, the multiplication result or (a 32-bit part of) the constant modulus p. Thanks to the highly regular modulus p—only a single bit is zero, all others are one—it is possible to hardcode this constant without any noteworthy area gain. The selected operand is then routed through two configurable shifters, the first one can shift its input up to 3 bits to the left and thus produces a 35-bit output, while the second shifter can shift this result by either 0, 16, or 32 bits to the left.

The multiplication part of the datapath consists of two multiplication operand registers A, B, and a 16×16-bit integer multiplier producing a 32-bit output. The operand registers are made up of 16-bit chunks, A consists of 3 parts A0 to A2, while B consists of 2 parts B0 and B1. The operand registers are used to perform a pipelined multiplication, as explained in the next section.

3.3 Pipelined Multi-precision Multiplication

To fully use the 32-bit single-ported memory interface, 32×32-bit multiplications are computed with the help of the dedicated 16-bit multiplier. A 32-bit multiplication takes four cycles and is done with a simple school-book multiplication algorithm, as illustrated in Fig. 3. Both 16-bit chunks of the first operand (A0 and A1) are multiplied with both chunks of the second operand (B0 and B1).

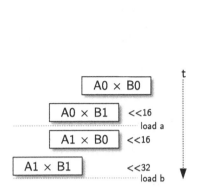

Fig. 3. Pipelined school-book multiplication scheme

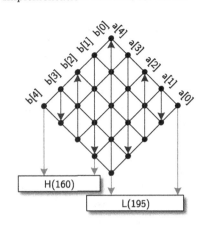

Fig. 4. Modular multiplication in $\mathbb{F}_p$

The 32-bit partial products are first shifted accordingly using the second shifter and then added to the accumulator, thus utilizing the multiply-and-accumulate (MAC) functionality of the datapath.

Prior to the start of the 32-bit multiplication, both operands need to be loaded into the designated operand registers. Dedicated operand load cycles would slow down the multiplication process, thus the operands for the next 32-bit multiplication are fetched during execution of the current one. As denoted by dotted lines in Fig. 3, operand B is replaced at the end of the fourth cycle, operand A after the second cycle. However, the 16 high-order bits of A (A1) are still needed in the third and fourth multiplication cycle. For this reason there are three 16-bit operand registers for A. The 16 high-order bits of operand A are alternately stored in the operand registers A1 and A2.

A product-scanning approach is used to perform 160-bit multiplications by means of 32-bit ones, this also utilizes the MAC functionality. 25 32-bit multiplications need to be computed, so a plain (non-modular) multiplication takes $25 \times 4 = 100$ cycles. Squarings can be sped up by using the commutative property of the multiplication, i.e., $a[i]a[j] = a[j]a[i], \forall i \neq j$, and hence $a[i]a[j] + a[j]a[i] = 2(a[i]a[j])$. Only 15 partial products need to be computed, this takes 60 cycles. The doubling operation is carried out by the first shifter in the datapath, thus the hardware cost of this simple optimization is almost equal to zero.

The following sections discuss the integration of modular arithmetic into this multiplication scheme.

Arithmetic in $\mathbb{F}_p$. The prime $p = 2^{160} - 2^{31} - 1$ is a so-called pseudo-Mersenne prime that permits fast reduction. An integer $x > p$ can be reduced by splitting it in $x = h2^{160} + l$ and then computing $x \equiv l + h + (h \ll 31) \bmod p$, i.e., reduction is achieved using shifts by 31 digits and additions. Unfortunately, 31 is not a multiple of the word size 32, thus disallowing shifting by simple addressing. Instead the datapath is modified to allow addition of a 32-bit word, i.e., a word of h, in two different locations of the accumulator concurrently.

The fast reduction algorithm is not only used in multiplication, but also for the basic operations addition, subtraction, and shifting. In the case of subtraction, a (fixed) multiple of the modulus is first added to the difference to ensure a positive intermediate result.

To gain higher speeds, the reduction is integrated into the multiplication process, this gives a time and storage space advantage. As seen in Fig. 4, multiplication is performed in two phases. First only the upper columns 5 to 8 are processed, the 160-bit result H is stored in RAM. Then multiplication continues with the lower columns, the addition of H is interleaved with the multiplication process. The 195-bit sum $L + H + (H \ll 31)$ is again stored in RAM. Finally, another round of reduction is performed, this produces the final 160-bit output. In total, modular multiplication or squaring requires 123 or 83 cycles, respectively.

Arithmetic in $\mathbb{F}_n$. The prime group order n is not of any special form, thus a general reduction process needs to be implemented in addition. We therefore decided to implement the Montgomery multiplication scheme [26]. It requires division and reduction by a chosen integer R, with $R > n$. We used the *Integrated Product Scanning* approach by Koç et al. [21] in this work.

One of n's properties makes implementing modular multiplication using the Montgomery method difficult: its bit length of 161. The implementation is geared towards handling of 160-bit integers, everything above that adds an area and time overhead. Also, 161 is not a multiple of the word size 32.

However, the structure of the modulus n—the MSB is followed by many zero bits—allows optimizations. The probability of a random element in field $\mathbb{F}_n$ being greater or equal to 2^{160} is 2^{-79}. So we can assume that all operands and results of the Montgomery multiplications performed throughout signing are restricted to 160 bits. If, despite the diminishing odds, a multiplication yields a 161-bit result, the outcome can not be used as input for the following multiplications. Such an occurrence is detected and an error is returned at the end of the signing process. Restricting all values to 160 bits allows setting $R = 2^{160}$. This does not satisfy the requirement of $R > n$, however, an R greater than both multiplication operands a, b suffices. Montgomery's argumentation includes the estimation $ab < Rn$, with $a, b \in \mathbb{F}_n$ and $R > n$. This is obviously also true with $a, b < R < n$.

The output of the algorithm t is in range $t < 2n$. Instead of avoiding the required conditional subtraction of n, as first suggested by Walter [29,30], it is always executed and both t and $t - n$ are stored in RAM. The runtime of a single multiplication is 197 cycles.

3.4 Optimized Prime Field Inversion Algorithms

Field inversions are performed by means of a modular exponentiation, i.e., by using $a^{-1} \equiv a^{p-2} \mod p$. Two inversions are performed during ECDSA, one after ECC scalar multiplication (to back-transform into affine coordinates) and one during the signing process (to invert the ephemeral key k).

Z^{-2} mod p. The exponent in $Z^{-2} \equiv Z^{p-3}$ contains only three 0 bits, so an optimization of the used left-to-right square-and-multiply exponentiation algorithm is possible. By iteratively computing $Z^{2^{\ell}-1}$, with $0 < \ell \leq 7$, and storing some intermediate values, one can retrieve the inverse in 159 squarings (S) and only 11 multiplications (M).

k^{-1} mod n. Here a highly customized window algorithm is used. During the initial precomputation selected powers of k (k^3, k^5, and k^9) are calculated, the actual multiplication is then performed in a simple square-and-multiply fashion. This inversion algorithm takes a total of 160S and 26M. The ideal set of powers was determined by means of a brute-force search.

4   Integration of KECCAK

The hashing modules are largely based on our previously presented KECCAK implementation [27]. Some changes are made to adapt the design to the different environment. The RAM interface is widened to 32 bits and the used interleaving scheme is changed from factor-2 to a factor-4 to achieve a higher bus-width utilization.

Combined Processing and Interleaving. KECCAK is defined for state sizes of $b = 25w$, with $w = 2^{\ell}$ and $0 \leq \ell \leq 6$. The KECCAK-f permutation internally organizes this state as a 3-D matrix with dimension $5 \times 5 \times w$. This matrix can be split into 25-bit slices and w-bit lanes. The KECCAK-f permutation is a round-based function, in each of its $12 + 2\ell$ rounds, five state mappings θ, ρ, π, χ and ι are executed. For a more thorough explanation of the components, we refer to the KECCAK reference [4].

Most software implementations process the lane state-wise, i.e., lane after lane is fetched and processed. Slice-wise processing, first proposed by Jungk and Apfelbeck [19], poses as a hardware-friendly alternative. The described design features both slice and lane-wise processing. The round function is rescheduled and split into a slice-processing and a lane-processing phase.

The combined-processing approach requires that both slices and lanes can be accessed efficiently. This is challenging when using a RAM for state storage. To achieve a high bus-width utilization, an interleaved storage scheme is used. Four consecutive lanes are bit-wise interleaved, these interleaved words are then stored in RAM. In [27], only two lanes are interleaved. Due to the wider memory bus and the restriction to an 800-bit state, a factor-4 interleaving is more suitable here.

The KECCAK Datapath. The KECCAK datapath consists of four 32-bit registers r0...r3, a slice unit, four rotation units required for the ρ transformation, and an interleave and deinterleave unit. During the lane-processing phase each register stores one lane, during slice processing four slices are stored. For a more detailed explanation we refer the reader to [27].

Keccak Integration. In order to save precious resources, the hashing modules are tightly integrated into the existing design.

One major shared part is obviously the RAM, during hashing the 800-bit state is stored in the same RAM used by other parts of the ECDSA algorithm.

It is also possible to merge the internal registers. The numbers of register bits included in the Keccak datapath and ECDSA datapath match up nicely, which is not a coincidence. In fact, the ECDSA datapath was designed with the Keccak memory requirements in mind. The registers are hence merged into a single shared register file, as previously seen in Fig. 1.

5   Protections Against Implementation Attacks

A chain is only as strong as its weakest link, so implementing a secure protocol like ECDSA without considering implementation attacks is grossly negligent (especially on easily accessible RFID tags). We implemented the following countermeasures to secure our design.

- Constant runtime and operation flow to provide protection against timing attacks and basic[2] Simple Power Analysis (SPA) attacks:
  - Constant runtime of modular reduction
  - Avoid negative results after subtractions by adding modulus p
  - Constant runtime of conditional negation of stored y coordinate. The implemented comb method requires a conditional negation of the y coordinate of a stored point. Here first $2y \bmod p$ is computed, then the desired result is retrieved as $y = 2y - y \bmod p$ or $-y = y - 2y \bmod p$.
  - No all-zero columns in comb
  - Inversion using Fermat's little theorem
  - Always execute final subtraction in Montgomery multiplication
- We applied the Randomized Projective Coordinates (RPC) [9] countermeasure to thwart Differential Power Analysis (DPA) attacks. The (affine) coordinates of the first referenced comb point are transformed to a projective representation with a random Z coordinate. Then the processed values are different even if the same k is used. RPC also offers protection against template-based SPA attacks.
- As a final countermeasure, the computation of $s = k^{-1}(e + dr) \bmod n$ is reordered as $s = k^{-1}e + (k^{-1}d)r$. Then, the private key d is multiplied with the inverse of the random nonce, multiplying it with the known signature part r would open the gate for DPA attacks [16].

---

[2] Constant runtime does not automatically make the implementation resistant against SPA attacks but often makes SPA attacks harder to perform because attackers are forced to exploit data-dependent leakage only instead of typically easier detectable operation-dependent leakage.

– ECDSA is not susceptible to refined power-analysis attacks (RPA) [12] and zero-value point attacks (ZPA) [1]. They require point multiplications with a fixed scalar and user-selectable base point (such as in ECDH schemes), neither is the case for ECDSA.

6   Results

The design was implemented in VHDL and then synthesized using a mixed tool design flow. The Synopsys Design Compiler 2013.03 generated a netlist targeting the *FSC0L_D* standard-cell library from Faraday. The 0.13 μm *low-leakage* process by UMC is the base for this library. Single-ported RAM macros by Faraday are used as storage elements. All circuit-area results are given as reported by the synthesizer. Circuit area is given in *gate equivalents* (GE), 1 GE is equal to the size a two-input NAND gate (5.12 μm² in the chosen process). An analysis with the Encounter Power System v8.10 yielded the power consumption, the operating frequency was set to 1 MHz to allow a fair comparison.

Figure 6 gives an overview of the area usage of different parts of the design. With 3 055 GEs, the RAM block takes up roughly 1/4 of the total area of 12 448 GEs. The datapath, including the ECDSA datapath (Fig. 2), the KECCAK datapath (Fig. 5), and the shared register file, amounts to 42 %. The EC-DP is dominated by the 16 × 16 multiplier with its 1 616 GEs. Interestingly, only 800 GEs are required for the ROM that is mainly used to store the pre-computed elliptic curve points (2 976 bits in total). This is a very small price to pay when considering the massive speed-up provided by the fixed-base comb method (factor 4 times faster).

Signing a 160-bit message takes only 139 930 cycles. The point-scalar multiplication is by far the most time-consuming operation, it requires 87.5 kCycles. The first field inversion Z^{-2} mod p uses 14.5 kCycles, due to the more expensive Montgomery multiplication scheme the second inversion k^{-1} mod n is twice

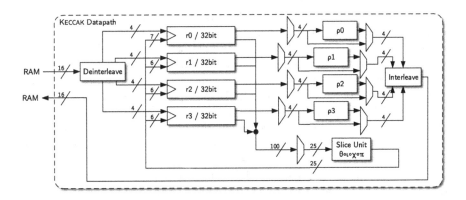

Fig. 5. KECCAK datapath

Component	Area	
	[GEs]	[μm²]
EC-DP	2 800	14 334
Multiplier	1 616	8 273
SHA-DP	823	4 211
Register File	1 662	8 509
Control	2 473	12 663
Other	816	4 178
ROM	820	4 198
Core Total	**9 393**	**48 093**
RAM	3 055	15 642
Total	**12 448**	**63 735**

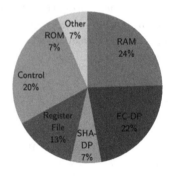

(a) Area of chip components   (b) Area distribution

Fig. 6. Area of chip components

as expensive (30.3 kCycles). A single 640-bit message block can be hashed in 5.5 kCycles, which is an improvement over the 7.6 kCycles given in [27].

Comparison with Related Work. In Table 1, we compare our design with other low-resource implementations. In [20], Kern et al. presented an ECDSA design using the same `secp160r1` curve but with SHA-1 instead of Keccak and a 350 nm CMOS technology. Compared to his implementation, we could improve the speed by a factor of about 3.6 (thanks to the use of the fixed-base comb method) and could reduce the area requirements by about 5 800 GEs (through the use of dedicated single-ported RAM macros). Recently, at the ECC workshop 2013, Roy et al. [28] reported a tiny ECC co-processor supporting both $\mathbb{F}_{p160}$ and $\mathbb{F}_{p192}$ arithmetic for a 32 nm IBM CMOS technology. Their design requires about 26 kGEs (in total) and 250 kCycles for a scalar multiplication over $\mathbb{F}_{p160}$. This is about twice as slow as our design.

ECDSA implementations over 192-bit prime fields have been, for example, reported by Wenger [31], Hutter et al. [16], and Fürbass et al. [11], They require more area, partly due to the larger prime field size, and are also significantly slower (in particular, our implementation is about 10 times faster than the work of Wenger [31]). Interestingly, our implementation can compete with many binary-field ECC processors. E.g., our ECDSA implementation is nearly as large as the work of Hein et al. [15] and Lee et al. [22] who reported an ECC implementation over $\mathbb{F}_{2^{163}}$. Compared to the results of Lee (with chosen multiplier digit-size $d = 1$), our implementation is about 2 times faster, includes Keccak, and allows computation of digital signatures.

Power consumption is extremely difficult to compare over different process technologies, so values are only given for designs using a 130 nm process. The 192-bit prime curve processor by Wenger—it uses the same 130 nm process technology used here—requires 39.54 μW/MHz and 55 μJ of energy. In comparison,

Table 1. Comparison of prime and binary field ECC implementations

	Techn. [nm]	Area [GEs]	Time [Cycles]	Power[a] [μW/MHz]	Field	Features[b]
This work[c]	**130**	**12 448**	**139 930**	**42.7**	$\mathbb{F}_{p160}$	**ECDSA, KECCAK**
Roy13 [28]	32	26 000	250 000	-	$\mathbb{F}_{p160}$	ECSM, dual field
Kern10 [20]	350	18 247	511 864	-	$\mathbb{F}_{p160}$	ECDSA, SHA-1
Wenger11 [31,32][c,d]	130	14 644	1 394 000	39.54	$\mathbb{F}_{p192}$	ECDSA, SHA-1
Hutter10 [16]	350	19 115	859 188	-	$\mathbb{F}_{p192}$	ECDSA, SHA-1
Fürbass07 [11]	350	23 656	500 000	-	$\mathbb{F}_{p192}$	ECSM
Lee08 [22] ($d=1$)	130	12 506	302 457	32.42	$\mathbb{F}_{2^{163}}$	ECSM, Schnorr
Hein08 [15]	180	11 904	296 000	-	$\mathbb{F}_{2^{163}}$	ECSM
Bock08 [5] ($d=4$)	220	12 876	80 000	-	$\mathbb{F}_{2^{163}}$	ECSM, DH

[a] Power values of designs using other process technologies are omitted.
[b] ECSM: Point-scalar multiplication only.
[c] Uses a RAM macro for storage.
[d] In [31], an area of 11.7 kGEs was achieved based on a 180 nm process. In [32], the same design requires 14.6 kGEs in a 130 nm process.

the power consumption of our design is slightly higher (42.7 μW/MHz), but due to the lower cycle count the energy consumption is considerably smaller (6 μJ).

6.1 Discussion

The following points invite to further discussion.

Advanced Single-Trace Attacks. While the used comb method provides a constant runtime and thus offers protection against basic SPA, it might still succumb to more sophisticated single-trace attacks, e.g., to Template Attacks or Horizontal SCA (e.g., [2]). These attacks were not considered in the context of comb methods in this paper, susceptibility to these techniques needs to be further evaluated.

Extension to Larger Curves. For applications with higher security demands the design could be extended to larger, e.g., 192 or 224-bit curves. The computation core could be mostly reused, only small adaptations are required. However, the memory requirements (RAM and ROM) would rise, in the case of a 192-bit curve by 20 % or roughly 1 kGEs. Also, computation time would increase to around 200 kCycles.

Acknowledgements. The work has been supported by the Austrian Science Fund (FWF) under the grant number TRP251-N23 (Realizing a Secure Internet of Things - ReSIT), the FFG research program SeCoS (project number 836628), and the European Cooperation in Science and Technology (COST) Action IC1204 (Trustworthy Manufacturing and Utilization of Secure Devices - TRUDEVICE).

A Explicit Doubling-Addition Formulæ

In Algorithm 2, the explicit doubling-addition formulæ are given. They are based on Longa and Miris formulæ and require 11M + 7S as well as 7 field registers $(X_1, Y_1, Z_1, R_{1...4})$. Availability of *in-place* multiplication is assumed, i.e., the result can overwrite an input operand.

Algorithm 2. Doubling-addition using 11M + 7S and 7 field registers, computes $2P + Q$, with $P = (X_1, Y_1, Z_1)$ and a precomputed comb point $Q = (X_{ROM}, Y_{ROM})$.

Require: $X_1, Y_1, Z_1, X_{ROM}, Y_{ROM}$
Ensure: X_1, Y_1, Z_1

1. $R_1 \leftarrow Y_{ROM}$
2. $R_2 \leftarrow 2Y_{ROM}$
3. $R_1 \leftarrow R_{1|2} - R_{2|1}{}^3$
4. $R_2 \leftarrow Z^2$
5. $R_3 \leftarrow Z \times R_2$
6. $R_1 \leftarrow R_1 \times R_3 - Y$
7. $R_3 \leftarrow X_{ROM} \times R_2 - X$
8. $R_4 \leftarrow R_3^2$
9. $Z \leftarrow Z + R_3$
10. $R_3 \leftarrow R_4 \times R_3$
11. $Z \leftarrow Z^2 - R_2 - R_4$
12. $R_2 \leftarrow X \times R_4$
13. $Y \leftarrow Y \times R_3$
14. $R_4 \leftarrow R_1^2$

15. $X \leftarrow 4R_4 - 4R_3 - 8R_2 - 4R_2$
16. $R_3 \leftarrow R_1 + X$
17. $R_3 \leftarrow R_3^2$
18. $R_1 \leftarrow X^2$
19. $Y \leftarrow 8Y$
20. $R_3 \leftarrow R_4 + R_1 - R_3 - 2Y$
21. $R_2 \leftarrow 4R_2$
22. $R_2 \leftarrow R_2 \times R_1$
23. $Z \leftarrow Z \times X$
24. $R_1 \leftarrow X \times R_1$
25. $X \leftarrow R_3^2 - R_1 - 2R_2$
26. $R_1 \leftarrow Y \times R_1$
27. $R_2 \leftarrow R_2 - X$
28. $Y \leftarrow R_3 \times R_2 - R_1$

return (X_1, X_2, Z)

References

1. Akishita, T., Takagi, T.: Zero-value point attackson elliptic curve cryptosystem. In: Boyd, C., Mao, W. (eds.) ISC 2003. LNCS, vol. 2851, pp. 218–233. Springer, Heidelberg (2003)
2. Bauer, A., Jaulmes, E., Prouff, E., Wild, J.: Horizontal collision correlation attack on elliptic curves. In: Lange, T., Lauter, K., Lisoněk, P. (eds.) SAC 2013. LNCS, vol. 8282, pp. 553–570. Springer, Heidelberg (2014)
3. Bertoni, G., Daemen, J., Peeters, M., Van Assche, G.: Cryptographic sponge functions. Submission to NIST (Round 3) (2011)
4. Bertoni, G., Daemen, J., Peeters, M., Van Assche, G.: The Keccak reference. Submission to NIST (Round 3) (2011)
5. Bock, H., Braun, M., Dichtl, M., Hess, E., Heyszl, J., Kargl, W., Koroschetz, H., Meyer, B., Seuschek, H.: A milestone towards RFID products offering asymmetric authentication based on elliptic curve cryptography. In: RFIDSec, July 2008

---

[3] Dependent on sign of operand Q (cf. Sect. 5) either R_1 or R_2 is subtracted.

6. Brown, M., Hankerson, D., López, J., Menezes, A.: Software implementation of the NIST elliptic curves over prime fields. In: Naccache, D. (ed.) CT-RSA 2001. LNCS, vol. 2020, pp. 250–265. Springer, Heidelberg (2001)
7. Certicom Research: Standards for Efficient Cryptography, SEC 2: Recommended Elliptic Curve Domain Parameters, Version 1.0., September 2000. http://www.secg.org/
8. Certicom Research: Standards for Efficient Cryptography (SECG), SEC 1: Elliptic Curve Cryptography, Version 1.0., September 2000. http://www.secg.org/
9. Coron, J.-S.: Resistance against differential power analysis for elliptic curve cryptosystems. In: Koç, Ç.K., Paar, C. (eds.) CHES 1999. LNCS, vol. 1717, pp. 292–302. Springer, Heidelberg (1999)
10. Faraday Technology Corporation: Faraday FSA0A_C 0.13 μm ASIC Standard Cell Library (2014). http://www.faraday-tech.com
11. Fürbass, F., Wolkerstorfer, J.: ECC Processor with low die size for RFID Applications. In: Proceedings of IEEE International Symposium on Circuits and Systems, IEEE, May 2007
12. Goubin, L.: A Refined power-analysis attack on elliptic curve cryptosystems. In: Desmedt, Y.G. (ed.) PKC 2003. LNCS, vol. 2567, pp. 199–211. Springer, Heidelberg (2002)
13. Goundar, R.R., Joye, M., Miyaji, A., Rivain, M., Venelli, A.: Scalar multiplication on Weierstraß elliptic curves from co-Z arithmetic. J. Crypt. Eng. 1(2), 161–176 (2011)
14. Hedabou, M., Pinel, P., Bénéteau, L.: Countermeasures for preventing comb method against SCA attacks. In: Deng, R.H., Bao, F., Pang, H.H., Zhou, J. (eds.) ISPEC 2005. LNCS, vol. 3439, pp. 85–96. Springer, Heidelberg (2005)
15. Hein, D.: Elliptic curve cryptography ASIC for radio frequency authentication. Master thesis, Technical University of Graz, April 2008
16. Hutter, M., Feldhofer, M., Plos, T.: An ECDSA processor for RFID authentication. In: Ors Yalcin, S.B. (ed.) RFIDSec 2010. LNCS, vol. 6370, pp. 189–202. Springer, Heidelberg (2010)
17. Hutter, M., Feldhofer, M., Wolkerstorfer, J.: A cryptographic processor for low-resource devices: canning ECDSA and AES like sardines. In: Ardagna, C.A., Zhou, J. (eds.) WISTP 2011. LNCS, vol. 6633, pp. 144–159. Springer, Heidelberg (2011)
18. Hutter, M., Joye, M., Sierra, Y.: Memory-constrained implementations of elliptic curve cryptography in co-Z coordinate representation. In: Nitaj, A., Pointcheval, D. (eds.) AFRICACRYPT 2011. LNCS, vol. 6737, pp. 170–187. Springer, Heidelberg (2011)
19. Jungk, B.: Area-efficient FPGA implementations of the SHA-3 finalists. In: 2011 International Conference on Reconfigurable Computing and FPGAs-ReConFig, November 30–December 2, Cancun, Mexico, pp. 235–241 (2011)
20. Kern, T., Feldhofer, M.: Low-resource ECDSA implementation for passive RFID tags. In: ICECS, 12–15 December 2010, Athens, Greece, pp. 1236–1239. IEEE (2010)
21. Koç, Ç.K., Acar, T., Kaliski Jr., B.S.: Analyzing and comparing montgomery multiplication algorithms. IEEE Microwave Mag. 16(3), 26–33 (1996)
22. Lee, Y.K., Sakiyama, K., Batina, L., Verbauwhede, I.: Elliptic-curve-based security processor for RFID. IEEE Trans. Comput. 57(11), 1514–1527 (2008)
23. Lim, C.H., Lee, P.J.: More flexible exponentiation with precomputation. In: Desmedt, Y.G. (ed.) CRYPTO 1994. LNCS, vol. 839, pp. 95–107. Springer, Heidelberg (1994)

24. Longa, P., Miri, A.: New composite operations and precomputation scheme for elliptic curve cryptosystems over prime fields. In: Cramer, R. (ed.) PKC 2008. LNCS, vol. 4939, pp. 229–247. Springer, Heidelberg (2008)
25. Meloni, N.: New point addition formulae for ECC applications. In: Carlet, C., Sunar, B. (eds.) WAIFI 2007. LNCS, vol. 4547, pp. 189–201. Springer, Heidelberg (2007)
26. Montgomery, P.L.: Modular multiplication without trial division. Math. Comput. **44**, 519–521 (1985)
27. Pessl, P., Hutter, M.: Pushing the limits of SHA-3 hardware implementations to fit on RFID. In: Bertoni, G., Coron, J.-S. (eds.) CHES 2013. LNCS, vol. 8086, pp. 126–141. Springer, Heidelberg (2013)
28. Roy, S.S., Yang, B., Rozic, V., Mentens, N., Fan, J., Verbauwhede, I.: Designing tiny ECC processor. Presentation at the 17th Workshop on Elliptic Curve Cryptography (ECC 2013) (2013). https://www.cosic.esat.kuleuven.be/ecc2013/files/sujoy.pdf
29. Walter, C.D.: Montgomery exponentiation needs no final subtractions. Electron. Lett. **35**, 1831–1832 (1999)
30. Walter, C.D.: Montgomery's multiplication technique: how to make it smaller and faster. In: Koç, Ç.K., Paar, C. (eds.) CHES 1999. LNCS, vol. 1717, pp. 80–93. Springer, Heidelberg (1999)
31. Wenger, E., Feldhofer, M., Felber, N.: Low-resource hardware design of an elliptic curve processor for contactless devices. In: Chung, Y., Yung, M. (eds.) WISA 2010. LNCS, vol. 6513, pp. 92–106. Springer, Heidelberg (2011)
32. Wenger, E., Hutter, M.: Exploring the design space of prime field vs. binary field ECC-hardware implementations. In: Laud, P. (ed.) NordSec 2011. LNCS, vol. 7161, pp. 256–271. Springer, Heidelberg (2012)

ePassport:
Side Channel in the Basic Access Control

Luigi Sportiello[✉]

European Commission, Joint Research Centre,
Via Enrico Fermi 2749, 21027 Ispra, VA, Italy
luigi.sportiello@jrc.ec.europa.eu

Abstract. An electronic version of the traditional passport (ePassport) is nowadays issued by many countries to their citizens. A contactless chip storing personal details of the document holder is embedded in the ePassport cover. To prevent unauthorized reads of the chip's content and to protect its communication with a legitimate reader the Basic Access Control (BAC) has been introduced. Thanks to the BAC, only those readers aware of the secret associated with an ePassport chip can access its content. In this paper we show that a side channel analysis can be carried out for some chips secured with the BAC. In particular we analyze the chip response time during BAC operations, showing how the collected data could be exploited to mount an attack in order to get access to the chip's content. We have verified the presence of such side channel in real ePassports and stress that electronic Driving Licences could be affected as well, since the same access control mechanism is adopted for them.

Keywords: ePassport · Basic access control · Side channel analysis · eDriving licence

1 Introduction

Nowadays many countries all over the world issue the electronic version of the passport (ePassport) [1,2] to their citizens, the international document used by people for their identification abroad. In contrast to the traditional passport, in the ePassport a chip is embedded in the cover of the document. Such electronic component stores personal data regarding the document holder and can be accessed by a contactless interface: a reader put in proximity of the document, following the RFID communication principle, powers the chip and exchanges messages with it. Due to the sensitivity of the involved data and the over-the-air nature of the communication, a mechanism to protect the access to the chip and the communication with it has been introduced, the Basic Access Control (BAC). The BAC is a mutual authentication protocol between chip and reader based on symmetric-key cryptography: every ePassport is featured by a secret string called Machine Readable Zone (MRZ) and a reader has to be aware of

N. Saxena and A.-R. Sadeghi (Eds.): RFIDSec 2014, LNCS 8651, pp. 173–184, 2014.
DOI: 10.1007/978-3-319-13066-8_11

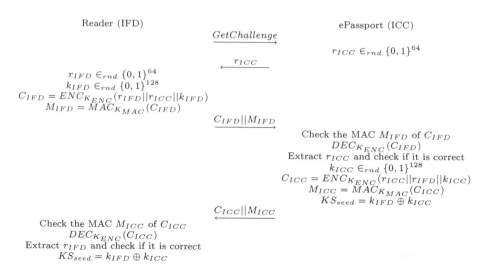

Fig. 1. Basic Access Control between Reader (also known as InterFace Device - IFD) and ePassport chip (also known as Integrated Circuit Card - ICC). ENC/DEC represent a cipher based on Triple-DES in CBC mode with zero IV, while MAC generates a 8-byte message authentication code according to the ISO/IEC 9797-1 MAC Algorithm 3 [2].

such string to successfully run the BAC with the document's chip and establish a communication with it. At the end of the BAC a couple of secret keys are agreed by the two parties and the following communication is then encrypted and authenticated.

In the literature different works highlighting some weaknesses of the BAC have been published. In particular, the majority of them reports that the entropy associated to the MRZ is quite low putting at stake the data stored in the chip. This has been pointed out for Belgian, Dutch, German, American and Italian ePassports [3–7]. In addition, the ePassports issued by a country over time could be featured by different chip versions, each associated to a subset of possible MRZs, so querying properly an ePassport chip its version can be identified associating it to a quite low entropy set of MRZs [7]. The authors of [6] show that in case of low entropy MRZs specific cracking machines can be used to attack a recorded BAC communication between a reader and an ePassport trying to get the relative MRZ.

In this paper we show that the BAC security could be also affected by the analysis of side channels. In cryptography the side channel analysis denotes the examination of information unintentionally leaked by a device regarding its internal execution of a cryptographic operation. Such analysis can be exploited to breach the security of cryptographic mechanisms. We have found out that timing analysis can be carried out during the execution of the BAC for some ePassport implementations. The first example of timing analysis against ePassports is reported in [8], where the authors analyzing the response times of ePassport chips were able to track them without breaking the relative cryptographic protocol. In our work we examine the response times of ePassports solicited with specific pre-formatted commands and show how such analysis, when combined with the MRZ low entropy issue, could be used to mount an attack against the BAC if no countermeasures are taken. We have detected the side channel in a subset of the examined ePassports, as it basically depends on the specific implementation of the adopted cryptographic algorithms in the chip, but for all of them a countermeasure was able to prevent the attack designed in this paper to exploit such timing side channel. We also point out that for such attack to be successful, an interaction of several days with the document's chip would be required, and this may be hard to achieve in practice. Nevertheless, the detected side channel analysis allows to retrieve data that the chip is not suppose to leak, that being so a security assessment of the current ePassport implementations is advisable.

The paper is organized as follows. Section 2 introduces the BAC. In Sect. 3 we present the side channel found out during the execution of the BAC in some ePassport implementations, while in Sect. 4 we show how it could be exploited to set up an attack against ePassport chips in case no specific countermeasures are adopted. We discuss some implications of our work in Sect. 5 and give conclusions in Sect. 6.

2   Basic Access Control

The BAC has been introduced to prevent the unauthorized read of the ePassport's chip content and to guarantee confidentiality during the communication with a reader. It is a mutual authentication protocol based on a common secret shared by a chip (Integrated Circuit Card - ICC) and a reader (InterFace Device - IFD) that intend to communicate together. Such secret is represented by a string, called Machine Readable Zone (MRZ), printed in an internal data page of the ePassport. The idea behind the MRZ is that only the ePassport holder can authorize the access to the chip of his document explicitly showing such page: the string can then be optically scanned or typed by an operator and given to the reader. Each ePassport is featured by a unique MRZ and its typical form is the following

```
P<UTOSURNAME<<NAME<<<<<<<<<<<<<<<<<<<<<<<<<<<<<
1234567897UTO6908061F9406236<<<<<<<<<<<<<<<04
```

where the information encoded in the second line, the only one used for the BAC, is the following: 9 characters representing the passport number (PN) followed by a check digit, 3 characters reserved for the nationality, 6 characters for the date of birth (DB) followed by a check digit, one character representing the gender of the holder, 6 characters for the document expiration date (DE) and in the end padding symbols (<) followed by two final check digits (the check digits are defined in [1]). The MRZ is used by the two parties to derive a key pair, K_{ENC} and K_{MAC}, as follows

D_{IFD}=[0xDD$_0$,0xDD$_0$,...,0xDD$_{31}$]
M_{IFD}=[0xMM$_0$,...,0xMM$_7$]

M_{IFD} is a valid MAC of D_{IFD} for the ICC

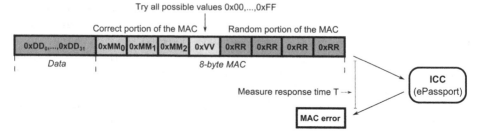

The measured T varies if the used 0xVV is the correct byte for the MAC (0xMM$_3$ in the example) or not.

Fig. 2. ePassport MAC checking: timing analysis of a specific MAC byte.

$$MRZ\_information=PN||DB||DE$$
$$K_{seed}=msb\_16(SHA\text{-}1(MRZ\_information))$$
$$K_{ENC}=msb\_16(SHA\text{-}1(K_{seed}||00000001))$$
$$K_{MAC}=msb\_16(SHA\text{-}1(K_{seed}||00000002))$$

where PN, DB and DE are respectively followed by their check digit and msb_N stands for "the N most significant bytes".

The full BAC protocol is shown in Fig. 1. K_{ENC} and K_{MAC} are respectively used to encrypt the data exchanged by the parties, relying on a Triple-DES in CBC mode with zero IV, and to compute a relative 8-byte message authentication code (MAC) according to the ISO/IEC 9797-1 MAC Algorithm 3 [2]. At the beginning the ICC, solicited by the IFD, generates and sends a random value. Such value is encrypted by the IFD along with an additional pair of generated random numbers obtaining C_{IFD}, which is sent to the ICC together with its MAC M_{IFD}. Firstly the ICC checks the MAC and, if valid, decrypts C_{IFD} verifying that the random number generated at the beginning is correctly returned. If so, the protocol continues in reverse order, with further random material generated by the ICC, which is encrypted, authenticated and sent to the IFD. If also the IFD checks are successful, the random values exchanged by the parties are used to set up a common secret KS_{seed}. From this agreed secret a session key pair is generated to encrypt and authenticate the following communication.

3   Side Channel Discovery

We focused our attention on the message $C_{IFD}||M_{IFD}$ sent by the reader to the chip during the BAC (Fig. 1). Upon the arrival of the message, the chip has to perform some checks on it and in case of failure an error message is returned. Measuring the response time of such error messages it is possible to extract some information concerning the internal checks carried out by the chip.

Given:
K_{MAC} = Valid MAC key for the ICC
$D_{IFD}[32] = [0xDD_0, \ldots, 0xDD_{31}]$ //Generic 32-byte vector
$M_{IFD} = MAC_{K_{MAC}}(D_{IFD})$ //Valid authentication code of D_{IFD} for the ICC

Consider the MAC sent by the IFD to the ICC during the BAC as an 8-byte vector. For each byte T ($T \in [0, 7]$) collect time statistics running $ByteStatistics(D_{IFD}, M_{IFD}, T)$.

$ByteStatistics(D_{IFD}, M_{IFD}, T)$:

T = MAC target byte to be analyzed
$MeanResponseTimes[256]$;

$for(V = 0x00\,to\,0xFF)$: //Try all possible values V in the byte T of the MAC
$\quad MeanResponseTime[V] = ByteValueStatistics(D_{IFD}, M_{IFD}, T, V)$;

Plot $MeanResponseTimes$;

$ByteValueStatistics(D_{IFD}, M_{IFD}, T, V)$:

Reader (IFD)	—	ePassport (ICC)

T = MAC target byte
$V = 0xVV$ //Value for the target byte
$M_{IFD}[8] = [0xMM_0, \ldots, 0xMM_7]$

$TestMAC = [0xMM_0, \ldots, 0xMM_{T-1}, 0xVV,$
$0xRR_{T+1}, \ldots, 0xRR_7]$ //$0xRR_i$ is a random byte

$\xrightarrow{\quad GetChallenge \quad}$

$\xleftarrow{\quad r_{ICC} \quad}$

Take time T_1

$\xrightarrow{\quad D_{IFD}\|TestMAC \quad}$

$\xleftarrow{\quad error \quad}$

Take time T_2
Record response time $T_2 - T_1$

Routine repeated N times
returning the mean
of the recorded response times

Fig. 3. Our timing analysis on the MAC checking of a given ePassport.

For instance, for some ePassport implementations, as already highlighted in [8], the error response time differs if there is an immediate failure during the MAC check or later during the verification of the returned random number r_{ICC}: the second case takes longer as also the C_{IFD} decryption is performed, while in the first case such computation is simply skipped.

We decided to perform a deeper timing analysis on the MAC check failure. Our idea is shown in Fig. 2. For a given chip we prepare messages of the form $C_{IFD}\|M_{IFD}$ with a partially erroneous 8-byte MAC, which is made of a series of correct bytes, followed by a target byte, appending in the end random bytes. The value of the so-called target byte is varied among all possible byte values, so 256 messages are generated for a given target byte. Such messages are sent to the chip, which will reply with MAC error messages, and the relative response times are measured. The response time should differ when the right value, considering the valid MAC that should be attached to the message, is used in the target byte.

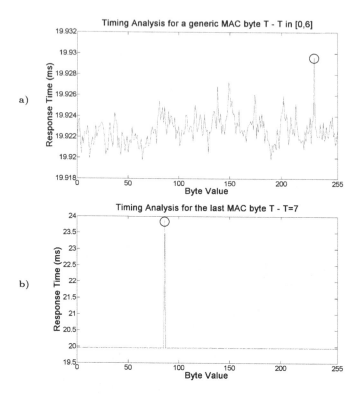

Fig. 4. MAC bytes value identification through MAC checking response times. A representative chart of the timing analysis on a generic byte of the MAC (excluded the last one) is presented in figure *a*: varying the byte value the MAC checking response time (mean on 5000 iterations) is affected and the highest peak identifies the correct byte value. In figure *b* a representative timing analysis (mean on 500 iterations) for the last byte of the MAC is shown: an outstanding peak clearly identifies the right byte value.

Note that to highlight the time difference a single attempt for each message is not sufficient and a statistics has to be created: each message is sent N times averaging its response times. Our full timing analysis considering in turn all the MAC bytes as target is summarized in Fig. 3.

We have successfully tested our analysis on four Italian ePassports issued between 2009 and 2010. We relied on the libnfc library [9] to develop our timing analysis software that was run on an Ubuntu machine, using an ACS ACR122 contactless reader to interrogate the chips. In our experiments, for a given ePassport with its MRZ, we set $D_{IFD} = ENC_{K_{ENC}}(0x00_0, \ldots, 0x00_{31})$ at the beginning of our timing analysis presented in Fig. 3. Two examples of timing analysis charts are presented in Fig 4. For a given target byte T of the MAC, a chart shows the average response time of the MAC checking operation performed by the chip varying the value of such target byte. We point out that a trimmed mean has been used to compute the average response time associated with each byte value, discarding 5 % of the measures equally distributed between lowest and highest times, to make the charts clearer and less affected by outliers.

In our experiments the timing analysis for each of the first seven bytes of the MAC of our examined ePassports presented similar results and a representative example based on $N = 5000$ iterations is given in the chart of Fig. 4a: some peaks are present with the highest one that identifies the right value for the byte under examination. We have verified that for a lower number of iterations the peak associated with the right value could not emerge remaining immersed at same level of others, so without revealing the correct byte value. In that regard, we have verified that in general a higher number of iterations allows to achieve more reliable analysis. The chart of Fig. 4b shows a representative timing analysis, based on $N = 500$ iterations, for the last byte of a MAC: the peak identifying the right byte value is clearly evident. We also ran our analysis on two Italian ePassports dating back to 2007, but for them no peaks appeared (apart from the last byte), so our analysis was not apparently applicable against them.

It is difficult to give an explanation for the chip behaviour regarding the first seven bytes of the MAC, because the details regarding the internal implemented solutions are not publicly released and we have to look at the chip as a black box. Despite that, according to the results, a tight relation with the specific MAC checking algorithm implementation in the chip seems evident. Indeed, the timing analysis is effective for a subset of documents but not for others issued in a different period of time, and as stated in [7] different versions of ePassport chips are issued by the country over time, each one probably featured by a specific hardware platform and ePassport software. We suppose that for the affected version the MAC value is somehow internally checked in a byte by byte manner starting from the first one and when a wrong byte is found some decision is taken. In that regard, we also point out that some tests sending to the chip a MAC with the correct value in the target byte and random values in the remaining seven bytes were attempted, but they did not produce good results, that is no peaks stood out. Therefore, probably, the peak shown in the chart of Fig. 4a is not linked to a single check of the target byte, but it is related to a sequential verification of the MAC. Differently, the situation appears clearer for the behaviour linked to the last byte of the MAC. When the correct value is used, the MAC check is passed and the received message is decrypted, then verifying the returned r_{ICC} (note that in the BAC attempts of our timing analysis this check basically fails, as in the preparation of D_{IFD} we have fixed a vector of 0x00 bytes for r_{ICC}, which will be essentially always different from the r_{ICC} sent by the chip at the beginning of the BAC attempt). So the outstanding peak is due to the extra decryption operation performed by the chip. Note that for this reason, a lower number of iterations is needed to make the peak stands out and in principle even one iteration could be enough.

We also have to point out a specific mechanism adopted by the examined Italian ePassports featured by the side channel. They counted the number of

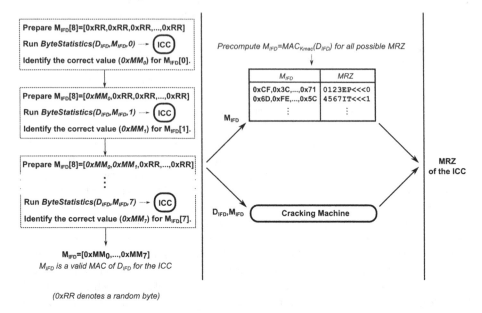

Fig. 5. Possible attack against the Basic Access Control exploiting the identified side channel.

consecutive unsuccessful BAC attempts, for instance due to MAC check failures, and when a specific threshold was reached the chip response was heavily delayed, basically preventing a correct time responses collection for our analysis. To overcome this issue, we periodically ran a successful BAC protocol within our analysis to reset the failure counter. We will discuss later how this feature represents a valid countermeasure against possible attacks that try to exploit the side channel just presented. We also report that for a given ePassport, at the beginning of our timing analysis over the MAC bytes, we recorded slightly higher response times during the first iterations, but this did not affect the validity of our analysis.

4   Possible Attack

An attack could be mounted against those ePassports that are featured by the highlighted side channel to obtain their MRZ. We present it in Fig. 5. In the attack scenario, for a given ePassport, differently from the timing analysis presented in the previous section, the relative MRZ is not known, so it is not possible to prepare a priori a MAC with some correct bytes. The idea is to use our timing analysis to retrieve byte by byte the valid MAC of a specific message. First, a generic 32-byte vector D_{IFD} is set. Then our timing analysis is launched, giving as input D_{IFD} and a random MAC of 8 bytes, selecting the first byte of the

MAC as the target one. The resulting chart will highlight the right value for the first byte of the correct MAC of D_{IFD}. The process is repeated preparing a MAC with the identified correct value for the first byte and setting the second byte as target, getting the right value for it from the timing analysis. Iterating such process over all MAC bytes as shown in Fig. 5 the full correct MAC of D_{IFD} for the given ePassport is obtained.

Such information could then be exploited in two different ways. The pair (D_{IFD}, M_{IFD}) could be given to a cracking machine where all possible MRZs are used to compute the MAC of D_{IFD} until the match with M_{IFD} is found [6]. Alternatively, since D_{IFD} can be fixed a priori, all its possible MACs are pre-computed using all possible MRZs, then exploiting the stored data as lookup table. Note that both approaches are feasible only if the attacked ePassport is featured by a low entropy MRZ, that is the full set of strings representing all possible MRZs is exhaustively manageable, but as reported in Sect. 1 this is the case for ePassports issued by different countries. For instance, it has been reported that the MRZ entropy for ePassports issued by some countries can be around 40 bits [4,7]. In such a case, considering that a cracking machine could be able to test $\approx 2^{28}$ BAC keys per second [6], ≈ 1 h would be required for getting the MRZ, while a lookup table would require some TBs of precomputed data.

We remark that this attack performs better than a brute force approach based on BAC attempts against the victim ePassport in terms of number of queries sent to the chip. Indeed, assuming 5000 iterations in the timing analysis for each of the first seven bytes of the MAC and 500 iterations for the last byte, ≈ 9 million queries would be needed in total (we remind that in our analysis, for each MAC byte, each possible byte value between 0x00 and 0xFF is tested N times, where N = 'number of iterations'), that is by far less than the number of possible MRZs. It also has to be noted that, according to the times experienced with our set-up, a timing analysis of 5000 iterations on a MAC byte requires an interaction of ≈ 85 h with the attacked chip, so some days would be required for a complete attack as the one estimated above, which could be not easy to achieve in practice even if we try to depict a couple of attack scenarios in the next section. In addition, for our statistical analysis to be successful and usable for the designed attack, the chip response times should not be affected by artificial behaviours as it was for our examined ePassports featured by the side channel. Indeed, for them, after roughly 250 failed BAC attempts the chip responses were artificially delayed by some seconds, de facto preventing any successful statistical analysis.

5   Discussion

Our experiments have been conducted by a lab set-up, with the examined chips interrogated through a contactless reader connected to a workstation. As real life attacking scenarios, we could think of NFC-enabled mobile phones used to mount attacks against BAC-protected chips. For instance two attack method-ologies could be adopted, one based on physical proximity and the other act-ing remotely. In the first case, a person regularly in proximity of the victim document holder (e.g., on means of public transport, at the workplace) could collect data day by day. If the holder keeps for instance his document in a bag or in a pocket, the attacker could silently put his phone close to such points running the timing analysis in chunks, retrieving in the end the MRZ of the victim's document. For the second methodology an attacker should be able to install the timing analysis software in the mobile phone of the document holder. This could be achieved in different ways, as for instance distributing the analysis software through phone application repositories (e.g., hiding the software in games) or using social engineering techniques. Then the timing analysis is carried on when the victim keeps his phone close to the document (e.g., many people tend to keep phone and wallet, where the document could be placed, close together). Note that with such an approach it is possible to think of massive attacks infecting a large number of phones. Once cracked the document could be partially copied reading its content or remotely used through a relay attack [10].

We have got our timing analysis results on documents currently in circulation. We hope that our results foster ePassport chip manufacturers to assess their implementations in order to identify the possible presence of the side channel presented here. The issue could be solved forcing the MAC check to be executed in constant time or simply adding a delay for the chip responses when a certain number of unsuccessful BAC attempts have been run, de facto preventing the timing analysis. We have verified that this second option was adopted by the ePassports examined during our experiments, basically protecting them from our attack (even if such mechanism was probably introduced to protect the chip against brute force attacks). Also the adoption of high entropy MRZs prevents the attack, but a change in the MRZ scheme should be decided by the administrations of the different countries. In addition we remark as for ePassports the BAC is going to be replaced by the PACE scheme [11] that relies on a different cryptographic protocol.

Another electronic document that could be affected by our results is the electronic Driving Licence (eDL), recently regulated in the EU [12]. Similarly to ePassports a chip can be embedded in the document. Whether a contactless chip is adopted (also contact chips are possible) the access to its data is protected by the Basic Access Protection (BAP) [13]. Also the BAP is based on a shared secret between chip and reader, called Scanning Area Identifier (SAI), to run an authentication protocol between the parties. The BAP can be configured to act exactly as the BAC, the BAP 1 configuration of [13] specifies the same cryptographic algorithms, and also the SAI can be set to be a machine readable string. Such arrangement is exactly the one adopted for European eDLs, in favor of interoperability with existing equipment already used to read similar documents like ePassports, and no alternative options are given. In light of this a check on the SAI entropy and an assessment of the eDL chip implementation would be advisable, in order to evaluate the feasibility of the attack presented here against eDLs.

6 Conclusion

In the paper we present a side channel analysis for electronic documents featured by a contactless chip protected through the Basic Access Control (BAC). In particular specific timing analysis during chip operations for the BAC can be carried out. We explain how such analysis could be exploited to mount an attack to retrieve the chip's BAC keys when no countermeasures are adopted in combination with low entropy secrets. We have verified the presence of such side channel in ePassport chips currently in circulation and we remind that the same access control mechanism is adopted for contactless electronic Driving Licences. We advice all those players in charge of manufacturing and issuing such electronic documents to assess their security in light of these new results.

Acknowledgments. We thank Philippe Teuwen for his suggestions about the use of libnfc.

References

1. International Civil Aviation Organization: Machine Readable Travel Documents. Part 1, vol. 1, Sixth Edition (2006)
2. International Civil Aviation Organization: Machine Readable Travel Documents. Part 1, vol. 2, Sixth Edition (2006)
3. Juels, A., Molnar, D., Wagner, D.: Security and privacy issues in e-Passports. In: Proceedings of the IEEE 1st International Conference on Security and Privacy for Emerging Areas in Communications Networks, pp. 74–88 (2005)
4. Avoine, G., Kalach, K., Quisquater, J.-J.: ePassport: Securing international contacts with contactless chips. In: Tsudik, G. (ed.) FC 2008. LNCS, vol. 5143, pp. 141–155. Springer, Heidelberg (2008)
5. Hoepman, J.-H., Hubbers, E., Jacobs, B., Oostdijk, M., Schreur, R.W.: Crossing borders: Security and privacy issues of the European e-Passport. In: Yoshiura, H., Sakurai, K., Rannenberg, K., Murayama, Y., Kawamura, S. (eds.) IWSEC 2006. LNCS, vol. 4266, pp. 152–167. Springer, Heidelberg (2006)
6. Liu, Y., Kasper, T., Lemke-Rust, K., Paar, C.: E-Passport: Cracking basic access control keys. In: Meersman, R. (ed.) OTM 2007, Part II. LNCS, vol. 4804, pp. 1531–1547. Springer, Heidelberg (2007)
7. Sportiello, L.: Weakening ePassports through bad implementations. In: Hoepman, J.-H., Verbauwhede, I. (eds.) RFIDSec 2012. LNCS, vol. 7739, pp. 123–136. Springer, Heidelberg (2013)
8. Chothia, T., Smirnov, V.: A traceability attack against e-Passports. In: Sion, R. (ed.) FC 2010. LNCS, vol. 6052, pp. 20–34. Springer, Heidelberg (2010)
9. libnfc: Public platform independent Near Field Communication (NFC) library, Version 1.7.0 (2014). http://nfc-tools.org/
10. Sportiello, L., Ciardulli, A.: Long distance relay attack. In: Hutter, M., Schmidt, J.-M. (eds.) RFIDsec 2013. LNCS, vol. 8262, pp. 69–85. Springer, Heidelberg (2013)
11. International Civil Aviation Organization: Supplemental Access Control for Machine Readable Travel Documents, version 1.01 (2010)

12. Commission Regulation (EU) No. 383/2012: Laying down technical requirements with regard to driving licences which include a storage medium (microchip), 4 May 2012
13. ISO/IEC 18013: Information Technology - Personal Identification - ISO-Compliant Driving Licence - Part 3: Access Control, Authentication and Integrity Validation (2009)

A Low Area Probing Detector for Power Efficient Security ICs

Michael Weiner[1]([✉]), Salvador Manich[2], and Georg Sigl[1]

[1] Institute for Security in Information Technology,
Technische Universität München, Munich, Germany
{m.weiner,sigl}@tum.de
[2] ETSEIB, Universitat Politècnica de Catalunya, Barcelona, Spain
salvador.manich@upc.edu

Abstract. In this paper, a new concept of a low cost, Low Area Probing Detector (LAPD) is presented. Probing or microprobing is an attack technique against integrated circuits implementing security functions, such as OTP tokens or smartcards. It allows intercepting secrets from on-chip wires as well as injecting faults for other attacks. Microprobing is invasive as classified by Skorobogatov in 2005 and requires opening the microchip package as well as removing the passivation layer. While it may sound complicated and expensive, Maier and Nohl showed in 2012 that microprobing is feasible for low-budget adversaries. However, existing protection techniques against microprobing, such as active shields, redundancy of core components, or analog detection circuits containing large capacitors, are still expensive.

The LAPD provides low-cost protection against microprobing. It measures minimal timing differences between on-chip wires caused by the capacitive load of microprobes. As a novelty, it is merely based on digital components and does not require analog circuitry, which reduces the required area and process steps compared to previous approaches.

1 Introduction

Microprobing is a highly powerful attack technique against security chips. Its purpose is to violate the tamper-resistance characteristics of a chip. Despite its higher cost compared to other types of attacks, it has the advantage to achieve direct reading of internal data or writing on control signals. Furthermore, attackers can use microprobing to manipulate the behavior of an attacked chip by forcing on-chip wires to arbitrary voltages [7].

When dumping the chip memory is the objective, buses are a more interesting target than memory cells because on buses, all relevant data passes through a few single lines. Worse than that, buses are difficult to hide in lower metal layers due to their extension [10].

For many years, buses and other chip structures have been protected by different means like active or passive shields, attack sensors and masking schemes. Shields are top layers of metal that usually cover the whole surface of the chip [1].

© Springer International Publishing Switzerland 2014
N. Saxena and A.-R. Sadeghi (Eds.): RFIDSec 2014, LNCS 8651, pp. 185–197, 2014.
DOI: 10.1007/978-3-319-13066-8_12

Planarization and a dense mesh of conductive routes complicate the access to lower layers of it. In active shields, routes are periodically tested to detect breaks in them [9].

The performance improvement and accessibility of specialized laboratory equipment, from micropositioners over high-end optical and electron microscopes up to Focused Ion Beams (FIBs) has put in danger protection measures like shields. FIBs can drill holes with the necessary depth between meanders of metal routes which access underlying lines of interest without damaging the shield. Later on, they can deposit conductive material to route initially inaccessible signals to the surface, which allows the right alignment and contact of microprobes [14]. Other protection mechanisms such as light sensors can be defeated as well, for example by using targeted laser pulses – or they are expensive to implement, such as masking which requires a huge area effort.

The aggregation of impediments against these attacks has forced attackers to search for other easier alternatives. Access through the backside of the chip has been recently investigated. Using the photonic emission of transistors, a mapping of transistors is elaborated and regions of interest located [8]. Then, the backside is thinned down close to transistors, approximately $50 \, \mu m$, and thereafter FIB machine edition completes the access to source and drain of the target ones. As formerly described, ad hoc metal contacts are added to ease the microprobe contacts [6]. In such a way, buses can be accessed too by locating the driving buffers, which usually produce larger photo-emission.

We present a novel concept to protect the lines of buses from the inside of itself. It is based on the fact that the timing behavior of bus lines is mutually similar under normal conditions, while attaching a microprobe to some lines makes this significantly different. A similar, much more resource-intensive approach called Probe Attempt Detector (PAD) was presented in [11]. An overview of its concept is presented in Sect. 3.

In this paper, the concept of a Low Area Probing Detector (LAPD) is presented which is implemented only using digital standard cells and achieves a sensitivity degree in the order of magnitude of the present commercial microprobes [12]. Owing to the digital scheme, the area requirement is much lower than the PAD as no analog components such as capacitors are required. In addition, the LAPD allows detecting probes in a single shot, while the PAD is slower and consumes more energy as it requires counting clock ticks of a ring oscillator.

The rest of the paper is organized as follows: In Sect. 2 the statement of the problem is formally presented. Related work is shown in Sect. 3. In Sect. 4 the LAPD is explained in detail and in Sect. 5 simulation results are shown. Finally concluding remarks are presented in Sect. 6.

2   Problem Statement

Consider an on-chip bus transmitting sensitive data that consists of n lines, to some of which an attacker can contact microprobes. Also assume that the test bench is static, i.e. the probes are not moved while the attacked chip is powered up.

If the attacker required k probes simultaneously attached to the chip instead of only one, his cost increase may appear linear in the first place – he needs to have access to k microprobes, micropositioners, amplifiers and other equipment. However, we assume it is more than linear, as he will also face additional and presumably time consuming practical challenges: the more probes are required, the more likely it is that different needles obstruct each other's way. Furthermore, it is difficult to position many micropositioners around the chip as they are orders of magnitude larger than the chip itself.

In order to minimize the harm of the information leakage by the bus, two possible strategies could be selected: masking the data transmitted through the bus or *detecting the microprobe presence* by electrical means. The first strategy needs very high resources in terms of chip area, power consumption and computation time, as well as price for certification. This is mainly used for the protection of high-value targets such as Pay TV smartcards [4,5]. It is, however, not feasible for mass-market low performance processors – for example, SIM cards or RFID based public transport tickets – while the second strategy can be implemented at a vastly reduced cost in terms of area and power consumption. We focus on the latter case because we target low-cost secure chips.

The *detection of the microprobe presence* could be performed online, while data is transmitted through the bus, or *offline*, at time instants when the bus is idle. Like before, the online mode will typically require more power because it will be in continuous operation while the *offline* mode will consume power only during its activation. For this reason, the selected mode is the *offline* mode.

In conclusion, the LAPD presented in this paper is of type *offline detector of microprobe presence* by electrical means. Since the test bench is assumed static, typically a detection run must be performed after reset and/or in bus idle cycles before critical data is transfered over the bus.

3   Related Work

The smartcard industry protects their chips against microprobing either by meshes, sensors, or by using area intensive masking schemes.

Shields, also known as meshes, are regular wiring structures located at the top layer of a smartcard chip. Passive shields obstruct the way to security critical signals but do not have any integrity verification – if an attacker is able to remove this shield, e.g. by means of polishing or FIB manipulation, the shield is completely defeated. Active shields, in addition, transmit random-looking patterns over the shield lines and verify whether the signal still arrives at the other end of the lines; if this is not the case, the chip can trigger an alarm that shuts the chip down or even erases its memory, depending on the level of security required. This mechanism is more difficult to defeat as it requires bridging all interrupted shield lines.

A different approach against microprobing and other attacks are using multiple instances of security-critical components such as memory or CPU cores that only know an obfuscated version of the data that is stored or processed, while

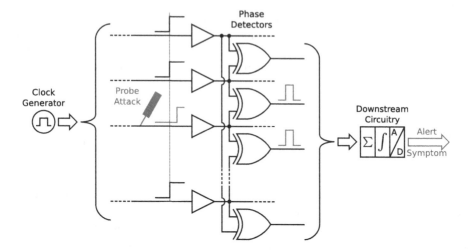

Fig. 1. Overview of the Probe Attempt Detector

only the combination of various pieces of data allows reconstructing the actual secret. This is called masking.

In 2012, another protection mechanism against microprobing was proposed in academia. The Probe Attempt Detector (PAD) [11] aims at protecting buses from the physical contact of probes.

This detector is embedded in the chip and exploits the increase of delay suffered by the line when its parasitic capacitance is enlarged due to the physical contact of the probe. In Fig. 1, an overview of the detector is shown. The PAD runs in off-line mode and when started, a periodic signal is sent simultaneously through all the lines. At the outputs, XOR gates compare the state of the lines and if transitions arrive with different propagation delays they generate pulses of a width proportional to the delay difference. A downstream circuitry adds all these pulses, integrates over time and generates a digital alert symptom. Because of the differential mode, the response of the PAD does not depend on the number of buffers inserted in the bus lines.

In Fig. 2, a simplified model of the downstream circuitry is shown. A tank capacitor C with the initial charge CV_{DD} is gradually discharged by the pulses coming from the XOR gates. When the pulses arrive, they switch on nMOS transistors which in turn extract some charge from C through a current source; therefore, the amount of charge discharged from the capacitor is proportional to the 'active' time of the nMOS transistors. Initially, when the detector starts, C is charged to the maximum voltage V_{DD} through switch S. Then, the switch is opened and the XOR gates start comparing signals coming from the bus during a given integration time. If the arrival times of the XOR inputs are mutually delayed by a probe, the XOR gates generate pulses accordingly which in turn gradually discharge the capacitor. A comparator CP raises its output when the voltage v_c goes below the threshold V_{ref}. A probing attack alert is activated when this signal is raised earlier than normal.

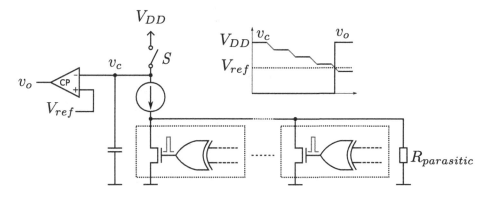

Fig. 2. Simplified model of the PAD downstream circuitry

4   The Low Area Probing Detector

Attaching a microprobe to a bus line increases its capacitive load. Different capacitive loads of equally sized lines lead to different delays of these lines. We present the Low Area Probing Detector (LAPD) that detects microprobing by observing the timing differences between two or more adjacent bus lines. This increases the complexity of a microprobing attack: If n lines are protected by the LAPD, $n - 1$ microprobe connections can be detected such that the adversary would need to attach the same capacitive load to all n protected lines. We assume to protect buses consisting of lines with similar dimensions and delays.

In order to achieve the maximum level of security, the LAPD shall protect all lines that either transfer sensitive information or can be used for forcing or fault injection. This work is focused on the protection of bus lines on a security microcontroller: these lines transfer sensitive information between different components on the chip and they are easy targets as they are presumably situated on the top metal layers due to the distance they need to cross. Furthermore, their structure is well suitable for our symmetry assumptions that are used for this work. Alternatively, the LAPD can be used to enhance the security of active shields such that they do not only evaluate the existence of proper connections, but also validate their timing behavior [10].

4.1   Principle of Operation

The LAPD protects a set of bus lines in a system, as shown in Fig. 3 for the example case of two lines. The lines to be monitored by the LAPD each have the parasitic capacitance C_L, while an attacker probing a line introduces the additional capacitance C_A, which increases the total capacitance of the probed line to $C_L + C_A$.

During the attack, the line capacitances are

$$C_1 = C_L + C_A \tag{1}$$

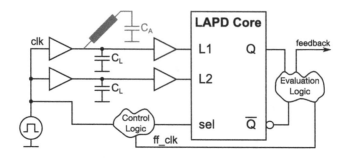

Fig. 3. Overview of a system using the LAPD

$$C_2 = C_L \tag{2}$$

where C_1 is the capacitance of the victim line **L1** and C_2 is the capacitance of the reference line **L2**. Assuming the alpha-power model for the transistors [3,13], the delay of the line buffers can be approximated by

$$d_i = \tilde{k}\frac{C_i\,V_{DD}}{(V_{DD} - V_t)^\alpha} \tag{3}$$

where α is the velocity saturation coefficient of the carriers, V_t is the threshold voltage of the transistors, $\tilde{k}$ is the trans-resistance including the remaining transistor parameters, V_{DD} the supply voltage and C_i the load of the driving buffer [2]. All technological parameters are balanced between nmos and pmos transistors. Equation (3), as explained in [2], assumes that signals approach voltage limits during swinging, which is the case when signals propagate through chains of gates.

After the attack the delay difference between lines **L1** and **L2** is

$$d_1 - d_2 = \tilde{k}\frac{(C_1 - C_2)V_{DD}}{(V_{DD} - V_t)^\alpha} = \Omega\,C_A \tag{4}$$

with

$$\Omega = \tilde{k}\frac{V_{DD}}{(V_{DD} - V_t)^\alpha} \tag{5}$$

As shown in (4), the delay difference is, in a first approximation, proportional to the amount of capacitance of the microprobe. This relationship is valid for small values of C_A which is the characteristic property of advanced microprobes. For probes with larger C_A, Eq. (4) tends to a saturation but in any case the increase of delay function is monotonic and therefore we expect the circuit to behave reliably.

The LAPD detects this delay difference by evaluating race conditions between the two inputs of an RS latch, as shown in Fig. 4. A clock signal drives lines **L1** and **L2**, while a control logic alternates inserting intentional delays t_D in the end of these lines and before the **R** and the **S** input, such that the latch output

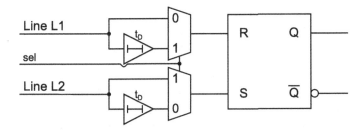

Fig. 4. Conceptual schematic of the LAPD core

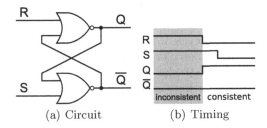

(a) Circuit   (b) Timing

Fig. 5. NOR RS latch

shall alternate between 0 and 1 every cycle. It is preferrable that the clock is not externally accessible to avoid attacks such as glitching. The delay t_D is chosen such that its value is above the intrinsic timing jitter between the R and S inputs and below the minimum timing delay that is expected to be introduced by the microprobe.

4.2 The LAPD Architecture

The LAPD is based on the timing behavior of a standard Reset-Set (RS) latch, as depicted in Fig. 5(a) for the NOR implementation. The *Basic Concept* section explains the most basic case protecting two lines, *Control and Evaluation Logic* describes the components required for operation, and *Protection of n Lines* explains how to protect more than two lines.

Basic Concept. An RS latch, as composed of two NOR or NAND gates, is a memory cell that can be set by activating the S input and reset by activating the R input. As shown in Fig. 5(b) for NOR RS latches, Q does not match $not(\overline{Q})$ during the time that R and S are active simulaneously – in other words, the output is inconsistent. However, as soon as the first of the two inputs returns to the inactive state, the other, still active input "wins the race" and the output becomes valid again.

The LAPD makes use of this behavior by providing both R and S with a square wave, e.g., a clock signal, where one of the R and S lines is alternately delayed. For our assumed case of balanced lines, the latch output Q will alternate

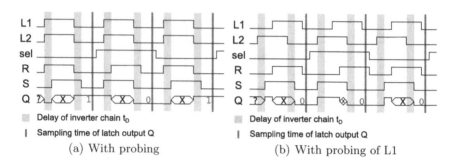

(a) With probing   (b) With probing of L1

Fig. 6. LAPD timing

between 0 and 1 every clock cycle if no probe is attached. The switchable delay driver is dimensioned to be smaller than the delay introduced by the target microprobe: If an adversary attaches such a probe, it will constantly delay one of the lines beyond the other line, such that Q will stop alternating and give a constant output of 0 or 1, depending on the line that is probed.

The timing of the LAPD is shown in Fig. 6. The inconsistent output state of the latch is denoted "X", and an unknown output state is denoted "?". Figure 6(a) shows its regular operation without any probe attached to L1 or L2. Inputs R and S are alternately delayed such that Q alternates between 0 and 1 at the sampling time every clock cycle. In Fig. 6(b), L1 is probed, which induces an additional delay to R. In this case, R is *always slower* than S, such that Q stops alternating and keeps a constant value of 0. The inconsistent output state of the latch is denoted "X", and an unknown output state is denoted "?". Figure 6(a) shows its regular operation without any probe attached to L1 or L2. Inputs R and S are alternately delayed such that Q alternates between 0 and 1 at the sampling time every clock cycle. In Fig. 6(b), L1 is probed, which induces an additional delay to R. In this case, R is *always slower* than S, such that Q stops alternating and keeps a constant value of 0.

Control and Evaluation Logic. The control logic provides the multiplexer input `sel` to the LAPD. `sel` controls whether latch input R or S shall be delayed. Figure 7 depicts a schematic of a sample control logic implementation. It is designed such that `sel` is generated by a toggle flip-flop clocked by a delayed, inverted clock signal. The rising edge of the T flip-flop clock `ff_clk` shall occur after the falling edge of the delayed LAPD latch input. An additional delay t_A ensures this condition.

On the output side of the latch, the evaluation logic shall provide feedback about the absence or presence of a probe. Conceptually, this is a PASS/FAIL signal where PASS means that Q toggles every cycle and FAIL indicates that Q remains at a constant value over two subsequent cycles. Implementing a single PASS/FAIL output line is dangerous, though: if an attacker would force such a line to a constant PASS, for example by the means of a second microbe, the LAPD would become obsolete.

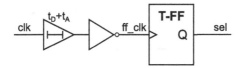

Fig. 7. LAPD control logic

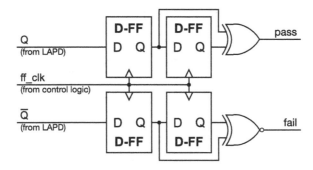

Fig. 8. Redundant LAPD evaluation logic

The circuit as provided in Fig. 8 has two redundant outputs **pass** and **fail** to avoid this single point of failure. It is fed by the signals Q and $\overline{\text{Q}}$ and uses the clock **ff_clk** coming from the control logic. As a positive side effect of the symmetry of the evaluation logic, both outputs of the LAPD latch are equally loaded, which avoids introducing a bias to the circuit.

Protection of Multiple Lines. So far, only the protection of two lines has been discussed. In order to protect a bus, it is necessary to extend the scheme to the protection of n symmetric bus lines.

Using "switches" such as pass transistors, transmission gates or a combination of AND and OR gates, n lines can be protected by connecting $n/2$ lines to the **L1** input of the LAPD through such a gate, while connecting the other half to **L2**. Then, several delay comparisons are performed such that for each comparison, *one* of the bus lines is passed through to **L1** and *one other* bus line is passed through to **L2**. A schematic is depicted in Fig. 9. With this approach, the LAPD protecting an n bit bus can detect up to $n - 1$ attached probes.

A full probe detection coverage is obtained by verifying that the delays of all bus lines are equal. Due to the transitivity of equality, it is sufficient to perform a pairwise comparison of adjacent lines.

In practice, the length of bus lines is not exactly balanced and therefore, the comparison of two adjacent lines is assumed to be slightly biased. In the case this bias has a magnitude that affects the measurement accuracy, it can be compensated by fine-tuning the individual line delays t_D: Instead of having one constant delay t_D for all bus lines, an individual t_{Di} can be used for each bus line.

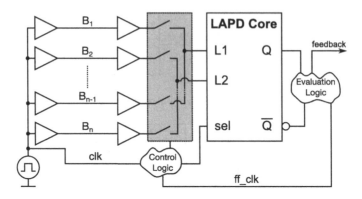

Fig. 9. Bus protected by the LAPD

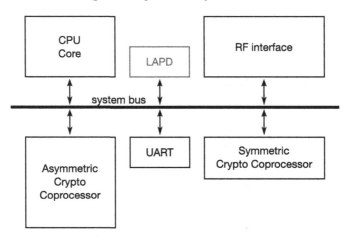

Fig. 10. LAPD system integration

4.3   System Integration Example

Given that the LAPD can take over control of the bus for a limited time, for example by using DMA, it can be attached to the bus of a microprocessor system just like any peripheral component. The CPU core can trigger a probe detection run, for example, by a read operation to the LAPD which would give the LAPD full access to the data bus until the LAPD signals the end of the read operation.

A probe detection run can be triggered during startup or prior to transferring critical information such as keys over the bus.

A top-level view of the LAPD integration into a low-power smartcard chip is shown in Fig. 10.

5   Simulation Results

We simulated the function of the LAPD on a STMicroelectronics 65 nm technology using standard cells in the Cadence environment with *spectre*.

We aimed at obtaining the dependency between the delay t_D and the minimum nominal capacity $C_{A,min}$ that can be detected. From that, the delay t_D shall be determined.

The dependency between t_D and $C_{A,min}$ is determined by simulating a system as shown in Fig. 3. For reasons of simplicity, the control logic is replaced by manually driving the sel input, while the evaluation logic is implemented in software that uses the *spectre* analog waveforms of Q as input data. Due to the symmetry of the RS latch, it is sufficient to simulate probing the line that is connected to the L2 input of the LAPD. We assume probe capacitance values of $C_A \in \{0\,fF, 5\,fF, 10\,fF, \cdots, 60\,fF\}$. The LAPD itself is implemented according to Fig. 4, but allows keeping the delay t_D variable. As an observation window, we chose values between 10 ps and 300 ps. Considering the line capacitance C_L, we assumed a value of 100 fF.

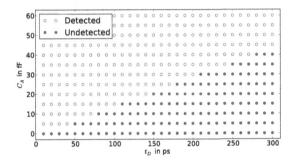

Fig. 11. Nominal LAPD detection coverage

Table 1. Nominal minimum detected C_A depending on t_D

t_D in ps	$C_{A,min}$ in fF	t_D in ps	$C_{A,min}$ in fF
10	5	160	25
20	5	170	25
30	5	180	30
40	5	190	30
50	10	200	30
60	10	210	35
70	10	220	35
80	15	230	35
90	15	240	35
100	15	250	40
110	20	260	40
120	20	270	40
130	20	280	45
140	20	290	45
150	25	300	45

Table 1 shows the nominal values of $C_{A,min}$ in dependency of the delay t_D. A graphical representation of the nominal detection coverage of probe attachments is shown in Fig. 11. The x axis points out the configured delay t_D of the delay gate, while the y axis denotes the capacitance C_A of the attached probe. Blue circles represent undetected capacitive loads, which means that the detector output still behaves as normal, while white circles denote the successful detection of a probe attachment – on a technical level, this means that the LAPD outputs Q and $\overline{\text{Q}}$ stop alternating and keep at a constant value. From this figure, 10 fF can be spotted as the minimal value of C_A to be detected. The microprobe with the smallest input capacitance we found on the market [12] has an input capacitance value of at least 20 fF and therefore could be detected by the LAPD.

6   Conclusion

In this paper, we present the concept of a Low Area Probing Detector (LAPD), a new approach to detect microprobing on symmetric lines such as buses. It is the first detector measuring capacitances to detect tampering without relying on analog circuitry. This avoids large analog components, which makes the area required for the LAPD circuitry lower than for any other delay-based probe detection scheme.

Our nominal simulations indicate that probes with parasitic capacitances in the range of 20 fF can be detected. The scheme can be used to enhance the security of low-cost security controllers, as found on cheap mass market products such as SIM cards, but it is also possible to apply its concepts to improve the security of – already well-protected – high end security controllers, as they are found in Pay TV smart cards, for example.

As the LAPD increases the complexity for a successful bus attack, adversaries continue to look for other attack vectors. For an effective and comprehensive protection of security chips, other components need to be protected as well – this includes, for example, memory controllers, address decoders, control logic and arithmetic-logic units (ALUs), but also the signalling mechanisms of attack detectors themselves. Therefore, analyzing other microprobing attack targets and providing appropiate protection mechanisms appears as an important field for future work. Another important piece of future work are monte-carlo simulations to evaluate the reliability of the LAPD.

Acknowledgements. This work was partly funded by the Spanish research program TEC2010-18384 as well as by the German Federal Ministry of Education and Research (BMBF) in the project SIBASE through grant number 01S13020A.

References

1. Anderson, R., Bond, M., Clulow, J., Skorobogatov, S.: Cryptographic processors-a survey. Proc. IEEE **94**(2), 357–369 (2006)
2. Balankutty, A., Chih, T.C., Chen, C.Y., Kinget, P.: Mismatch characterization of ring oscillators. In: Custom Integrated Circuits Conference, CICC '07, pp. 515–518. IEEE (2007)

3. Bowman, K.A., Austin, B.L., Eble, J.C., Tang, X., Meindl, J.D.: A physical alpha-power law MOSFET model. In: Proceedings of the 1999 International Symposium on Low Power Electronics and Design, ISLPED '99, pp. 218–222. ACM, New York (1999). http://doi.acm.org/10.1145/313817.313930

4. Buchmüler, H.U.: Security Target M7820 A11 and M11, August 2012. http://www.commoncriteriaportal.org/files/epfiles/0829b_pdf.pdf. Accessed 16 Jan 2014

5. Common Criteria for Information Technology Security Evaluation, Part 3: Security assurance components (2012). https://www.niap-ccevs.org/Documents_and_Guidance/cc_docs.cfm. Accessed 25 Aug 2013

6. Helfmeier, C., Nedospasov, D., Tarnovsky, C., Krissler, J., Boit, C., Seifert, J.P.: Breaking and entering through the silicon. In: Proceedings of the 2013 ACM SIGSAC Conference on Computer and Communications Security, CCS '13, pp. 733–744. ACM, New York (2013). http://doi.acm.org/10.1145/2508859.2516717

7. Kömmerling, O., Kuhn, M.G.: Design principles for tamper-resistant smartcard processors. In: Proceedings of the USENIX Workshop on Smartcard Technology on USENIX Workshop on Smartcard Technology, WOST'99, p. 2. USENIX Association, Berkeley (1999). http://dl.acm.org/citation.cfm?id=1267115.1267117

8. Krämer, J., Nedospasov, D., Schlösser, A., Seifert, J.-P.: Differential photonic emission analysis. In: Prouff, E. (ed.) COSADE 2013. LNCS, vol. 7864, pp. 1–16. Springer, Heidelberg (2013)

9. Ling, M., Wu, L., Li, X., Zhang, X., Hou, J., Wang, Y.: Design of monitor and protect circuits against FIB attack on chip security. In: 2012 Eighth International Conference on Computational Intelligence and Security (CIS), pp. 530–533 (2012)

10. Maier, P., Nohl, K.: Low-Cost Chip Microprobing. 29th Chaos Communication Congress (29C3), November 2012. http://events.ccc.de/congress/2012/Fahrplan/attachments/2247_29C3-Dexter_Nohl-Low_Cost_Chip_Microprobing.pdf. Accessed 16 Jan 2014

11. Manich, S., Wamser, M.S., Sigl, G.: Detection of probing attempts in secure ICs. In: Hardware-Oriented Security and Trust (HOST), pp. 134–139 (2012)

12. Picoprobe Model 18C & Picoprobe Model 19C. Datasheet. http://www.ggb.com/PdfIndex_files/mod18c.pdf. Accessed 16 Jan 2014

13. Sakurai, T., Newton, A.R.: Alpha-power law MOSFET model and its applications to CMOS inverter delay and other formulas. IEEE J. Solid-State Circuits **25**(2), 584–594 (1990)

14. Tarnovsky, C.: Deconstructing a 'Secure' Processor. Blackhat DC (2012)

Non-Linear Collision Analysis

Xin Ye[(⊠)], Cong Chen, and Thomas Eisenbarth

Worcester Polytechnic Institute, Worcester, MA, USA
{xye,cchen,teisenbarth}@wpi.edu

Abstract. As an unsolved issue for embedded crypto solutions, side channel attacks are challenging the security of the Internet of things. Due to the advancement of chip technology, the nature of side channel leakage becomes hard to characterize with a fixed leakage model. In this work, a new non-linear collision attack is proposed in the pursuit of the side channel distinguishers with minimal assumption of leakage behavior. The attack relies on a weaker assumption than classical DPA: it does not require a specific leakage model. The mechanism of collision generation enables independent recovery of partial keys so that for the first time the collision attack can be fairly compared with other standard side channel distinguishers. The efficiency of this attack has been verified by experiments on an unprotected microcontroller implementation of AES. Its immunity to modeling errors is confirmed through simulation of a broad range of leakage functions.

1 Motivation

Side channel attacks (SCA) such as Power and EM analysis remain as a major concern for embedded cryptographic systems. The mostly wireless connection of devices and appliances makes security and hence reliable embedded crypto engines a necessity for the entire Internet of things. Only affordable countermeasures and robust evaluation methods can assure a widespread protection against SCA. In general, SCA achieves its key recovery objective through exploring the data dependency between side channel observables and the internal state or the system. Such data dependency has usually been described with a particular leakage model by the classical Differential Power Analysis (DPA) [8] and Correlation Power Analysis (CPA) [4]. Models range from Hamming weight/distance models to more complicated toggle count models depending on the a-priori knowledge about the implementation. Consequently, the error from leakage modeling assumption or the lack of detailed a-priori knowledge can aggravate or even prevent successful attacks. Recent studies [6,9,13] call for generic distinguishers that do not rely on a-priori knowledge about the implementation and have minimum assumption on the leakage distribution. Although non-parametric statistic methods such as Mutual Information Analysis [7] and Kolmogorov-Smirnov test [20] are well suited to estimate the unknown leakage behavior, the cost is a huge loss of efficiency: many more measurements are needed for probability density estimation or empirical distribution comparison. Whitnall et. al. showed in [21]

© Springer International Publishing Switzerland 2014
N. Saxena and A.-R. Sadeghi (Eds.): RFIDSec 2014, LNCS 8651, pp. 198–214, 2014.
DOI: 10.1007/978-3-319-13066-8_13

that generic univariate attacks with a leakage model exist only for a very limited selection of target functions. It is indicated that profiled attacks such as template attacks [5] and stochastic modeling attacks [14] are necessary for security evaluation. Although those attacks achieve great efficiency, the requirement of the profiling stage is sometimes demanding except for evaluating labs.

An alternative side channel strategy are *side channel collision attacks* [16] where the adversary recovers the key with the combined benefit from the algebraic property and the leakage similarity of internal collisions. Another attractive feature of collisions is the *self-templating* property: instead of estimating or assuming a leakage model, leakages observed from different queries are directly compared. In other words, side channel collision attacks do not even require a leakage model. This satisfies the need of generic side channel distinguishers that assume as little about the leakage function as possible.

Contribution. In this work we propose a new side channel collision attack to recover secret information without prefixing a leakage model or estimating leakage distributions. The attack derives side channel collisions between internal states that do not have a simple linear relationship. The approach allows us to collide the same partial state at two different stages, e.g. the input and output of an S-Box, and hence retrieve the secret information by exploiting the bivariate leakage samples reflecting the two stages. Results are verified experimentally and through simulation. Of independent importance is the quantitative analysis of the sensitivity of collision attacks to leakage mismatch in the colliding states. The proposed attack is efficient, immune to leakage modeling errors and robust against high inhomogeneity of the leakage behavior of non-linear collisions.

The rest of the paper is organized as follows: After a review of related prior work in collision attacks in Sect. 2 we explain in Sect. 3 how to exploit non-linear collisions for more efficient key recovery. Section 4 details on experiments as well as simulations and highlights the applicability and convenience of non-linear collision attacks.

2   Background

We briefly revisit the existing proposals in side channel collision attacks.

2.1   Collision Attack

Side channel collision attacks were introduced in [16] against DES and extended in [15] against AES. Works of [1–3, 22] further improved the collision attacks for different scenarios. They have a common definition of collisions being the same internal state computed from different inputs. A collision tells the adversary that targeted key parts satisfy certain algebraic equalities which are employed to reduce the space of valid key hypotheses. Collision attacks take advantage of both side channel leakage and the algebraic property of the cipher and hence can recover the key with fewer traces. However, such benefit stands on two prereq-uisites: (1) the adversary should have chosen plaintext capability as mentioned in [15]; (2) the adversary can detect the occurrence of collision with as low proba-bility of false positive decision as possible. This is because the algebraic property can be used only after a collision is successfully detected and it is easy to under-stand that using a wrongly detected collision yields misuse of invalid algebraic property and hence risks missing the correct key.

2.2 Linear Correlation Collision Attack

In [11], an interesting algorithm has been proposed to attack AES using corre-lation enhanced linear collision. It is different from the classical collision attack since it does not use collision *detection* to reduce the total number of valid key hypotheses. In fact, it works more like classical DPA/CPA style attacks that firstly make hypothesis and then use distinguisher to determine the correct key that actually *generates* collisions. But unlike classical DPA/CPA, the lin-ear correlation collision attack (LCCA) does not recover each subkey directly, but instead it tests hypothesis of the difference between subkeys as shown in Fig. 1(a). More specifically, if the adversary aims at recovering the difference $\Delta = k_a \oplus k_b$ between subkey k_a and k_b at byte a and b, she needs to test all possible hypotheses δ of the subkey difference. For each hypothesis δ, the adversary computes the correlation $\rho(M_a^X, M_b^{X \oplus \delta})$ between the averaged leak-age trace M_a^X of the byte-a-plaintext $X_a = X$ and the averaged leakage trace $M_b^{X \oplus \delta}$ of the byte-b-plaintext $X_b = X \oplus \delta$. Upon completion of all hypotheses, the adversary makes the decision of the hypothesis that gives highest correlation, i.e. $\delta^* = \text{argmax}_\delta \{\rho(M_a^X, M_b^{X \oplus \delta})\}$. The attack works because when testing the correct hypothesis $\delta = \Delta = k_a \oplus k_b$, the Sbox outputs of the two bytes cause collisions as seen from below.

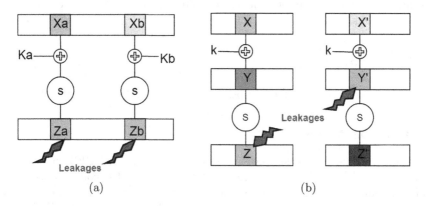

(a)   (b)

Fig. 1. Simplified schematic for linear correlation collision attack (LCCA) (a) vs non-linear collision attack (NLCA) (b). While LCCA exploits linear collision of two *different* state bytes at the same stage in the cipher round, NLCA can exploit the non-linear collision of the *same* state byte at two different stages of the cipher round.

$$X_a \oplus X_b = X \oplus X \oplus \delta = \Delta = k_a \oplus k_b$$
$$\Longleftrightarrow X_a \oplus k_a = X_b \oplus k_b$$
$$\Longleftrightarrow S(X_a \oplus k_a) = S(X_b \oplus k_b)$$

Therefore the averaged leakage traces M_a^X and $M_b^{X \oplus \Delta}$ gives high correlation. If a wrong hypothesis $\delta \neq \Delta$ is assumed, the above equalities do not hold any more, neither have collisions be generated. Therefore a wrong hypothesis results in low correlation.

3 Non-Linear Collision Attack

Non-linear collisions take advantage of the fact that processing two internal states of the same value yields similar leakage behavior—especially for software implementations. The concept of exploitable collisions is extended so that they occur for different internal states, even if processed under different operations. We first explain the idea of generating non-linear collisions and then detail how to exploit them and use them to build a side channel distinguisher called Non-Linear Collision Attack (NLCA). Its validity, complexity and relation to other side channel attacks are also discussed.

3.1 Existence of Non-Linear Collisions

Let two internal states of the target implementation be denoted by Y and Z for the NLCA. The first state $Y = f_k(X)$ is the output of a function of the plaintext X with the secret key k. The keyed function f_k is part of the crypto algorithm that is executed in the target device. For notational convenience, we use $f_k^{-1}(Y)$ to denote the set of all pre-images of plaintexts that lead to the internal state Y. The second state $Z = \phi(Y)$ is mapped through an intermediate non-linear function ϕ from the predecessor state Y. It is clear that the state Z is a functional composition output, represented as $Z = \phi \circ f_k(X)$. Note that both of Y and Z should produce observable side channel leakage to be exploitable by the side channel adversary. We use L_Y and L_Z to denote the observed leakages for processing the two respective states Y and Z.

The goal of NLCA is to generate collisions between state Y and state Z and to exploit them by detecting the correlated leakage behavior. That is, for a given plaintext X, we want to find another X' such that the induced internal states Y, Y', Z, Z' satisfy the cross-state collision of either $Y' = Z$ or $Z' = Y$. Without loss of generality, we explore the first type $Y' = Z$, i.e.

$$f_k(X') = \phi \circ f_k(X) \tag{1}$$

Clearly, if X' is chosen as one of the pre-images of $\phi \circ f_k(X)$, then it is a solution to Eq. (1). In other words, $X' \in f_k^{-1}(\phi \circ f_k(X))$ implies that the internal state $Y' = f_k(X')$ is guaranteed to be colliding with the internal state $Z = \phi \circ f_k(X)$. Hence the observed leakage behavior of L_Z and $L_{Y'}$ can be expected to be very similar.

3.2   Building a Non-linear Collision Attack

We now show how this idea can be used and converted to a side channel attack on AES. The described approach can be easily adjusted to target many other block ciphers. We choose the non-linear operation ϕ as the first round[1] SubBytes. More precisely, we only consider ϕ as a single Sbox $S\left(\cdot\right)$ in the following context. The states Y and Z are then the input and output of the same Sbox respectively. The function f_k is the initial key addition (xor) operation. Figure 1(b) visualizes the idea of NLCA in this setting. The cross state collision in Eq. (1) becomes $X' \oplus k = S\left(X \oplus k\right)$ and clearly it has a unique solution

$$X' = k \oplus S\left(X \oplus k\right) \tag{2}$$

In other words, if the AES encryption algorithm is executed with plaintexts X and X' computed from Eq. (2), the produced side channel leakages $L_{Y'}$ and L_Z (with $Y' = X' \oplus k$ and $Z = S\left(X \oplus k\right)$) will be closely correlated. The adversary, however, does not know the subkey k and therefore cannot directly plug it into the equation and find such X'. Nevertheless, all possible subkey hypotheses can be checked to find the correct subkey k. Algorithm 1 shows the detailed procedure for the attack on AES. Basically, the adversary makes a total of 256 subkey hypotheses $g \in \{0,1\}^8$. For each hypothesis g, she computes $X'_g = g \oplus S\left(X \oplus g\right)$ for all possible plaintext bytes X. The resulting list of plaintext pairs X and X'_g is assumed to generate cross-state collisions $Z = Y'_g$, under this hypothesis g. The respective average leakage signals $L_Z, L_{Y'_g}$ are stored in vectors α, β_g. The Pearson correlation coefficient $\rho(\alpha, \beta_g)$ between them is finally computed for testing the subkey hypothesis g. After testing all subkey hypotheses, the adversary picks the subkey hypothesis k^* that yields the highest correlation coefficient and determines it as the correct subkey k, i.e. $k^* = \text{argmax}_g \{\rho(\alpha, \beta_g)\}$.

Validity. If the hypothesis is correct, i.e. $g = k$, the computed $X'_g = X'_k$ has the same format as in Eq. (2). It follows that

$$X'_g = g \oplus S(X \oplus g) = k \oplus S(X \oplus k)$$
$$\Longleftrightarrow X'_g \oplus k = S\left(X \oplus k\right)$$
$$\Longleftrightarrow Y'_g = Z$$

Hence the respective mean signals α, β_g of the observed leakage should be similar and have high correlation. However if the hypothesis is wrong, i.e. $g \neq k$, then the above equations do not hold anymore. Hence Y'_g does not collide with Z and their respective leakage should only give low correlation.

Adaptable with Higher Order Statistical Moments. Generic distinguisher has low assumption on the leakage distribution. In certain scenario, leakage cannot be captured with the first order statistical moment (empirical mean) but

---

[1] It can easily be translated to last round SubBytes with known ciphertexts.

Algorithm 1. Non-Linear Collision Attack on AES

Input: Number of Traces q, plaintext-byte values $X = [X_1, ..., X_q]$ Leakages $L_Y = [L_{Y,1}, ..., L_{Y,q}]$ and $L_Z = [L_{Z,1}, ..., L_{Z,q}]$
Output: Subkey Decision k^*
 1: **for** x = 0 to 255 **do**
 2:      $U_x = \{i \mid X_i = x, i \in [1:q]\}$ ▷ the set of indices where plaintext is x
 3:      $\alpha[x] = \text{avg}\{L_{Z,i} \mid i \in U_x\}$ ▷ mean leakage for processing Z
 4:      $\gamma[x] = \text{avg}\{L_{Y,i} \mid i \in U_x\}$ ▷ mean leakage for processing Y
 5: **end for**
 6: **for** g = 0 to 255 **do**
 7:      **for** x = 0 to 255 **do**
 8:          $x'_g = g \oplus S(x \oplus g)$ ▷ x and x'_g cause hypothetical collision $z = y'_g$
 9:          $\beta_g[x] = \gamma[x'_g]$ ▷ get the leakage for processing Y'_g
10:      **end for**
11:      $R[g] = \rho(\alpha, \beta_g)$ ▷ Pearson correlation coefficient
12: **end for**
13: $k^* = \text{argmax}_g \{R[g]\}$
14: **return** k^*

---

is able to be detected through higher order moments (e.g. empirical variance, skewness, etc.) as pointed out by [10]. The proposed non-linear collision attack can easily be extended to capture such hidden leakages. The adjustment is on line 3 of Algorithm 1. The original vector α is used to precompute the mean signal (i.e. 1st order moment) of leakage L_Z. That is

$$\alpha[x] = \text{avg}\{L_{Z,i} \mid i \in U_x\} = \frac{1}{|U_x|} \sum_{i \in U_x} L_{Z,i}$$

with U_x defined in line 2 of the algorithm. The d-th order moment $_d\alpha$ of leakage L_Z can also be precomputed for any integer $d > 1$

$$_d\alpha[x] = \frac{1}{|U_x|} \sum_{i \in U_x} (L_{Z,i} - \alpha[x])^d$$

Similarly $_d\gamma$ can be computed on line 4 to store the d-th order moment of leakage L_Y. Finally, one can finish the changes by replacing the first order moment terms α, β_g in line 9 and 11 with d-th order $_d\alpha, _d\beta_g$ respectively. The adjusted algorithm can then distinguish subkey hypothesis using higher order statistical moments. A detailed description of the methods as well as the benefits can be found in [10].

3.3   Comparison with Other SCA

In the following we explore possible benefits and drawbacks of NLCA when compared to other attacks.

Comparing NLCA with DPA, CPA. The big difference between NLCA and DPA, CPA lies in the fact that NLCA does not rely on a particular leakage model, e.g. Hamming weight model. DPA and CPA correlate leakage sample to the leakage model of hypothesis, while NLCA make correlation between leakage samples. In fact, NLCA only requires the minimal assumption that processing the same internal state results in similar leakage behavior. If the leakage behavior is precisely captured by the leakage model assumed in the DPA and CPA, NLCA might not show advantage. However, if the leakage model deviates from the physical observables, the two classical methods are more likely to fail while the NLCA is still robust. More details can be found in Sect. 4.2.

On the negative side, NLCA requires identifying the bivariate leakage samples for processing states Y and Z respectively, prior to the attack. With a known implementation this is not an issue. As $Z = S(Y)$ is processed after Y with a fixed offset of clock cycles, finding the two critical time samples is equivalent to locating the first sample for L_Y and adding the offset to get the second sample for L_Z. For unknown implementations the location and offsets have to be guessed. This can be easy, e.g. if it is highly likely that the non-linear function is implemented as a table-lookup, resulting in an offset of a few clock cycles. But this might not always be the case.

Comparing NLCA with Collision Attacks. The earlier works of side channel collision attacks [1–3,15,16,22] define collisions as the same value of one target state from different inputs. The NLCA extends the definition such that collision occurs on two different targets Y and Z of the same value. The second difference is that the previous works belong to the chosen plaintext attacks since only plaintexts in certain pattern can make sure to cause collisions. The NLCA is not a chosen plaintext attack. It works with traces associated with random plaintext inputs and hence belongs to the known plaintext attacks. It sorts traces into different bins U_x and uses all of them. The last but not the least difference is that previous works rely on successfully *detecting* the collisions from traces before making use of their algebraic property to shrink the space of key hypotheses. The NLCA works in a CPA manner that it tests different subkey hypotheses and ensures that only the correct hypothesis *generates* collisions – not just a few collisions, but all the resulting input pairs x, x' cause collisions. In other words, previous works exploit leakage similarity of collisions prior to the use of its algebraic property, while the order reverses for NLCA. The benefit is to avoid the false acceptance of collision detection and hence to reduce the risk of misuse of algebraic property in earlier proposals.

Comparing NLCA with the Linear Correlation Collision Attack. The NLCA and LCCA have one common feature that they do not require a leakage model. This is because both are computing the correlation amongst leakage samples rather than comparing leakage samples to model values. Their complexity is also at the same level. For LCCA, there are totally 15 independent subkey differences amongst the 16 bytes in AES. It means that there is a remaining 8 bit key entropy even after disclosing all subkey differences. Therefore, the total complexity for recovering a full AES key using LCCA is 15×2^8 recoveries of subkey relations plus 2^8 full key verification. While on the other side, the NLCA recovers all subkeys independently. Its total complexity is 16×2^8 in subkey recoveries. Yet there are critical differences between the two. Firstly, the LCCA is categorized by [18] as non-standard side channel attack because it hypothesizes on relation between two subkeys rather than a subkey itself. While NLCA follows a more straightforward divide-and-conquer approach. Secondly, the collision exploited in the LCCA reveals the *homogeneity* of leakage behavior under the *same* operations. More specifically, both states Z_a and Z_b are the output of Sbox as seen from Fig. 1(a). Hence they are derived from the same routine in the embedded system. For example, both are loaded from program memory into the state registers. The collisions generated from the correct hypothesis results in homogeneous leakage that should have high magnitude of correlation, which is shown in [11]. The NLCA, however, explores the *similarity* of leakage behavior caused by *different* operations. As can be seen from Fig. 1(b) that Y' is the output of key xor and Z is the output of Sbox. It means they are processed with different instructions. For instance, Y' is xored or moved to a register and Z is loaded from program memory onto a register. Such operational difference results in leakages of non-linear collisions behaving similarly but not homogeneously. Therefore, it is not surprising that the level of correlation obtained from NLCA is lower than from LCCA. However, especially in the case of software implementations, it can be assumed that locating the second colliding state is easier for NLCA, as both leakages are more likely to occur close to each other.

Some Limitations. The non-reliance of leakage model does not come for free. One prerequisite of the non-linear collision attack is the existence of the bivariate leakages: it is satisfied in the situation of software implementation but not in the hardwares. This restricts the applicability of the NLCA. In addition, it is not clear whether the NLCA can be extended such that it can also overcome countermeasures such as masking schemes.

4 Experiments

Three different groups of experiments are described in the following. The first group is the NLCA attack performed on power measurements of an 8-bit microcontroller executing AES-128. It also compares the performance of NLCA and CPA on the real measurements. The second group discusses situations where NLCA has significant advantage over CPA. The experiments are performed on simulated leakage traces for well-chosen leakage models. The third group focuses on the impact of the similar but inhomogeneous leakage behavior caused by exploiting leakages at different stages of a round.

4.1   Experiments on Smart Card Power Measurements

We first run the proposed NLCA using real measurements of the power consumption of an 8-bit AVR microcontroller, i.e. the ATXMEGA 256A3B processor. The microcontroller runs the Rjindael Furious [12]– a popular and efficient software implementation of AES-128 for AVR. A Tektronix digital sampling oscilloscope is used to measure power leakage traces. The sampling rate is set to 200M Samples per second which provides 100 sampling points per clock cycle. The Rjindael Furious implements the SubBytes operation on each byte as an S-box look up table (LUT). It firstly takes 1 clock cycle to move the input Y of Sbox into a particular register for relative addressing the LUT, then uses 3 cycles to load the output Z of Sbox from program memory into another register. It is therefore expected that there is an offset of 3 clock cycles (approximately 300 time points) between processing input state Y and the output state Z of Sbox.

Using Algorithm 1, we test all 256 subkey hypotheses over all time samples. That is, testing at time sample t refers to assuming L_Y occurring at sample t and L_Z occurs at sample $t + 300$. As can be seen from Fig. 2, the correct subkey hypothesis (red) stands out remarkably from wrong hypotheses (gray) at the time sample around 6500, which means Y is processed around that time instance and Z around 6800. More importantly, it is observed that only the correct hypothesis results in a distinguishable correlation coefficient. This verifies the validity of the non-linear collision attack. It also indicates that leakages of collisions at different states under different instructions also behave similarly.

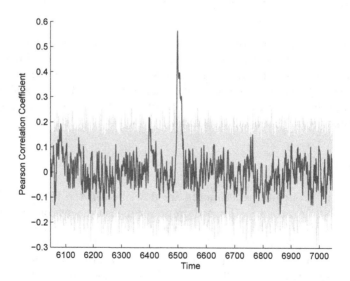

Fig. 2. Pearson correlation coefficient (y-axis) computed from non-linear collision attack over all time samples (x-axis). 1000 traces have been used in the experiments. Gray curves indicate correlation for the wrong subkey hypotheses; red (dark) represents the correct hypothesis (Color figure online).

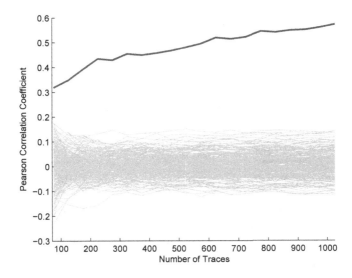

Fig. 3. Pearson correlation coefficient (y-axis) computed for the non-linear collision attack over the number of utilized leakage measurements (x-axis). NLCA is performed only over the most remarkable time sample disclosed in Fig. 2. Gray curves represent wrong subkey hypotheses and the red (dark) curve represents the correct hypothesis (Color figure online).

Next, the number of traces needed for a successful NLCA is explored. The correlation experiment is repeated on the discovered critical time point, as visualized in Fig. 2, using 75 to 1000 traces. The observed trend is depicted in Fig. 3. The correct hypothesis (red/dark) always features a higher correlation than the wrong ones (gray). The correlation computed from the correct subkey increases with the number of used traces, and seems not to have reached the limit with 1000 used traces. The counterparts from the wrong hypotheses, however, are bounded from -0.2 to 0.2. It is clear that the distinguishability in NLCA becomes increasingly remarkable with more traces. Note that the performance of NLCA using fewer traces is not covered in the plot. One might be interested in the performance of NLCA when, for example, only 20 or traces are available. However, NLCA requires finding a sequence of pairs (X, X') such that the resulted Y' and Z collide. With limited availability of leakage traces, it is very likely that intermediate states cannot be paired with the colliding counterpart. In other words, too few pairs or even no pairs of $L_{Y'}$ and L_Z can be used for computing correlation, which is easily biased or even undefined.

Next, the performance of NLCA and correlation based DPA (CPA) are compared on the same measurement setup. The attacks use the same set of 500 leakage measurements. The NLCA is tested on the critical time point discovered in Fig. 2. The CPA assumes the Hamming weight leakage model of the output Sbox and it is therefore only performed on the most relevant time point for looking up the output state Z of the Sbox. As can be seen from Figs. 4(a) and

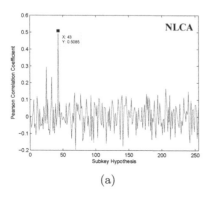
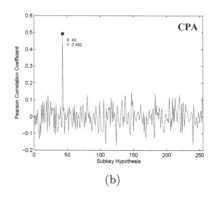

(a)   (b)

Fig. 4. Pearson correlation coefficient (y-axis) for all subkey hypotheses (x-axis) computed from NLCA (a) and from classical CPA (b). The latter assumes Hamming weight model of the Sbox output. The two attacks use the same set of 500 traces, applied to the most related time samples disclosed in Fig. 2. The correct subkey 43 gives highest correlation in both scenarios.

(b), both NLCA and CPA work well in this setting, outputting the correct subkey 43 with the highest correlation coefficient. It is hard to determine which attack performs better simply from the two plots. The NLCA gives the correlation for the correct subkey a little higher than the CPA. But the level of correlation for wrong hypotheses in NLCA (roughly between -0.2 to 0.2) is also higher than the CPA (roughly between -0.15 to 0.15). Nevertheless, the CPA assumes the Hamming weight leakage model. The experiment only indicates that the behavior of leakage obtained from the target microcontroller is well captured by the leakage model in CPA. In general, if the leakage does not behave according to the assumed leakage model, CPA might fail due to the modeling error. This effect is studied in greater detail in the following simulations.

4.2 Experiments on Simulations: Immunity to Modeling Errors

In this section, we run experiments to test the robustness of the proposed NLCA under different simulations of the leakage function. We show situations where the NLCA has significant advantage over the CPA and Mutual Information Analysis (MIA).

Adversarial Model. We consider four non-profiling adversaries: the classical CPA, the univariate MIA (UMIA), the multivariate MIA (MMIA), and our NLCA. The univariate target of CPA and UMIA is the output of Sbox. While for the MMIA and NLCA the targets are both the input and the output of Sbox. The CPA and the two mutual information based distinguishers all assume Hamming weight leakage model[2]. All probability densities for UMIA and MMIA

---

[2] As pointed out in [19], the near generic 7LSB power model for AES does not perform well for the MIA and it even fails catastrophically in strong signal setting.

are estimated through the histogram method using 9 bins. The NLCA does not assume any power model.

Leakage Simulation Design. We follow the design proposed in [19] of three situations of simulation—the optimistic, the realistic and the challenging scenario. The optimistic scenario assumes the leakage behaves proportionally to the Hamming weight of the state value. I.e.

$$\lambda^{op}(Z) = \text{HW}(Z) + \epsilon$$

where $\epsilon \sim \mathcal{N}(0, \sigma^2)$ is the additive white Gaussian noise that has variance σ^2. The realistic scenario assumes an unevenly weighted Hamming weight model. That is, the least significant bit (LSB) of the intermediate data has a relative weight of 10 while all the other bits have weight of 1. So the leakage function is expressed as

$$\lambda^{re}(Z) = \text{HW}(Z >> 1) + 10\text{LSB}(Z) + \epsilon$$

The third case, i.e. the challenging scenario, assumes a non-linear leakage function, and it is instantiated as Sbox mapping composition with the Hamming weight function. That is when the state Z is processed, the leakage function evaluated at Z is

$$\lambda^{ch}(Z) = \text{HW}(S(Z)) + \epsilon$$

In other words, processing state Z gives a leakage of the Hamming weight of the Sbox output of Z. It is clear to see that the modeling bias for CPA, UMIA and MMIA become increasingly severe in the three simulation scenarios.

Performance Comparison. We use the first order success rate and the guessing entropy [17] to evaluate the subkey recovery performance of the four distinguishers as shown in Fig. 5. All metrics are derived empirically from 1000 independent experiments. In each experiment, the two correlation based distinguishers i.e. CPA and NLCA are fed with 256 simulated traces while the two mutual information based adversaries use 2560 traces because of the demand of pdf estimation.

It can be seen that only NLCA and MMIA survived from all three simulation scenarios: both their first order success rate and guessing entropy converge to 1. The CPA and UMIA are efficient when the Hamming weight model captures the simulated leakage functions very well. However, they become increasingly impacted by the leakage modeling errors. They succeed in the realistic scenario at a much higher SNR and remain as failure in the challenging scenario no matter how SNR varies. Interestingly, in the challenging situation, the guessing entropy of CPA and UMIA grow much higher than 128 – the quantity for a random guess without using side channel leakages– even if provided with strong signal. It indicates that the impact of false leakage model can be as catastrophic as misleading the adversary.

A first glance at the behavior of the two remaining distinguishers MMIA and NLCA appears to tell that former has some advantage over the latter. But

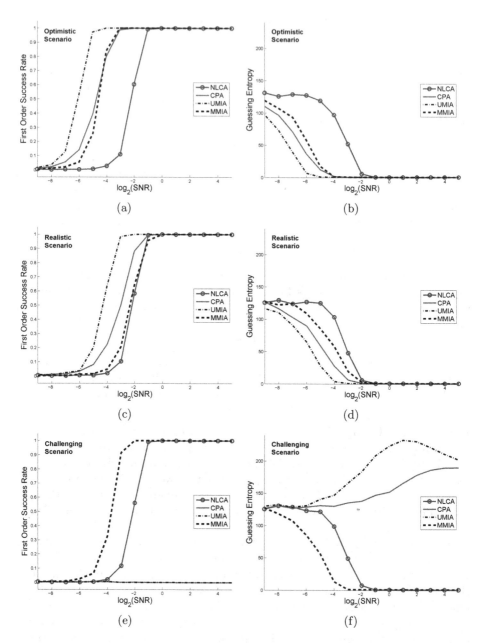

Fig. 5. Performance comparison of NLCA, CPA, UMIA and MMIA using first order success rate (left) and guessing entropy (right) under three leakage function assumptions: optimistic (upper), realistic (middle), and challenging (lower). Experiments are simulated at different Signal-To-Noise ratios (x-axis). Leakage modeling error has negligible impact on NLCA, slight but noticeable impact on MMIA and severe impact on CPA and UMIA.

one should consider that firstly the MMIA requires 10 folds of simulated traces than the NLCA because of the need of pdf estimation. Secondly, the behavior of MMIA at optimistic and challenging situations are much more similar, while at the realistic scenario it actually becomes worse. Such observation shows that the leakage modeling error still have some impact on its performance, just not in the same way as one could expected. On the contrary, the NLCA remains an unchanged pattern in all the three cases. Therefore, NLCA is robust with respect to different leakage functions and is immune to leakage modeling errors.

4.3   Impact of the Inhomogeneity of Leakages

As mentioned in Sect. 3.3, processing Y with a move instruction and Z with a load instruction results similar but not homogeneous leakage behavior even if the values of the two states collide. Abstractly, it can be viewed as the leakage functions over the state Y domain and state Z domain are different. The impact of the inhomogeneity of the bivariate leakage needs to be investigated. The last group of experiments shows the robustness of non-linear collision attacks against different levels of inhomogeneity in the leakage. We first define the homogeneity coefficient τ as the number of bits that both states Y and Z are leaking in the same manner. It induces the following leakage functions.

$$\lambda_\tau (Y) = \lambda (Y_L \| Y_R) = \lambda (U) + \lambda (Y_R) \tag{3}$$

The Y_R represents, for example, the rightmost τ bits of state Y, which are assumed to be leaking normally (i.e. with the same constant weight). The Y_L is respectively the remaining bits of Y that are assumed to be leaking in a different way. More precisely, in Eq. (3), the Y_L is independent[3] of the leakage function, and it is replaced by an independently generated random $8 - \tau$ bit value U, which then generates leakage. A corresponding leakage function is defined for state Z such that $\lambda_\tau(Z) = \lambda (V) + \lambda (Z_R)$ with a different random V. It is easy to see that when Y' collides with Z in the NLCA, the part Y_R' is the same as Z_R leading to $\lambda (Y_R') = \lambda (Z_R)$ while $\lambda (U) \neq \lambda (V)$. In other words, the collisions are detected only from the common τ bits that are leaking in the same way. The remaining bits contribute only as noise. The lower the homogeneous coefficient τ, the more the leakages between the two leaking states will deviate from one another.

In our experiments the leakage function λ is instantiated with the Hamming weight function. In the τ homogeneous setting, this means that the leakage function $\lambda_\tau (Y) = \mathrm{HW} (U) + \mathrm{HW} (Y_R)$ generates Hamming weight of τ bits Y_R as signal, and the remaining random $8 - \tau$ bits U give binomially distributed noise. The equivalent is true for Z. A total of 400 independent experiments is performed. Each experiment uses 256 simulated traces generated from the above defined leakage functions. The result in Table 1 shows that for homogeneity coefficient $\tau \geq 3$, the NLCA gives 100 % success rate even for a single subkey trial. When $\tau = 1, 2$

---

[3] It can also be considered that Y_L is mapped non-linearly to U before generating leakages. This is similar to the challenging scenario discussed in Sect. 4.2.

Table 1. The robustness of NLCA against various levels of homogeneity of leakage behavior for the two sensitive states.

	Homo. Coef. $\tau = 0$	Homo. Coef. $\tau = 1$	Homo. Coef. $\tau = 2$	Homo. Coef. $\tau = 3$ to 8
1st order success rate	0.3 %	23.0 %	89.3 %	100.0 %
4th order success rate	1.5 %	43.0 %	97.8 %	100.0 %
Guessing entropy	126.13	19.18	1.35	1.00

which are the fairly low level of homogeneity, the adversary can still achieve success rates more than 40 % and more than 95 % respectively by making 4 trials. The last line of the table uses the security description Guessing Entropy defined in [17] that quantifies the expected number of subkey guesses until finding the correct subkey. It is not surprising to see that 2 trials can guarantee the adversary finding the correct subkey when $\tau \geq 2$. Even at the lowest homogeneity level, it can still be achieved with 20 trials. To sum up, the NLCA shows very strong robustness against inhomogeneity of leakages for the two states. This result is not restricted to NLCA and apply in the same way to inhomogeneity of leakages in LCCA.

5   Conclusion

This work proposes the non-linear collision attack as another variety of collision-based side channel attacks. The attack exploits leakages of collisions of different states and does not rely on accurate leakage modeling. Experimental results show that the leakage behavior for different states are similar enough to be exploited by NLCA especially in the software implementation situations. It also shows that inhomogeneous leakages generated by different operations have only low impact on the performance of the proposed attack.

Acknowledgments. This material is based upon work supported by the National Science Foundation under Grant No. #1261399 and Grant No. #1314770. We would like to thank the anonymous reviewers for their helpful comments.

References

1. Bogdanov, A.: Improved side-channel collision attacks on AES. In: Adams, C., Miri, A., Wiener, M. (eds.) SAC 2007. LNCS, vol. 4876, pp. 84–95. Springer, Heidelberg (2007)
2. Bogdanov, A.: Multiple-differential side-channel collision attacks on AES. In: Oswald, E., Rohatgi, P. (eds.) CHES 2008. LNCS, vol. 5154, pp. 30–44. Springer, Heidelberg (2008)
3. Bogdanov, A., Kizhvatov, I.: Beyond the limits of DPA: combined side-channel collision attacks. IEEE Trans. Comput. PP(99), 1 (2011)

4. Brier, E., Clavier, C., Olivier, F.: Correlation power analysis with a leakage model. In: Joye, M., Quisquater, J.-J. (eds.) CHES 2004. LNCS, vol. 3156, pp. 16–29. Springer, Heidelberg (2004)

5. Chari, S., Rao, J., Rohatgi, P.: Template attacks. In: Kaliski Jr., B.S., Koç, Ç.K., Paar, C. (eds.) CHES 2002. LNCS, vol. 2523, pp. 13–28. Springer, Heidelberg (2003)

6. Durvaux, F., Standaert, F.-X., Veyrat-Charvillon, N.: How to certify the leakage of a chip?. Cryptology ePrint Archive, Report 2013/706 (2013). http://eprint.iacr.org/

7. Gierlichs, B., Batina, L., Tuyls, P., Preneel, B.: Mutual information analysis. In: Oswald, E., Rohatgi, P. (eds.) CHES 2008. LNCS, vol. 5154, pp. 426–442. Springer, Heidelberg (2008)

8. Kocher, P.C., Jaffe, J., Jun, B.: Differential power analysis. In: Wiener, M. (ed.) CRYPTO 1999. LNCS, vol. 1666, pp. 388–397. Springer, Heidelberg (1999)

9. Mather, L., Oswald, E., Bandenburg, J., Wójcik, M.: Does my device leak information? an *a priori* statistical power analysis of leakage detection tests. In: Sako, K., Sarkar, P. (eds.) ASIACRYPT 2013, Part I. LNCS, vol. 8269, pp. 486–505. Springer, Heidelberg (2013)

10. Moradi, A.: Statistical tools flavor side-channel collision attacks. In: Pointcheval, D., Johansson, T. (eds.) EUROCRYPT 2012. LNCS, vol. 7237, pp. 428–445. Springer, Heidelberg (2012)

11. Moradi, A., Mischke, O., Eisenbarth, T.: Correlation-enhanced power analysis collision attack. In: Mangard, S., Standaert, F.-X. (eds.) CHES 2010. LNCS, vol. 6225, pp. 125–139. Springer, Heidelberg (2010)

12. Poettering, B.: Rijndael furious. Implementation. http://point-at-infinity.org/avraes/

13. Renauld, M., Standaert, F.-X., Veyrat-Charvillon, N., Kamel, D., Flandre, D.: A formal study of power variability issues and side-channel attacks for nanoscale devices. In: Paterson, K.G. (ed.) EUROCRYPT 2011. LNCS, vol. 6632, pp. 109–128. Springer, Heidelberg (2011)

14. Schindler, W., Lemke, K., Paar, C.: A stochastic model for differential side channel cryptanalysis. In: Rao, J.R., Sunar, B. (eds.) CHES 2005. LNCS, vol. 3659, pp. 30–46. Springer, Heidelberg (2005)

15. Schramm, K., Leander, G., Felke, P., Paar, C.: A collision-attack on AES. In: Joye, M., Quisquater, J.-J. (eds.) CHES 2004. LNCS, vol. 3156, pp. 163–175. Springer, Heidelberg (2004)

16. Schramm, K., Wollinger, T., Paar, C.: A new class of collision attacks and its application to DES. In: Johansson, T. (ed.) FSE 2003. LNCS, vol. 2887, pp. 206–222. Springer, Heidelberg (2003)

17. Standaert, F.-X., Malkin, T.G., Yung, M.: A unified framework for the analysis of side-channel key recovery attacks. In: Joux, A. (ed.) EUROCRYPT 2009. LNCS, vol. 5479, pp. 443–461. Springer, Heidelberg (2009)

18. Veyrat-Charvillon, N., Gérard, B., Standaert, F.-X.: Security evaluations beyond computing power. In: Johansson, T., Nguyen, P.Q. (eds.) EUROCRYPT 2013. LNCS, vol. 7881, pp. 126–141. Springer, Heidelberg (2013)

19. Whitnall, C., Oswald, E.: A fair evaluation framework for comparing side-channel distinguishers. J. Cryptogr. Eng. $\mathbf{1}(2)$, 145–160 (2011)

20. Whitnall, C., Oswald, E., Mather, L.: An exploration of the Kolmogorov-Smirnov test as a competitor to mutual information analysis. In: Prouff, E. (ed.) CARDIS 2011. LNCS, vol. 7079, pp. 234–251. Springer, Heidelberg (2011)

21. Whitnall, C., Oswald, E., Standaert, F.-X.: The myth of generic DPA and the magic of learning. In: Benaloh, J. (ed.) CT-RSA 2014. LNCS, vol. 8366, pp. 183–205. Springer, Heidelberg (2014)
22. Ye, X., Eisenbarth, T.: Wide collisions in practice. In: Bao, F., Samarati, P., Zhou, J. (eds.) ACNS 2012. LNCS, vol. 7341, pp. 329–343. Springer, Heidelberg (2012)

Author Index

Printed in the United States
By Bookmasters